LIVING
in the
KINGDOM
of GOD

LIVING
in the
KINGDOM
of GOD

A Biblical Theology for the
Life of the Church

SIGURD GRINDHEIM

Baker Academic
a division of Baker Publishing Group
Grand Rapids, Michigan

Published by Baker Academic
a division of Baker Publishing Group
PO Box 6287, Grand Rapids, MI 49516-6287
www.bakeracademic.com

Printed in the United States of America

Library of Congress Cataloging-in-Publication Data
Names: Grindheim, Sigurd, 1968– author.
Title: Living in the Kingdom of God : a biblical theology for the life of the church / Sigurd
    Grindheim.
Description: Grand Rapids : Baker Publishing Group, 2018. | Includes bibliographical references
    and index.
Identifiers: LCCN 2018015634 | ISBN 9781540960320 (pbk.)
Subjects: LCSH: Church. | Kingdom of God. | Jesus Christ—Kingdom.
Classification: LCC BV600.3 .G745 2018 | DDC 231.7/2—dc23
LC record available at https://lccn.loc.gov/2018015634

In keeping with biblical principles of creation stewardship, Baker Publishing Group advocates the responsible use of our natural resources. As a member of the Green Press Initiative, our company uses recycled paper when possible. The text paper of this book is composed in part of post-consumer waste.

18 19 20 21 22 23 24   7 6 5 4 3 2 1

Contents

Abbreviations

New Testament

Matt.	Matthew	1–2 Thess.	1–2 Thessalonians
Mark	Mark	1–2 Tim.	1–2 Timothy
Luke	Luke	Titus	Titus
John	John	Philem.	Philemon
Acts	Acts	Heb.	Hebrews
Rom.	Romans	James	James
1–2 Cor.	1–2 Corinthians	1–2 Pet.	1–2 Peter
Gal.	Galatians	1–3 John	1–3 John
Eph.	Ephesians	Jude	Jude
Phil.	Philippians	Rev.	Revelation
Col.	Colossians		

1

The Dream of Utopia

The Kingly Rule of God in the Old Testament

The most important words in Jesus's vocabulary are nowhere to be found in the Old Testament. "The kingdom of God" is not mentioned at all, and there are only two references to the "kingdom of the LORD" (1 Chron. 28:5; 2 Chron. 13:8). But these statistics are deceptive. Jesus's language about the kingdom builds on the idea that God is king, a point that is made explicitly or implicitly on almost every page of the Old Testament.

The psalmist praises God as the perfect king. "The King is mighty, he loves justice—you have established equity; in Jacob you have done what is just and right" (Ps. 99:4). As a ruler, God is always fair; he ensures that his society is a just one. His people live in safety, knowing that their king is able to provide for them. "For the LORD is our judge, the LORD is our lawgiver, the LORD is our king; it is he who will save us" (Isa. 33:22).

This king eliminates the powers of evil. "But God is my King from long ago; he brings salvation on the earth. It was you who split open the seas by your power; you broke the heads of the monster in the waters. It was you who crushed the heads of Leviathan and gave it as food to the creatures of the desert" (Ps. 74:12–14). "The seas" and "Leviathan" probably refer to the spiritual enemy of God and his people, later referred to as the devil. (The book of Revelation draws on the image of Leviathan to portray the dragon, which represents Satan; see Rev. 12:3.)

1

Where God rules as king, there are no evil powers. I often dream of such a society, a society without evil, a society ruled by God. I imagine what the world would be like if everyone did good all the time, if every individual always did what God wants us to do, if everyone obeyed the golden rule: "Do to others what you would have them do to you" (Matt. 7:12).

First of all, many people would be out of work. Take locksmiths, for example. You would never again need to lock your door. No one would ever steal anything, and people would come to visit only when you really wanted to see them.

In a society like that, all insurance companies would be unnecessary. You simply would not need insurance. If you needed anything at all, your friends and neighbors would provide it for you, free of charge. Those who had to go to the doctor would not need health insurance because the doctor would always give them all the care they needed. If your house were to burn to the ground, your neighbors would rebuild it for you while you were away on vacation, without asking for any compensation.

For the same reason, there would be neither banks in this society nor any form of money. Money would be completely superfluous and therefore utterly worthless. When you wanted something, your fellow citizens would give it to you. If someone from the United States got a hankering for Ethiopian coffee, someone from Ethiopia would travel across the ocean and give it to them. They would not need to be asked, and they would not charge anything.

If you think that no one who lived in such a world would ever want to work, since they could have everything for free, you would be mistaken. People would work harder than ever, not out of a desire to acquire more wealth for themselves but in order to give everything away to those in need. This kind of society would provide a life of luxury for all people. Every individual in the world would have thousands of servants ready to do anything they could imagine.

But there is something else that excites me even more than this imaginary life of wealth and abundance. That is the thought of what kind of relationships you could have with other people. You would be able to trust everyone you met and to confide fully in them without any reservation. They would never do anything to hurt you. Nothing you said would ever be used against you. Your words and your actions would never bring shame on you. The whole concept of shame would not exist. You could share all your most intimate thoughts and feelings with everyone you met without having to fear. Every person you ever knew would show you unconditional acceptance. No one would judge you, despise you, belittle you, or secretly think they are better than you. Every person in your life would be your best friend.

There would be no conflicts with anyone. There would be no competitiveness, no jealousy, no envy. There would be no slander, no ridicule, no humiliation. There would be no falsehood. No one would ever deceive you by telling you something they didn't really mean. We would know a fellowship with other people at a level we can hardly imagine.

In a world like this, no one would ever be treated differently than others because of the color of their skin or because of their country of origin. No one would look at someone else with suspicion because their appearance was different. No one would be denied a job or a house or any other privileges because they came from the wrong country or the wrong side of town. People would extend the same level of kindness to perfect strangers as they would to their own family. They would trust foreigners as unreservedly as they would trust their own parents. They would show the same kind of generosity toward people from different cultures as they would toward their own children. If all people always did the will of God, the world would be a happy place. If God would rule as king and everyone would do as he says, our planet would be a paradise.

God Is King

The Bible insists that God is the king. He is the ruler of both heaven and earth. With the lofty words of Psalm 103, we are told, "The LORD has established his throne in heaven, and his kingdom rules over all" (103:19). The Psalms return to this point again and again as they praise the Lord: "For the LORD Most High is awesome, the great King over all the earth" (47:2). "For God is the King of all the earth; sing to him a psalm of praise. God reigns over the nations; God is seated on his holy throne" (47:7–8).

These psalms are beautiful, but do they have any connection with the world in which we live? In David's time, this language was appropriate for use in worship, and it makes us feel better when we repeat the same language in church. But does it say anything meaningful about our world? Or are these words merely pious, wishful thinking? If we watch the news, we see little evidence that God reigns over the nations. The opposite seems to be the case. When we receive the latest updates from our extended family, it would not appear that God's dominion endures through all generations.

It may be comforting to take refuge in the words of the Bible when I am faced with the misery in this world, but are the words of Psalms true, in the sense that they correspond to anything I can experience around me? Or do they just help me dream of a better world, a world that is not real but that nevertheless enables me to live my life without losing all hope? To modern Christians, it has become more and more challenging to see what the God of the Bible has to do with the life we live every day. From biblical times until a couple hundred years ago, things were very different. If you were sick, you prayed to God and turned to a Spirit-filled healer to help you. We may do the same today, but only as an afterthought, after we have gone to the doctor and exhausted all the resources afforded by modern medicine. In the past, if you were curious to learn about the origin of the earth, you would read about it in the Bible. We may do the same today, but only in consultation with biblical scholars who could explain how nothing in the Bible contradicts what we know from science. When Israel was at war in Old Testament times, the people would be successful only if God went with them. On occasion, God would send most of their soldiers home, thus showing them that the victory was his alone (Judg. 7:1–25). We may trust that God is with our nation at war today as well, but we can only be sure that he will give us victory if we have the most powerful military in the world.

In more and more areas of life, the Bible is not the first place to which we turn. We still maintain that God is important in our lives, but he has increasingly been relegated to a restricted sphere, the sphere of religion. Our faith has come to occupy a smaller and smaller area of our lives. When the Bible makes its grand claims about God, we experience a form of disconnect. We say and think we believe them, but they no longer determine the way we go about our daily lives. And they no longer seem to make sense as the way we understand the world in which we live.

If it is true that God's kingdom rules over all, how does it apply to the world I inhabit, when I go to work, when I go to school, when I read the news, when I go shopping, when I engage with social media, when I interact with my neighbors and my family, and when I am involved in my community and in the local government? It is my firm conviction that the lofty words of the Psalms speak directly into every aspect of our lives and that we cannot make sense of anything that is happening in this world unless we grasp what the Bible has to say about the kingly rule of God. To understand that, we need to pay attention to the full biblical account. What we see will surprise us.

The Bible—in both the Old and the New Testaments—tells a rich story of the kingdom of God. However, we often misunderstand the words of the Bible because the English translation "kingdom of God" is only partly correct. In English, the word "kingdom" refers to a territory that is ruled by a king, as in the phrase "Kingdom of Denmark," "Kingdom of Thailand," or "United Kingdom." The Greek and Hebrew words that are used in the Bible may have this meaning also, but most frequently they mean something different. These words refer not to a piece of land or to a territory but to the rule of the king. We might therefore translate them "kingly rule." This is a dynamic concept. It has to do with the fact that someone rules, that someone issues commands and sees them carried out by their subjects, that someone makes laws and sees them obeyed by the people.

Although the term "kingdom of God" does not occur in the Old Testament, there are countless references to God acting and ruling as king. And when Jesus talks about the kingdom of God, he thinks of the kingly rule of God, as the Old Testament tells us about it. In many cases it would be better if we read "the kingly rule of God" instead of "the kingdom of God."

Psalm 145 may serve as an illustration. In verse 13, the psalmist proclaims: "Your kingdom is an everlasting kingdom, and your dominion endures through all generations." The word "dominion" functions here as a synonym for "kingdom," making clear that the psalmist thinks of God's rule, not of God's land. His rule is eternal.

Humans as Vice-Regents

What does God's rule look like? We might expect that a God who is the ruler of heaven and earth would dispatch an army of angels to ensure conformity to his laws or that he would use his almighty arm to enforce his will and make sure that everyone does his bidding. Occasionally he does so, but the Bible teaches that he prefers to rule in a different way. God chooses to exercise his kingly rule through the people he has created. Humans represent the pinnacle of God's work, and he wants them to be his coworkers. He created them to enjoy genuine fellowship with him. He created them to participate in his government of creation. That is the amazing value God has placed on humans.

In Psalm 8, the psalmist praises God for his creation:

> When I consider your heavens,
>   the work of your fingers,
> the moon and the stars,
>   which you have set in place,
> what is mankind that you are mindful of them,
>   human beings that you care for them?
> You have made them a little lower than the angels
>   and crowned them with glory and honor.
> You made them rulers over the works of your hands;
>   you put everything under their feet:

> all flocks and herds,
>   and the animals of the wild,
> the birds in the sky,
>   and the fish in the sea,
> all that swim the paths of the seas. (vv. 3–8)

This psalm is a commentary on the creation account. It explains what it means that humans are created in the image of God, as we learn in Genesis 1:27: "So God created mankind in his own image, in the image of God he created them; male and female he created them."

In antiquity, kings and potentates typically erected statues of themselves at strategic places in their kingdom so that all their subjects would be reminded of who their ruler was. To take a modern example, recall Saddam Hussein. He made sure to have a gigantic statue of himself right in the middle of Baghdad so that the people would always remember that he was their ruler. The image of Hussein was constantly hovering over the Iraqi people. As soon as Hussein was deposed, the first thing the Iraqis did was to start tearing down his statue. When his power was gone, his image was gone too; the image represented his power.

As God's image, we are such representatives—not of an evil ruler but of the creator of heaven and earth, the only true God. To be a bearer of God's image means to be God's vice-regent; it means to govern on God's behalf. That is why the mandate follows immediately after the declaration that we are created in the image of God. Genesis 1:28 tells us: "God blessed them and said to them, 'Be fruitful and increase in number; fill the earth and subdue it. Rule over the fish in the sea and the birds in the sky and over every living creature that moves on the ground.'"

The Fallout

God's plan was for his kingly rule to be executed by humans. He left his creation in the hands of the people he had created, and he entrusted to them the task of carrying out his dominion. It was a risky plan. It was a plan that shows us the magnitude of God's investment in the people he had formed. He had no interest in making robots with no will of their own, robots who blindly did what he had programmed them to do. God wanted his people to be his coworkers, and he loved them so much that he was willing to risk everything on one grand gesture of love. He left his entire creation in their care.

The potential for disaster was great, and therefore so was the fall. Humans did not prove themselves to be worthy vice-regents; they turned and rebelled against the one they were intended to serve. They did not want God as their king. God had placed Adam and Eve in the garden of Eden. God gave them all the fruit of the trees in the garden; they never lacked anything. Only the tree that was in the middle of the garden was off-limits; they were not allowed to eat from it. This simple commandment would allow Adam and Eve to show that they would obey God and submit to his rule. But the serpent tempted them to doubt God's good purposes. He enticed them to think that God was depriving them of something good when he commanded them not to eat from the tree (Gen. 3:4–5). When Adam and Eve no longer trusted God's good designs, they had already turned away from him in their hearts. Eating the forbidden fruit was the inevitable consequence of their internal rebellion (3:6).

They had enjoyed life under God's rule and had seen his good gifts in abundant supply, but through their revolt, they forfeited these blessings. Because of their sin, they were banished from the garden. Humans have rebelled against the kingly rule of God, but their rebellion does not change the fact that God is king. He has never been deposed, and the rebellion of humans does not represent a threat against God and who he is. The psalmist paints a vivid picture:

> Why do the nations conspire
>   and the peoples plot in vain?
> The kings of the earth rise up
>   and the rulers band together
>   against the LORD and against his anointed, saying,
> "Let us break their chains
>   and throw off their shackles."
> The One enthroned in heaven laughs;
>   the Lord scoffs at them.
> He rebukes them in his anger
>   and terrifies them in his wrath, saying,
> "I have installed my king
>   on Zion, my holy mountain." (Ps. 2:1–6)

God is still king, but the human rebellion causes dissonance in creation. His kingly rule is no longer respected by his subjects. The world has become like a territory that wants to assert its independence from the country to which it belongs. We might compare this world to the Somali region in Ethiopia. According to international law, the territory toward the east of Ethiopia, which is populated mainly by ethnic Somalis, belongs to the country of Ethiopia.

Whether this is a just law is a question for another day, but legally this territory is subject to the Ethiopian government and accountable to Ethiopian law. Yet the people of the Somali region do not always accept the fact that they belong to Ethiopia. They do not feel that they are a part of this country, and they tend to live according to their own customs and not according to whatever the government in Addis Ababa decides. Ethiopian money, for example, has no value in the Somali region. The authority of Ethiopia is not acknowledged, and nobody wants their currency. If there are local conflicts in this area, the Ethiopian court system is powerless to restore order. Nobody respects the verdicts passed by Ethiopian judges. Instead, the locals live by their own justice system. Conflicts are handled internally in the family and clan. The real power is that which is exercised by people with social authority, those recognized as leaders by the community. Legally, the Somali region is ruled by Ethiopia, but in practice it is often very different. In the same way, humans have disrespected God's authority and turned our world into God's Somali region. By right, he is the ruler, but his rule is routinely ignored.

God at War

God is not sitting idly by. He restores his kingly rule, and in order to do that, he goes to war against the powers that have revolted against him. The first time we see God reestablishing his kingly rule is when he delivers Israel from slavery in Egypt. Pharaoh stands as the archetype of earthly powers that buck God's rule and refuse to submit to his will. He mistreated the Israelites, who had come to Egypt as economic refugees, fleeing from the famine in Canaan. Initially, things went very well for them in Egypt: "The Israelites were exceedingly fruitful; they multiplied greatly, increased in numbers and became so numerous that the land was filled with them" (Exod. 1:7).

The Egyptians did not look kindly on the growth and success of their new neighbors. Like so many other demagogues after him, Pharaoh knew to take advantage of the people's fear and stoked their hostility toward the foreigners. "'Look,' he said to his people, 'the Israelites have become far too numerous for us. Come, we must deal shrewdly with them or they will become even more numerous and, if war breaks out, will join our enemies, fight against us and leave the country'" (Exod. 1:9–10). With this pretext, he smeared the Israelites as a danger to society and began his economic oppression. The Israelites were forced into slave labor. When Moses confronted Pharaoh and asked for lenience, Pharaoh answered by tightening the screws. He told his slave drivers: "You are no longer to supply the people with straw for making bricks; let them go and gather their own straw. But require them to make the same number of bricks as before; don't reduce the quota. They are lazy; that is why they are crying out, 'Let us go and sacrifice to our God.' Make the work harder for the people so that they keep working and pay no attention to lies" (Exod. 5:7–9).

Like oppressed people tend to do, the Israelites cried out to God (Exod. 2:23), seemingly to no avail. Even Moses lost patience; he held God responsible for Israel's misfortune and accused him of not caring: "Why, Lord, why have you brought trouble on this people? Is this why you sent me? Ever since I went to Pharaoh to speak in your name, he has brought trouble on this people, and you have not rescued your people at all" (5:22–23).

God allowed Pharaoh's obstinacy to play out for a long time, but in the end God made an example of him. The ruler who thinks he will not have to answer to God has another thing coming. The story of Pharaoh is the story of the world's superpower at the time, and it is the story of its crushing defeat by the far superior power of God, the king of heaven and earth. God showed his power by splitting the sea and leading the Israelites dry-shod across the ocean floor, while the waters were standing as a wall on each side. When the Egyptians were trying to follow them, the waters rushed back and swallowed them all. When God says, "Let my people go," you ignore God at your peril.

God had emerged as the king, and the world was on notice. When the people were brought to safety, Moses wrote a song of praise to the Lord, and concluded: "The LORD reigns for ever and ever" (Exod. 15:18). The exodus had showed that God was not a lame-duck ruler. He would not accept opposition to his rule. God had showed himself as a mighty military king, a theme that is essential to the idea of God's kingship in both the Old and New Testaments.

> The LORD is a warrior;
>   the LORD is his name.
> Pharaoh's chariots and his army
>   he has hurled into the sea.
> The best of Pharaoh's officers
>   are drowned in the Red Sea.
> The deep waters have covered them;
>   they sank to the depths like a stone.
> Your right hand, LORD,
>   was majestic in power.
> Your right hand, LORD,
>   shattered the enemy. (15:3–6)

God is king, and he will use his military might to restore his kingly rule.

The Good Society

When God had showed himself as king at the Red Sea, he once again decided to outsource his government to humans. God entered into a contract with the Israelites and announced: "Now if you obey me fully and keep my covenant, then out of all nations you will be my treasured possession. Although the whole earth is mine, you will be for me a kingdom of priests and a holy nation" (Exod. 19:5–6). The translation of these verses is difficult, but there are good reasons to read them as saying that Israel was called to be priests and to rule as kings. To be a priest means to be someone who serves as the intermediary between God and humans. The people of Israel are especially chosen by God, and they have a unique relationship with him. God doesn't deal directly with the other nations, but he deals directly with Israel. As his people, they have the role of priests, and they are given the task to rule as kings on his behalf.

God did not leave the government to the people's own devices, however; he gave them a set of laws to ensure that their society was ruled in the way he wanted. Unlike the legal codes of other nations, the laws of Israel did not give unbridled authority to the privileged and the powerful. Even the king was subject to the rule of law, to prevent excessive use of his power (Deut. 17:14–20). The laws of Israel guaranteed equity among its citizens. Land could not be permanently transferred out of the family, precluding the concentration of wealth in a few hands (Lev. 25:23–28). There were provisions for the poor so that they should not need to go hungry (19:9–10). Food could not be sold for profit, and loans had to be interest free (25:36–37). Punishment for crimes should not be excessive (Exod. 21:18–22:15).

Those familiar with the story of the Bible know that the utopia outlined in the laws of Moses never materialized. The people failed at their responsibility. Israel rejected the laws of God as soon as he had given them. While Moses was still on the mountain, receiving the laws from God, the people violated the first of his commandments; they made a graven image of a calf and bowed down to worship it (Exod. 32:1–8). After Moses had interceded for them, God did not reject his people, but his continued presence among them served as a reminder that their relationship was not as intimate as it could have been. God's dwelling was in the tabernacle's holy of holies, but only the high priest could enter, only once a year, and only when he brought the right gifts.

The Epistle to the Hebrews explains: "But only the high priest entered the inner room, and that only once a year, and never without blood, which he offered for himself and for the sins the people had committed in ignorance. The Holy Spirit was showing by this that the way into the Most Holy Place had not yet been disclosed as long as the first tabernacle was still functioning. . . . Those sacrifices are an annual reminder of sins" (Heb. 9:7–8; 10:3). The institutions of Israel demonstrated the distance that still existed between the people and their God. The laws reminded them of what could have been: a perfect society ruled by God. But reality taught the people that they were far from this.

After they had entered the promised land, the failure of the people was magnified by the failure of their rulers. The kings in Israel did not accept the God-ordained limits to their power. They used their position to take advantage of those less privileged and to enrich themselves at their expense. Israel's kings were supposed to be instruments of God's rule, but they sought other counsel and followed the ways of their pagan neighbors.

By the sixth century BCE, Israel had definitively turned away from God and given their allegiance to idols and political alliances with ungodly nations. As they had rebelled against the kingship of God, they also lost the good land that he had given to them. In 586 BCE, Jerusalem was destroyed by the Babylonians, and the people were led into exile.

The Messiah

God responded to Israel's downfall by preparing them for the arrival of a new king, a just king who would rule with the mercy of God. The prophet Isaiah offers an impressive panegyric:

> A shoot will come up from the stump of Jesse;
>   from his roots a Branch will bear fruit.
> The Spirit of the LORD will rest on him—
>   the Spirit of wisdom and of understanding,
>   the Spirit of counsel and of might,
>   the Spirit of the knowledge and fear of the LORD—
> and he will delight in the fear of the LORD.
> He will not judge by what he sees with his eyes,
>   or decide by what he hears with his ears;
> but with righteousness he will judge the needy,
>   with justice he will give decisions for the poor of the earth.
> He will strike the earth with the rod of his mouth;
>   with the breath of his lips he will slay the wicked.
> Righteousness will be his belt
>   and faithfulness the sash around his waist.
> The wolf will live with the lamb,
>   the leopard will lie down with the goat,

the calf and the lion and the yearling together;
and a little child will lead them.
The cow will feed with the bear,
their young will lie down together,
and the lion will eat straw like the ox.
The infant will play near the cobra's den,
and the young child will put its hand into the viper's nest.
They will neither harm nor destroy
on all my holy mountain,
for the earth will be filled with the knowledge of the LORD
as the waters cover the sea. (11:1–9)

Out of the ruin that is David's dynasty, a new day will dawn. The prophet uses the image of a tree that has been cut down so that only a stump is left. He associates the tree with Jesse, the father of David, the great king of Israel. Out of this seemingly fruitless tree, a new branch will sprout; a new glorious king will emerge. This king will be different from the worthless kings in Israel. He will not be partial to the rich and the privileged, but he will ensure that the poor and the needy get their rights. He will not be duped by appearances and smooth-talking lobbyists. His counsel will be the Spirit of the Lord. He will rule with wisdom.

This king will show mercy to the weak and unprivileged, and he will strike down all opposition against God's kingly rule. As God did with Pharaoh, so will he punish the wicked, those who rebel against God. When he appears, the kingly rule of God will be established once again.

Under such a rule, it will be wonderful to live on earth. What the prophet envisions is so magnificent that we see the contours of an entirely new world order. Enemies will be reconciled, and peace will rule, not only between humans but also throughout all creation. Even "the wolf will live with the lamb, the leopard will lie down with the goat, the calf and the lion and the yearling together; and a little child will lead them." When God's rule is reestablished, it will be a new world. It will be a world without evil of any kind. Humans and animals will be kind to each other. People will be able to live without fear because their reasons for fear have ceased to exist. We will no longer see news reports about wars, conflicts, natural disasters, floods, hurricanes, climate change, and destruction of the environment.

Isaiah's prophecy shows that God will intervene decisively in this world and change the very conditions under which this universe exists. The reestablishment of his rule entails not only a better way for humans to live in peace and harmony with each other but also a realignment of the forces of nature. God's benevolent rule will be executed throughout creation.

New Creation

The prophet Isaiah gives us his most detailed picture of this great new future in chapters 24–27. Isaiah looks forward to a day when God once again will show his awesome might:

> In that day the LORD will punish
>   the powers in the heavens above
>   and the kings on the earth below.
> They will be herded together
>   like prisoners bound in a dungeon;
> they will be shut up in prison
>   and be punished after many days.
> The moon will be dismayed,
>   the sun ashamed;
> for the LORD Almighty will reign
>   on Mount Zion and in Jerusalem,
>   and before its elders—with great glory. (24:21–23)

As was the case when God intervened to deliver the Israelites from Egypt, so does this ultimate and final reestablishment of his rule begin with the defeat of his enemies. We now understand, however, that there are not only humans among God's adversaries. They also include "the powers in the heavens above." There are heavenly entities, angels and spiritual beings that have risen up against God and caused the misery that we experience in this world every day. These spiritual powers present themselves in a number of different forms: the power of addiction, the degenerative influence of peer pressure, the violent proclivities of mob mentality, the debilitating inefficiency of bureaucratic institutions, the corrupting influence of power held by political entities, the curse that is passed on from one generation to the next in dysfunctional families. These powers, however impressive they may seem now, will meet their doom. Even the moon will be dismayed and the sun ashamed, proclaims the prophet. These are metaphorical expressions, designating the most powerful entities in our universe. The day will come when they will fade in comparison with the one and only power, the power of God, who will force every opposing might into complete submission. On that day, the Lord Almighty will rule as king on Mount Zion and in Jerusalem. God's kingly rule will be a reality with great glory.

That day is not only a day of punishment. More than anything else, it is a day of joy and celebration. It is the day when the Lord will throw a great party:

> On this mountain the LORD Almighty will prepare
>   a feast of rich food for all peoples,
> a banquet of aged wine—
>   the best of meats and the finest of wines.
> On this mountain he will destroy
>   the shroud that enfolds all peoples,
> the sheet that covers all nations;
>   he will swallow up death forever.
> The Sovereign LORD will wipe away the tears
>   from all faces;
> he will remove his people's disgrace
>   from all the earth.
>   The LORD has spoken.
>
> In that day they will say,
>
> "Surely this is our God;
>   we trusted in him, and he saved us.
> This is the LORD, we trusted in him;
>   let us rejoice and be glad in his salvation." (Isa. 25:6–9)

The prophet describes something he has seen in order to explain something he has not seen. He has not experienced the joy of God's salvation, but he knows it will be the most joyous event in history, so he paints a picture of the most lavish party known to man, a feast with the most exquisite food and drink. But we soon understand that this event is of a different kind than any party we have ever witnessed before. It is a party to celebrate that God is doing something spectacular, something previously unheard of. He will swallow up death forever. That is what will happen when he deals with the powers that stand against him, not only the human powers but also the spiritual powers. All evil forces that bring pain and suffering and misery will be destroyed. On that day, there will be no more sorrow because all reasons for sorrow will no longer exist. No one will ever lose their loved ones. No one will have their life ruined by poor health. No one will experience heart-wrenching relationship breakups. The prophet looks forward to a day of unbridled happiness, a happiness that will not give way to disappointment, as happens with all our happiness in this world. This is an eternal joy, the joy that our Lord will bring to those who trust in him.

Isaiah was a man of great vision. He lived in an era when injustice and ungodliness were rampant, and he addressed the situation when the Babylonians waged war against Israel. Their military machinery would conquer Jerusalem, take the people captive, and raze the city. Even the holy temple of God would be bulldozed. In the midst of this cruel reality, Isaiah took comfort in looking forward to a different time, a time when God would rule as king and his kingdom would appear on earth.

God's Kingdom and the Kingdoms of the World

It is easy to identify with the prophet Isaiah. We live in a time when God's good will for humanity is being rejected. In countries such as Rwanda, Sri Lanka, and Myanmar, people groups have sought to eradicate each other because of ethnic differences. In Syria, millions of people have been forced to flee from their homes in fear of violence. In Qatar, thousands of migrant workers have paid with their lives for labor conditions that fail to meet the most basic safety requirements. In places like North Korea, Iraq, Eritrea, and Afghanistan, Christians are killed because of their faith. Warfare in Chechnya, Iraq, South Sudan, and other places has taken the lives of thousands, and most of them have been civilians.

In many other ways, people suffer injustice all over the world. The so-called untouchables in India have been excluded from normal participation in society. In Europe and North America, people with foreign-sounding names and people of color experience discrimination both in the job market and in the housing market, as well as in the way they are treated by law enforcement. Women are victims of unprovoked violence and unwanted sexual advances. Children grow up in fear of violence from the people who should be their most zealous protectors, their own parents. Unborn children have little or no legal protection.

What has become of the dream of God's kingdom? Is it just a dream and nothing more? Is God really "the great King over all the earth"? Does his kingdom rule over all, as the psalms would have it (Pss. 47; 103:19)? If so, why are evil people in control everywhere? Why do those who step on other people rise to the top, while those who care for other people are taken advantage of? Why do bullies succeed and become millionaires, while people who devote their lives to showing compassion need to rely on public aid to get by? Why do ruthless and megalomaniacal people become heads of state? If God is king, what was he thinking when he appointed his cabinet?

The problem was just as painful for the people of Israel, the people God had chosen. They were supposed to experience the benefits of God's benevolent rule. Instead, they experienced being oppressed by Assyrian, Babylonian, Persian, Greek, and Roman rulers. Among the Old Testament writings, the prophet Daniel addressed this paradox most directly.

Daniel had a dream of four great beasts. Biblical scholars agree that these four beasts symbolize four of the major empires in world history, beginning with the Babylonians of Daniel's own time and continuing with the Medes, the Persians, and the Greeks. All the empires are represented by predatory animals. "The first was like a lion, and it had the wings of an eagle" (Dan. 7:4). The second "looked like a bear" (7:5) and the third "like a leopard" (7:6). The fourth was so terrifying that it didn't resemble anything Daniel had ever seen before. "It had large iron teeth; it crushed and devoured its victims and trampled underfoot whatever was left. It was different from all the former beasts, and it had ten horns" (7:7). These empires were cruel and merciless, oppressing other nations and devouring their resources. They were so drunk on their own power that they did not think they were accountable to anyone but themselves. The law was whatever they said it should be. They did not even respect the authority of God or consider that they had to answer to him for the way they had exercised their rule.

The fourth beast had ten horns on its head, probably symbolizing the ten Greek kingdoms that emerged after the conquests of Alexander the Great. One of these kings would subdue three others, and would "speak against the Most High and oppress his holy people and try to change the set times and the laws" (Dan. 7:25). The king in question is Antiochus IV Epiphanes, who went to unprecedented extremes in his cruelty toward Israel. His army entered Jerusalem in the year 167 BCE, destroyed the city walls, and plundered the temple. In his attempt to eradicate the Jewish religion and turn Jerusalem into a Greek city, he dedicated the Jerusalem temple to the Greek god Zeus. With a flair for the provocatively dramatic, he sacrificed a pig—the most unclean of all the animals—on the temple altar. This is what Daniel refers to as "the abomination that causes desolation" (11:31). Antiochus made observance of the Jewish law illegal, and circumcision became a capital offense.

In the Bible, Antiochus stands as the archetype of human rulers who think they are above God's law and who try to obliterate his people. Jesus uses the language from Daniel's prophecy when he describes the Romans' destruction of the temple as "the abomination that causes desolation" (Mark 13:14). John also alludes to Daniel when he refers to the end-time tribulation as lasting three and a half years (Rev. 11:2, 3; 12:6, 14), which was roughly the duration of Antiochus's rule of terror over Jerusalem.

Throughout history, there have been many rulers like Antiochus, tyrants who are better described as beasts than as humans, dictators who respect no one or nothing except their own ego, not even God. In the twentieth century, Adolf Hitler initiated the most organized attempt at exterminating the Jewish people. In our own time, more Christians are being martyred than at any other time in history. In North Korea, an estimated 50,000 to 70,000 Christians are being tortured in labor camps. The country's supreme leader,

Kim Jong-un, makes his people honor him in a way that looks more like worship than anything else. Saudi Arabia's government, tacitly supported by the
United States, violently oppresses the country's Shiite minority. In several cities
in the United States, police have systematically ignored the rights of African
Americans, have incarcerated people without due process, and in some cases
have even been able to get away with murder.

As these beastly forces appear to be able to operate with impunity, the
people of God wonder what has become of the kingly rule of God. Will he
forever remain passive while these ungodly rulers enrich themselves and bring
destruction on the weak and defenseless? The vision of Daniel shows that
the time of the beasts is running out. God explained the vision of the fourth
beast to Daniel and told him that "the holy people will be delivered into his
hands for a time, times and half a time" (Dan. 7:25). The beast was allowed
to exercise its power and even to torment the people of God. But God was
still in control, even of the terrible fourth beast, even of the rulers who had
no respect for God and made a parody of justice. They only had the time that
had been allotted to them, and their time was about to be up.

Besides the four beasts, Daniel's dream had shown him a different character, a character that appeared before him as a human: "There before me
was one like a son of man, coming with the clouds of heaven" (Dan. 7:13).
This character also corresponds to a kingdom, a kingdom of a completely
different nature. It is therefore not represented by any kind of animal at all.
In contrast to the predatory oppression and destruction of the world's many
empires, this kingdom is represented by a human. This is a kingdom in which
compassion and justice will rule.

Whereas the beasts only had a very limited rule, the son of man "was
given authority, glory and sovereign power; all nations and peoples of every
language worshiped him. His dominion is an everlasting dominion that will
not pass away, and his kingdom is one that will never be destroyed" (Dan.
7:14). The good news announced by the prophet Daniel is that the evil empires
had been given a limited time; they would be replaced by a good kingdom,
an eternal kingdom, a kingdom that would have no end. The empires of
this world are transitory; the kingdom of the son of man will last forever.
God promised Daniel, "Then the sovereignty, power and greatness of all the
kingdoms under heaven will be handed over to the holy people of the Most
High. His kingdom will be an everlasting kingdom, and all rulers will worship and obey him" (7:27).

All the oppressive kingdoms of the world would come to an end, but what
or who would appear in their place? The prophecy proclaimed that their sovereignty, power, and greatness "will be handed over to the holy people of the

Most High," so we may conclude that God would bring his plan to completion. He would establish his rule, and he would exercise his rule through humans, through the people he had chosen, his holy people. But there is more. In the next sentence, the prophet refers to "his kingdom." The kingdom in question must be the kingdom he just announced, which belonged to the people of God. But if he was talking about the people's kingdom, why didn't he say "their kingdom"? Why is this kingdom said to be "his"? Who is the person hiding behind this personal pronoun? The person can be none other than the human that Daniel had seen in his vision, the "one like a son of man, coming with the clouds of heaven" (Dan. 7:13).

In this subtle way, Daniel teaches that the kingdom is simultaneously the kingdom of God's people and the kingdom of the one like a son of man. In other words, the one like a son of man and the people of God are closely identified, so closely that many scholars have concluded that the one like a son of man is simply a symbol for the people of God. In light of the New Testament, however, we understand that this interpretation is not entirely correct. The son of man is none other than Jesus Christ, who talked about himself as the Son of Man and announced to the high priest that he "will see the Son of Man sitting at the right hand of the Mighty One and coming on the clouds of heaven" (Mark 14:62). What Daniel's prophecy shows, therefore, is that the people of the kingdom are closely united with the head of the kingdom. This is not a hierarchical kingdom where the king forces his will on reluctant subjects. This is not an oppressive kingdom that milks the resources from the common people and channels them to the top. This is a kingdom in which the authority belongs to the people. This is a kingdom that may equally well be said to belong to the people as to their ruler.

The king and the people appear to be indistinguishable, not because they are one and the same but because the people are so closely united with the king. The king is one of the people and identifies completely with them. The people define their own identity by their loyalty to their king. If you ask them who they are, they will answer, "We are the people who belong to the king." They identify with their king much in the same way sports fans identify with their team. Their self-respect, their feeling of worth, and their emotions are determined by the performance of their team. When their side wins, they are proud and happy because they have their identity tied to the team. They refer to the players as "we" and claim the team's victories as their own. The people of God's kingdom have their identity tied to their king, and they claim his victory as their own victory. But unlike the average sports fan, this shared identity is a two-way street. Most sports fans will never experience their heroes even knowing who they are. With God's kingdom, it is different. The king is one with the people, just as the people are one with him. He knows their names, and they mean just as much (or more) to him as he means to them. He is a king who identifies with his people.

A New Relationship

While Daniel looks forward to the final victory of God, one of the richest pictures of this ultimate triumph is found in the prophet Zechariah. In his fourteenth chapter, the prophet proclaims that "a day of the LORD is coming" (v. 1). "Then the LORD will go out and fight against those nations, as he fights on a day of battle" (v. 3). He will defeat all the nations, and the world as we know it will come to an end. It will be the day when he brings his salvation to earth. As Zechariah states, "On that day living water will flow out from Jerusalem, half of it east to the Dead Sea and half of it west to the Mediterranean Sea, in summer and in winter" (v. 8). God's good gift of life will flow freely, without interruption. On this day, when God's enemies are defeated and the gifts of salvation are freely available, "the LORD will be king over the whole earth. On that day there will be one LORD, and his name the only name" (v. 9). There has never been more than one Lord; there has never been any other God than the God who reveals himself in the Bible. However, humans have given their allegiance to other lords; they have obeyed other masters. As long as God's enemies have been at large, God's authority has not been acknowledged by all. But that will change when the Lord comes to be king over the whole earth.

On the day when God comes as king, he will once again elevate his people to be coregents with him. The rupture that existed between God and his people will be mended. The best way Zechariah knows to describe it is to use the language of the temple, the dwelling of God: "On that day HOLY TO THE LORD will be inscribed on the bells of the horses, and the cooking pots in the LORD's house will be like the sacred bowls in front of the altar. Every pot in Jerusalem and Judah will be holy to the LORD Almighty, and all who come to sacrifice will take some of the pots and cook in them" (14:20–21).

The institution of the temple had taught the people that God was a holy God. He was highly exalted above humans, but he was present among the people of Israel. He was present in the inner chamber of the temple, the holy of holies. God's presence held the potential for great blessings, but it was also fraught with danger. Encountering sinful humans, God was a consuming fire. No one could approach him. God's dwelling was among the Israelites, but no one except the high priest could enter it, and he had to prepare himself carefully. He had to sanctify himself so that he could be acceptable in the presence of God. He wore holy vestments with a special turban. It had a plate of pure gold attached to it. This plate bore an engraving: "HOLY TO THE LORD" (Exod. 28:36). No one but the high priest could ever bear this plate. No one but the high priest could ever be endowed with this kind of holiness, the holiness required in the presence of God.

In Zechariah's vision, this level of holiness is everywhere. It is not restricted to the high priest for a single appearance once a year. Even horses—animals not usually associated with cleanness and holiness—will be as holy as the high priest. Every pot in Jerusalem will be as holy as the pots in the temple. In other words, the holiness of the temple will extend throughout Israel. The holiness that is necessary for God to dwell in the temple will not be limited to the holy of holies. It will be everywhere, so that God's presence may be everywhere. Not only the high priest may be in God's presence once a year, but the whole people may be close to him every day. As in the garden of Eden, God and his people may be together without awkwardness. The distance manifested by the temple institution is overcome. People may see God and talk to him as they would talk to their best friend or a close family member. Their relationship has been restored. The kingly rule of God has brought harmony back into creation. People can approach God without shame or fear. They no longer feel unworthy of being in his presence. God's holiness fills the land. His people are with him. The prophets had a stunningly beautiful vision of God's kingly rule. What would it take for such a vision to become reality?

Further Reading

The study on the kingdom of God in the Old Testament on which all others depend is found in **Gustaf Dalman**, *The Words of Jesus: Considered in the Light of Post-Biblical Jewish Writings and the Aramaic Language*, trans. D. M. Kay (Edinburgh: T&T Clark, 1902). Dalman shows that the meaning of the term is "the kingly rule of God."

In *The Kingdom of God: The Biblical Concept and Its Meaning for the Church* (New York: Abingdon, 1953), **John Bright** famously argues that the idea of God's kingdom is the center of the Old Testament.

Bright's thesis has not commanded much consent among other interpreters, but **Stephen Dempster**, in *Dominion and Dynasty: A Biblical Theology of the Hebrew Bible*, New Studies in Biblical Theology 15 (Downers Grove, IL: InterVarsity, 2003), maintains that kingly rule and kingdom constitute the unifying theme of the Old Testament. The biblical story proceeds from creation to exile and restoration.

Based on the connections between Genesis 1–3 and Revelation 20–22, T. Desmond Alexander argues in *From Eden to the New Jerusalem: An Introduction to Biblical Theology* (Grand Rapids: Kregel, 2009) that the biblical story line is framed by accounts of God's presence in the world and that this concept ties the whole Bible together. Much like **G. K. Beale** in *The Temple and the Church's Mission*, New Studies in Biblical Theology 17 (Downers Grove, IL: InterVarsity, 2004), Alexander sees the garden of Eden as a temple that is renewed in the new creation.

In *A New Testament Biblical Theology: The Unfolding of the Old Testament in the New* (Grand Rapids: Baker Academic, 2011), 29–116, **G. K. Beale** maintains that the story of the Old Testament moves toward God's establishment of his "new-creational kingdom."

An overview of the Old Testament teaching on God's kingship may be found in **Sigurd Grindheim**, *God's Equal: What Can We Know about Jesus' Self-Understanding?*, Library of New Testament Studies 446 (London: T&T Clark, 2011), as well as in **John P. Meier**, *Mentor, Message, and Miracles*, vol. 2 of *A Marginal Jew: Rethinking the Historical Jesus*, Anchor Bible Reference Library (New York: Doubleday, 1994).

Important studies of the messianic idea in the Old Testament include **Sigmund Mowinckel**, *He That Cometh*, trans. G. W. Anderson (New York: Abingdon, 1954); **James H. Charlesworth**, ed., *The Messiah: Developments in Earliest Judaism and Christianity* (Minneapolis: Fortress, 1992); **Antti Laato**, *Josiah and David Redivivus: The Historical Josiah and the Messianic Expectations of Exilic and Postexilic Times*, Coniectanea Biblica: Old Testament Series (Stockholm: Almqvist, 1992); **Walter C. Kaiser Jr.**, *The Messiah in the Old Testament*, Studies in Old Testament Biblical Theology (Grand Rapids: Zondervan, 1995); **Joseph A. Fitzmyer**, *The One Who Is to Come* (Grand Rapids: Eerdmans, 2007). A brief account is found in the introductory chapter of **Sigurd Grindheim**, *Christology in the Synoptic Gospels: God or God's Servant?* (London: T&T Clark, 2012).

2

The Surprising Fulfillment

Jesus Establishes the Kingly Rule of God

"The time has arrived; the kingdom of God is upon you. Repent, and believe the gospel" (Mark 1:15 REB). With this brief statement, Mark summarizes Jesus's message: the kingdom of God is here! Most Christians have heard this line many times and have become so used to thinking they know what it means that the significance of Jesus's words is almost completely lost on them. Preachers from the tradition of the great revivals have announced that Jesus came to offer us personal salvation, a place in his heavenly kingdom, a kingdom that will become reality sometime in the distant future (or maybe very soon) when Jesus comes back to earth. Others insist that this is an individualistic misunderstanding of Jesus's message. To them, the kingdom of God becomes a reality when justice prevails in our society here and now.

Both of these interpretations are inadequate, but there is a simple reason why they are so popular: they allow us to domesticate Jesus's message. They make it possible to continue our lives more or less as if nothing has happened. If Jesus came to ensure that the gates of heaven are open when we die, our life here on earth doesn't need to change much. We'll make sure to thank Jesus for what he has done for us before we go to bed every night, but for the most part our life stays the same. If Jesus came to propel us in our work for justice, we'll just keep doing that, only with even more conviction.

Jesus's words change everything we think we know about the world. If what he says is true, it is impossible to carry on with life as we are used to doing. To understand him, we must read his words in light of the Old Testament. Jesus uses the term "kingdom" with the same meaning it has in the Old Testament, referring not to a territory but to the rule of a king. Thus when Jesus speaks of the kingdom of God, it would be better translated as "the kingly rule of God."[1]

When Jesus proclaims the presence of God's kingly rule, he announces that the dreams of the prophets have come to fulfillment. God himself has come down from heaven and stepped onto the face of the earth. He has come to put an end to all his enemies, once and for all. All evil powers that do not submit to his will are meeting their demise. God's rule has been established on earth. God has come to the world as king. "The kingdom of God is upon you."

This sounds like crazy talk. We all know that the world is not the paradise it would be if God's will prevailed. The world is not ruled by love and kindness. Families are breaking up. Societies are torn apart by conflicts between different ethnic groups. Millions of people are targets of violence because of their ethnicity or religion. Many of them are forced to flee from their homes, chancing everything, often their own lives, seeking basic safety for themselves and their families. To speak of God's kingly rule in this world seems delusional if not offensive.

The people who first heard Jesus were confused too. The Jewish people were expecting a whole new world to emerge when God's kingly rule was established. They were waiting for all the injustice in the world to come to an end. Most of all, they were thinking of the brutal, alien power that had conquered Israel and now ruled their land: the Romans. There was hardly any clearer proof that God's kingly rule was not established. The Romans were disrespecting God's rule and spurning his laws. The Roman governor of Judea, Pontius Pilate, had his soldiers carry the Roman standards into the Holy City of Jerusalem. These standards bore the emperor's effigies. According to the law of God, "You shall not make for yourself an image in the form of anything in heaven above or on the earth beneath or in the waters below" (Exod. 20:4). Pilate was not acting out of ignorance but was intentionally seeking to provoke the Jews. This Roman official was in effect telling them, "I don't care about you or the sovereignty of your nation any more than I care about your God and his laws. I am the one who rules here, not you or your God, and I will do whatever I want to do." He relented only when a Jewish delegation pleaded with him, refusing to back down even under threat of death.

---

1. However, in contrast to the English translations, the Greek term *basileia* is capable of both meanings. Sometimes, especially when Jesus talks about entering the kingdom, it would be more appropriate to think of a territory.

The Jews thought that when God established his rule, he would put an end to this abomination, the Roman rule of God's own people. We can understand why they were puzzled when Jesus talked about God's kingly rule. They didn't see it. Tiberius was still the emperor, and the Roman army was still exercising its unmitigated authority in the Holy Land. Where is this kingly rule of God? they wondered.

Jesus Brings the Kingly Rule of God

Luke gives an account of one of the exchanges between Jesus and the Pharisees. "Once, on being asked by the Pharisees when the kingdom of God would come, Jesus replied, 'The coming of the kingdom of God is not something that can be observed, nor will people say, "Here it is," or "There it is," because the kingdom of God is in your midst'" (Luke 17:20–21). As so often, Jesus and the Pharisees were on different wavelengths. The Pharisees were using the same language as Jesus, but they did not understand him. They were looking for the kingly rule of God, but they could not see it. "When will it come?" they wondered. "When can we see it?" You cannot see it, Jesus explained; it is not something that can be observed. The Pharisees were probably expecting spectacular cosmic phenomena, as when God revealed himself to Moses on Mount Sinai and covered the mountain in smoke (Exod. 19:18). The kingly rule of God does not manifest itself in this way. Nevertheless, it is right in your midst.

Jesus's point can only be that he himself brings the kingly rule of God. Where Jesus is, there God rules. When you see the person of Jesus Christ, then you see God's rule on earth. Where Jesus is, there is salvation, there is the new creation. Where Jesus is, there the world is the way God wants it to be. Evil must flee. Justice is established. There is life. There is blessedness. Everything is good. God's rule is there.

Many Christians will respond to this: Yes, when Jesus comes again, he will do all this. He will bring salvation and the new creation. He will establish justice, and God's will shall be carried out perfectly. God's kingdom is something we are still waiting for. It is not here, but it will come. We are eagerly expecting it. But Jesus is saying that the kingdom or kingly rule of God is in our midst now. He is not saying that it is coming later. He is not saying that it will be here in a few thousand years, and we have to just sit tight and wait. No. He is saying that it is in our midst. It is here. Now.

When Jesus came, he said that he was establishing the kingly rule of God. He did not lie, and he did not fail. He did what he said he did. He established the kingly rule of God. He brought the new creation. He brought salvation. It is already here. Where Jesus is, there is the kingly rule of God. There is salvation.

John Doesn't Understand

The Pharisees were not the only ones puzzled by Jesus's statement; John the Baptist was also perplexed, and it is not hard to see why. John the Baptist was one of the most fiery revival preachers the world has ever seen. He told people that the time was short. The great king was coming, and he was going to hold his people accountable. God was coming, and the people needed to get ready for his final judgment.

When I served in the Norwegian military, we frequently had to get ready for inspection. Some officer was coming, and this officer was going to examine us and see if we had fulfilled all our duties. Was our room clean? Was our closet tidy? Was our uniform in order? We knew that this officer was making his rounds every morning, so every day when we got out of bed, we were only focused on one thing: what we had to do to get ready for inspection. We made sure every square inch of our little room was completely clean. We started with mop and water and cleaned up everything as well as we could. And when we were done, we would get down on our hands and knees and go over everything with our bare hands to make sure that there was not a single speck of dust in our entire room. We had to be ready for the visitation by our superior officer. That inspection is nothing compared to the big inspection that John the Baptist was talking about. God himself, the creator of heaven and earth, the judge of the living and the dead, was coming to earth. And he was going to do an inspection. You'd better get ready, John the Baptist said, for this is serious.

We read about it in the Gospel of Luke: "John said to the crowds coming out to be baptized by him, 'You brood of vipers! Who warned you to flee from the coming wrath? Produce fruit in keeping with repentance. And do not begin to say to yourselves, "We have Abraham as our father." For I tell you that out of these stones God can raise up children for Abraham. The ax is already at the root of the trees, and every tree that does not produce good fruit will be cut down and thrown into the fire'" (Luke 3:7–9). God is coming, and he is going to judge the evildoers. "The ax is already at the root of the trees," and he is ready to swing it. He is going to chop down everyone who does not do his will. You'd better get your house in order for this inspection. You'd better get ready, because God is coming to judge, warned John.

When he saw Jesus, John knew: this is the one. This is the one who is coming. This is the one who is going to put everything in order. This is the one who is going to take care of everything. He will punish the wicked. He will bring justice and righteousness. But it didn't pan out exactly as John the Baptist thought it would. John was waiting for God's justice to be carried out, but instead John was thrown into prison. I am sure he was thinking: If Jesus is the one who would come and bring God's justice, what am I doing in prison? And why is King Herod still on the throne? If Jesus is the one who is coming with judgment and righteousness, he surely would take care of King Herod and punish him. That has got to be on the very top of his to-do list. But Herod is still on the throne, and I am in prison. There is something wrong with this picture. I must have gotten something wrong. I'd better ask Jesus about this.

Luke tells us that John sent two of his disciples to Jesus with a question:

> When the men came to Jesus, they said, "John the Baptist sent us to you to ask, 'Are you the one who is to come, or should we expect someone else?'"
> At that very time Jesus cured many who had diseases, sicknesses and evil spirits, and gave sight to many who were blind. So he replied to the messengers, "Go back and report to John what you have seen and heard: The blind receive sight, the lame walk, those who have leprosy are cleansed, the deaf hear, the dead are raised, and the good news is proclaimed to the poor. Blessed is anyone who does not stumble on account of me." (Luke 7:20–23)

John was wondering, Is this really what we have been waiting for? Is Jesus the one who was to come? Is he the one who is establishing the kingly rule of God and bringing God's justice? Look at what you have seen and heard, Jesus replied. "The blind receive sight, the lame walk, those who have leprosy are cleansed, the deaf hear, the dead are raised, and the good news is proclaimed to the poor." The significance of Jesus's answer would have been crystal clear to John the Baptist, who knew the Old Testament prophets well. In his reply, Jesus quoted from three different prophecies in the book of Isaiah (26:19; 35:5; 61:1). All these prophecies concern the time of salvation and the new creation that would become a reality when God intervened in the world to establish his kingly rule. I am doing it, Jesus said. The prophecies regarding the new creation are being fulfilled right before your eyes. Sickness and suffering are taken away. There is health. There is blessing. There is salvation. The new creation is here. Now. You can see it with your own eyes. Paralytics are playing football. Blind people have become stargazers. Dead people are jumping out of their graves. The new creation is here, the world as God intended it to be. The kingly rule of God is here.

There is a more subtle point that Jesus also is making in his reply to the Baptist. He is quoting from several passages in Isaiah, and all these passages have something to say about salvation and the new creation, but they also contain some serious words about God's judgment. When God comes to bring salvation, he is also going to punish the evildoers. But Jesus is not quoting any of these statements about judgment. He is quoting only words about salvation. The message is subtle but clear: Jesus fulfills the prophecies but in a different way than the Baptist expected. God's salvation is here at this moment, but his judgment on evildoers is not being carried out. The fulfillment of the promises looks different from what the Baptist had envisioned. Jesus brought God's kingly rule, but he did not come as a violent ruler. He came with kindness and humility, bringing healing and restoration.

Jesus brought the kingly rule of God while John the Baptist and his disciples were watching. That is the main point of Jesus's response to the Baptist, but his answer also contains an implied warning: "Blessed is anyone who does not stumble on account of me." It is possible to stumble on account of Jesus and to miss the fact that he is coming with the gifts of God. Those who do will lose out on the blessing he brings and place themselves under judgment.

A Present and Future Kingdom

While Jesus emphasizes that he brings salvation in the present, he also lets us know that he will come with judgment in the future. He announces his future coming as the Son of Man, when he will reward his people and punish the wicked (Matt. 25:31–46). Corresponding to this emphasis on the future, Jesus also speaks of the future emergence of God's kingly rule.

He teaches his disciples to pray, "Your kingdom come." This petition presupposes that in a certain sense the kingdom is not yet here. Otherwise there would be no reason to pray for it to come. On another occasion, when he is sharing the Last Supper with his disciples, he tells them that he "will not drink again from the fruit of the vine until the kingdom of God comes" (Luke 22:18). Once again, the presupposition is that the kingdom of God in some sense is not yet here: it is coming.

God's kingly rule is therefore both present and future. In one sense, we are still waiting for it to come. And it will come, when Jesus comes in the clouds with his holy angels. Then he will come in his glory, and he will establish God's kingly rule in such a way that everyone can see it, when he judges the evildoers. And yet, the kingly rule of God is already here. The new creation is already here. The gifts of salvation are already here. Where Jesus is, there is the kingly rule of God.

Defeat of Evil

For God's kingly rule to be reestablished, the powers that stand against him have to be defeated. The Old Testament hinted that the real enemies of God and his people are not Pharaoh or the king of Babylon but the spiritual powers that stand behind these evil empires. In the Gospels, this point is even clearer. King Herod and the emperor in Rome are not the ultimate adversaries. The real enemy is Satan and his army of evil spirits, the army that stands behind the leaders and power structures of this world, the spiritual forces that influence our world for their oppressive and destructive purposes. In the Gospels, we also see that these powers can control individual humans. There are people who have an evil spirit, and this spirit has so taken over their faculties that their behavior and their speech are controlled by that spirit.

When Jesus came, he defeated these spirits. He not only cast them out of people; he also brought about their complete downfall. This is why the spirits were so terrified whenever Jesus approached. The first account of Jesus's encounter with the demons that we find in Mark's Gospel is particularly instructive. When the man with an unclean spirit met Jesus, he cried out, "What have you to do with us, Jesus of Nazareth? Have you come to destroy us? I know who you are—the Holy One of God" (Mark 1:24). In a different account in Mark's Gospel, we hear about a man who had a number of evil spirits, but there is no indication in this story that Jesus was dealing with more than one such spirit. Nevertheless, the spirit spoke on behalf of not only himself but other spirits as well: "What have you to do with us?" He spoke like that because he knew what was happening. Jesus was coming, and he was taking down not only this spirit but all the evil spirits. "Have you come to destroy us?" the spirit cried. Yes, exactly. The great warrior God had come. He was waging war against his enemies, and he was going to destroy them. The time of their downfall was now. Jesus's victory was complete.

When he encountered the spirits, there was no extended conflict. Jesus was not fighting with the demons to see who would come out on top. There was no battle; there was no struggle. Jesus is so superior that there is no room for that. Jesus comes. The spirits run. That's all. Where Jesus is, the kingly rule of God is. There is no room for evil there. Where Jesus is, God's victory over evil is a fact. Evil has to flee. God's kingly rule is reestablished. The time is up for those who stand against God. Jesus brings the kingly rule of God, the new creation, the new world order in which God's will happens. Evil is history.

A Surprising Victory

Jesus's victory is won in a surprising way—so surprising that many people fail to realize that he has won. The nature of his victory is explained by Matthew and Luke, who offer a more detailed account of Jesus's confrontation with the devil. After his baptism, Jesus was in the wilderness where he was fasting for forty days and forty nights and where Satan came to tempt him. The tempter had three challenges for Jesus: (1) Turn stones to bread, (2) Throw yourself down from the highest point of the temple, and (3) "Bow down and worship me" (Matt. 4:3–9).

In the first challenge, Satan was reminding Jesus of what had just happened at his baptism, when God had spoken from heaven and declared that Jesus was his Son. "This is my Son, whom I love; with him I am well pleased," God had said (Matt. 3:17). Now Satan was daring him to prove it. "Are you really God's Son?" he challenged Jesus. "Then it would be a small task for you to take these stones and turn them into bread." Satan knew what he was doing. He knew that many Jews expected the Messiah to do something like what he was suggesting to Jesus. God had promised to raise up another prophet like Moses (Deut. 18:18), and since Moses was famous for his role in the provision of manna from heaven, the Messiah was also expected to perform a food miracle. When Jesus later did feed the multitudes, many Jews thought he might be the end-time prophet and wanted to make him king (John 6:14–15). If Jesus had taken Satan's suggestion, he could have made people understand that he really was the Messiah they had been waiting for. He really was the Son of God. What God had said at his baptism was really true. This would have been an easy way for Jesus to have been recognized as the Messiah. If Jesus had turned the stones into bread, he could have gone straight into his glory as king.

For the second challenge, Satan was taking Jesus to the highest point of the temple, the social, political, and religious center of Israel. Whatever happened at the temple would get the attention of the entire nation. It was the first-century equivalent to announcing something on the evening news or to seeing something go viral on social media. Everyone would know. Once again, the devil was daring Jesus to prove that he was the Son of God. "'If you are the Son of God,' he said, 'throw yourself down. For it is written: "He will command his angels concerning you, and they will lift you up in their hands, so that you will not strike your foot against a stone"'" (Matt. 4:6). What a perfect way for Jesus to show that he was the special one, the one God had chosen. If the angels came swooping in and flew him to safety as he fell down from the temple precipice, all Israel would see that Jesus enjoyed a special protection from God. He would have to be the Messiah, the Son of God. Once again, if Jesus had done what the devil proposed, he could have gone straight into his glory as the Messiah.

In the end, it seems as though the devil became a little desperate, because as the third challenge he asked Jesus to fall down and worship him. "The devil took him to a very high mountain and showed him all the kingdoms of the world and their splendor. 'All this I will give you,' he said, 'if you will bow down and worship me'" (Matt. 4:8–9). But this temptation is really the same as the other two. The devil was offering Jesus the chance to have all the glory of the Son of God, all the glory of the world.

It was God's plan that Jesus would receive all the world's glory. This plan entailed that Jesus would die on a cross for all the sins of the world. In this way, he would save his people from sin and death. By doing this, Jesus would enter into his glory. After his resurrection, Jesus explained it to two disciples on the way to Emmaus: "Did not the Messiah have to suffer these things and then enter his glory?" (Luke 24:26). God's plan was that Jesus would go into his glory through suffering. Satan's temptation was simple: Don't you want to have all that glory without the suffering? Just fall down and worship me. Just become my kind of Messiah. Just become the kind of Messiah that the people are waiting for, an impressive Messiah, someone who dazzles people with a spectacular display of power and strength, the kind of Messiah who turns stones into bread and commands an army of angels to carry him on their wings as he jumps from the pinnacle of the temple.

If Jesus had chosen to be a Messiah like that, he might have become more popular among the people. He might have gained a greater following than he did. He might have had an easier time getting the people to accept that he was indeed their Messiah. But he would have become a satanic Messiah. His glory would have been a satanic kind of glory. Satan's sin was that he wanted to be God; he wanted to take God's place. He was not content with the role that God had assigned to him.

Jesus's glory is of the exact opposite kind. From the beginning, Jesus was equal to God and shared all his glory. He did not have to reach for something that did not belong to him. But instead of reveling in his exalted status, Jesus made himself small. He came to the world not in great, obvious glory but in weakness, as the Father had assigned to him (cf. Phil. 2:6–8). He did not reach for the visible glory that the devil dangled before him. Even though Jesus, unlike

Satan, had a rightful claim to such glory, he chose to appear in weakness and suffering instead. And in this way, he completely defeated the devil. Against this kind of power, the devil is helpless. He has nothing to put up against the superior force of Jesus, the force that he demonstrated when he willingly put himself under suffering so that he could bring salvation to his people.

Jesus's way on this earth did not go straight into glory, as the devil tempted. Instead, his way went to the cross. His path led to a humiliating death. When he was hanging on the cross, his detractors were confident that they were right to condemn him. "He saved others; let him save himself if he is God's Messiah, the Chosen One," they said (Luke 23:35). They meant to make fun of him, but without knowing it they spoke a profound truth. Jesus had saved others, but he couldn't save himself. It was precisely because he had saved others that he could not save himself. He had brought salvation and new creation to the people. He could do that only because he had taken their place of suffering. He had taken their sins on himself. If he had stepped down from the cross, he could not have saved others. He would not have died for their sins and brought life and salvation into their lives. He could have gone straight into his glory, as Satan had suggested, but then he would not have been the Savior of the world.

Jesus won his decisive victory over the devil when he came to earth. It was a victory that was won through defeat. It was a victory that was won through suffering, by choosing the way of the cross, by giving up his own life. The power that proved superior to that of the devil was the power of sacrifice, the power that consisted in offering himself to die for his people. The devil was defenseless against this power.

A student once asked me why Jesus didn't just rebuke the devil and chase him away when he was tempted in the wilderness. I think we know the answer. Jesus is stronger than the devil, not because he matches the great power of the devil with something even greater of the same kind. It is not as if Jesus brings a gun to the fight when the devil brings a knife. Jesus's power is of a different nature. It is not a more impressive display of the strength that is admired in this world. It is the power of sacrifice. It is the power that was demonstrated when Jesus breathed his last on the cross, when even his heavenly Father had abandoned him because he had to suffer the punishment for all the sins in the world. With that power he disarmed the devil and made him crumble. With that power, he proved triumphant. The Roman officer who presided over Jesus's execution was the first one to affirm it. "When the centurion, who stood there in front of Jesus, saw how he died, he said, 'Surely this man was the Son of God!'" (Mark 15:39). The moment of Jesus's death was the moment of his perfect victory over evil.

The apostle Paul speaks of Jesus's crucifixion in the same way: "Having disarmed the powers and authorities, he made a public spectacle of them, triumphing over them by the cross" (Col. 2:15). From the Epistle to the Hebrews, we learn that "by his death he might break the power of him who holds the power of death—that is, the devil—and free those who all their lives were held in slavery by their fear of death" (Heb. 2:14–15; cf. 1 John 3:8). All evil powers were destroyed by Jesus; they lost their power and were exposed in their defeat. The time when Jesus won his victory over them is not some moment in the future, when Jesus will return; it was when Jesus was nailed to the cross. When it appeared that the powers of evil had triumphed over Jesus, neutralized him, and humiliated him, that was the time of Jesus's complete victory. That was the time when the powers and authorities were rendered utterly powerless. It was a surprising victory. Yet it was complete.

Jesus Deals with the Root Problem

The power of Jesus's sacrifice is the power that truly changes the world. It is the power that brings salvation and the new creation. And it began right away. Where Jesus was, the power of healing was present. People just had to touch him, and the healing power would emanate from him and cure them of their diseases (cf. Mark 5:25–34). Jesus could do such miracles because he had dealt with the problem of evil once and for all. To deal with sickness, suffering, and disaster, Jesus had to go to the heart of the matter. The root cause is that the world has turned against its Creator; humans have sinned against God and ignored his righteous rule.

It may appear confusing that the effects of Jesus's victory were on display before he died, even though the New Testament clearly shows that Jesus won his victory when he died on the cross (John 12:31; Col. 2:15; Heb. 2:14). From the New Testament, we learn that Jesus triumphed through suffering and that his cross represents his victory, but his defeat of evil forces may also be associated with his earthly ministry in general (Luke 10:18; 11:22; 2 Tim. 1:10; 1 John 3:8). The New Testament is focused more on explaining the nature of Jesus's victory than on associating it with a particular date in history.

On one occasion, some men carried a paralyzed man to Jesus. When they could not get close to him because of the crowd, they hauled the man up to the roof of the house, and proceeded to tear it open so they could lower the man down in front of Jesus. When he addressed the man, Jesus showed that he was curing both the sickness and the underlying issue of human sin. Before he did anything with the fact that the man was bedridden, he told him:

"Son, your sins are forgiven" (Mark 2:5). Later he also healed the man, and he explained that the healing was a consequence of the forgiveness. He told those who were sitting there: "'But so that you may know that the Son of Man has authority on earth to forgive sins'—he said to the paralytic—'I say to you, stand up, take your mat and go to your home'" (2:10–11 NRSV). The healing demonstrated that the man had already been forgiven.

This does not mean that there was a connection between the man's individual sin and his personal suffering. He was not paralyzed because he was a greater sinner than other people. We must not think that when people are suffering from some particular disease, it is because they have committed some particular sin. Jesus repeatedly warns us against such a misunderstanding (Luke 13:1–5; John 9:1–5). Instead what Jesus means is that there is a fundamental connection between sin and suffering. The reason why people are sick and suffer is that there is sin in the world. And the reason why Jesus can do something about our suffering is that he has suffered for our sins and forgiven them.

Jesus has triumphed over evil because he has taken care of the problem of sin once and for all. "Christ was sacrificed once to take away the sins of many" (Heb. 9:28). He has won his victory by the superior power of sacrifice and forgiveness. He has conquered evil by choosing the way of suffering, so that he could bring salvation to his people. He died so that he could give us life. He suffered the punishment for sins so that he could forgive them.

In this way, he has banished evil. Wherever Jesus is, evil must flee because Jesus brings forgiveness and new life. He transforms every situation. He brings healing where there is sickness. He brings forgiveness where there is sin. He brings peace where there is discord. He brings love where there is hatred. He brings joy where there is bitterness. John the Baptist said that Jesus is "the Lamb of God, who takes away the sin of the world" (John 1:29). He takes our sin—away.

As the powers of evil are deposed, the rightful king is taking his place on the throne. As the regime of evil has been toppled, a new government is being installed. Christ's rule is of an entirely different nature than any other government the world has seen. This king is a different kind of king.

Further Reading

To scholars such as **Adolf von Harnack**, the kingdom of God means that God rules in the soul of the individual, but there is now broad agreement that God's kingly rule comes through divine intervention in history. **Johannes Weiss** in *Jesus' Proclamation of the Kingdom of God*, trans. and with an introduction by Richard Hyde Hiers and David Larrimore Holland, Scholars Press Reprints and Translations Series (Philadelphia: Fortress, 1971; originally published in German in 1892) and **Albert Schweitzer** in *The Mystery of the Kingdom of God: The Secret of Jesus' Messiahship and Passion*, trans. Walter Lowry (New York: Dodd, Mead, 1914; originally published in German in 1901) are famous for arguing that Jesus expected God's kingly rule to arrive sometime in the near future and to put an end to the current world order.

The pendulum of scholarship swung to the opposite extreme through the work of **Charles Harold Dodd**, who claimed in *The Parables of the Kingdom* (London: Nisbet, 1936) that Jesus understood God's kingly rule to be breaking into the world in the present through his own ministry. Dodd is known for the phrase "realized eschatology," which means that the end has already arrived. Dodd had little room for a future fulfillment of the kingdom.

Dodd has been influential, but his one-sided emphasis on the present nature of the kingdom has been modified by subsequent scholars. In *Christ and Time: The Primitive Christian Conception of Time and History*, trans. Floyd V. Filson (Philadelphia: Westminster, 1950)—a book that proved influential for later evangelical scholarship—**Oscar Cullmann** compares the establishment of the kingdom to an earthly war, in which the decisive victory may be won before the war is officially over. World War II provides an illustration: the Allied forces secured their victory on D-Day, June 6, 1944, even though the Germans did not formally surrender until May 8, 1945.

In his famous study *The Parables of Jesus* (London: SCM, 1954, originally published in German in 1947), **Joachim Jeremias** describes Jesus's teaching on the kingdom as "eschatology in the process of realization."

To explain the nature of the kingdom, **Norman Perrin** in his book *Jesus and the Language of the Kingdom: Symbol and Metaphor in New Testament Interpretation* (Philadelphia: Fortress, 1976) uses the term "tensive symbol" to indicate that the kingdom has a multifaceted meaning.

George Eldon Ladd in *Jesus and the Kingdom: The Eschatology of Biblical Realism* (New York: Harper & Row, 1966) and **George Beasley-Murray** in *Jesus and the Kingdom of God* (Grand Rapids: Eerdmans, 1986) have argued that God's kingly rule is already present yet also awaits its full manifestation in the future.

In his influential work *Jesus and the Victory of God*, vol. 2 of *Christian Origins and the Question of God* (Minneapolis: Fortress, 1996), **N. T. Wright** argues that Jesus's proclamation of the kingdom represents the culmination of Israel's story but in an unexpected way. On Wright's reading, Israel was still in exile, but the coming of the kingdom meant the end of the exile and victory over evil. Through the ministry and death of Jesus, God was coming as king to Zion.

In reaction to an excessive emphasis on the future nature of the kingdom, **N. T. Wright** in *How God Became King: The Forgotten Story of the Gospels* (New

York: HarperOne, 2012) also emphasizes the present nature of the kingdom in the ministry of Jesus, who came to earth to rule as king and form a renewed people of God. He brought his rule through his crucifixion and calls his people to rule through their suffering.

In contrast, **Dale Allison** in *Jesus of Nazareth: Millenarian Prophet* (Minneapolis: Fortress, 1998) and *Constructing Jesus: Memory and Imagination* (Grand Rapids: Baker Academic, 2009), much like Weiss and Schweitzer, argues that the historical Jesus expected God's kingdom to arrive in the imminent future.

E. P. Sanders also maintains in *Jesus and Judaism* (Philadelphia: Fortress, 1985) that the kingdom was primarily a future entity in the teaching of Jesus.

For interaction with many other scholars as well, see **Sigurd Grindheim**, *God's Equal: What Can We Know about Jesus' Self-Understanding?*, Library of New Testament Studies 446 (London: T&T Clark, 2011), where I emphasize that Jesus established God's kingly rule through his ministry. This book provides the more technical arguments for the interpretations adopted in this chapter.

In *Temptations of Jesus in Early Christianity*, Journal for the Study of the New Testament Supplement Series 112 (Sheffield: Sheffield Academic, 1995), **Jeffrey Gibson** shows that the nature of Jesus's temptations was to choose the way of glory rather than suffering.

G. K. Beale in *A New Testament Biblical Theology: The Unfolding of the Old Testament in the New* (Grand Rapids: Baker Academic, 2011), 227–316, ties the inauguration of God's kingdom and the new creation to Christ's resurrection. He argues that the theology of the New Testament should be understood in light of the fact that Christ has inaugurated this kingdom.

In his textbook *A Theology of the New Testament*, ed. Donald A. Hagner (Grand Rapids: Eerdmans, 1993), **George Eldon Ladd** describes the kingdom in light of the contrast between the present age and the age to come. The kingdom represents the inbreaking of the age to come.

Udo Schnelle, in his textbook *Theology of the New Testament*, trans. M. Eugene Boring (Grand Rapids: Baker Academic, 2009), discusses the future and present nature of the kingdom and speaks of the "proleptic presence of the future" (61–162).

Thomas R. Schreiner in *New Testament Theology: Magnifying God in Christ* (Grand Rapids: Baker Academic, 2008), 41–79, understands the kingdom as the saving power of God, in fulfillment of his promises. In the Gospel of John, he argues, "eternal life" represents a similar idea (80–95), and the rest of the New Testament uses other concepts—such as two ages, new creation, and the gift of the Holy Spirit—to express the same thought (96–116).

3

A Different King

Christ's Kingship

Most Jews in Jesus's time did not see much evidence of God's kingly rule in their midst. Their land was controlled by the Romans, who did not respect the laws of Israel's God. Many Jews felt that their own leaders were to blame. As their history had shown, ungodly leadership brought God's judgment on the nation. If only God would raise up the right leader for them, as he had done so many times in ancient days!

Pious Jews looked to the sayings of the prophets, to God's promises that he would give them a king like David once again. The prophet Isaiah had foretold that this messianic king would be called

> Wonderful Counselor, Mighty God,
> Everlasting Father, Prince of Peace.
> Of the greatness of his government and peace
> there will be no end.
> He will reign on David's throne
> and over his kingdom,
> establishing and upholding it
> with justice and righteousness
> from that time on and forever. (Isa. 9:6–7)

The leaders Israel had, both secular and religious, fell woefully short of this poetic description. Justice and righteousness were not the means by which they established and upheld their throne. They relied on corruption instead. Colluding with the Romans, they secured their power by oppressing their own people. With such leaders, Israel could not experience the blessings of God.

Today as well, poor leadership prevents us from enjoying the blissful rule of God. The reasons why poor countries are poor are very complex, but in many cases dysfunctional governments bear a lot of the responsibility. Development aid does not reach those who need it because government officials misdirect the funds, making sure the money ends up with their own family members rather than with the intended recipients.

In countries with stronger democratic traditions, the people choose their leaders. Elections are a reflection of the faith the people have in their politicians. Those who are elected tend to be those who promise to make the world, or at least their own country, a better place. Education will improve, and health care will be better and more affordable. Jobs will be more available, be better, and will offer higher pay. We will all enjoy more wealth, and in general we will be better off than we were last year.

The promise of economic gain often takes center stage at elections, but some politicians try to focus on ethical values as well. They promise more economic equality, better treatment of women and minorities, and a responsible stewardship of the environment. Others emphasize their efforts in supporting family values, lowering crime, ensuring law and order, making the country safe, and keeping out unwanted elements.

After so many promises and such meager results, many people have lost faith in their politicians. Many countries have seen a veritable rebellion against the political class, and candidates without political experience have benefited by emphasizing their "outsider" credentials. But whether people turn to experienced politicians or unconventional candidates, one underlying assumption stays the same. People believe that political leaders hold the power to make their lives and their world better. If they are disappointed with the development of their community or the opportunities they see in their personal lives, their political leaders are to blame. People think that if they could only get the right leaders—whether those with the right ideology, the right experience, and the right intelligence and temperament or those able to distinguish themselves by their lack of conventional credentials—things would be different.

The election of the right leader will prove to be, in the words of President Obama's acceptance speech, "the moment when the rise of the oceans began to slow and our planet began to heal; . . . the moment when we ended a war and secured our nation and restored our image as the last, best hope on

Earth." It will be the time when every individual in the country, in the words of President Trump's acceptance speech, "will have the opportunity to realize his or her fullest potential. The forgotten men and women of our country will be forgotten no longer. . . . We will double our growth and have the strongest economy anywhere in the world. . . . No dream is too big, no challenge is too great. Nothing we want for our future is beyond our reach."

The Messiah

In New Testament times, several individuals aspired to be the God-ordained leader who would bring better times to Israel. In some cases, people even believed that these individuals were the Messiah. The most famous of them was the leader of the Second Jewish Revolt against Rome in 132–135 CE, Simon bar Kokhba (Simeon bar Koziba). Rabbi Akiba declared him to be the Messiah. When Emperor Hadrian decided to make Jerusalem a pagan city and outlaw the practice of circumcision, Simon organized a military rebellion against the Roman troops in Judea. It is possible that Simon was able to gain control of Jerusalem for a limited time, but the available historical sources are not entirely clear about that. In any case, to crush the revolt, Hadrian sent his best military officers to Jerusalem and even traveled there himself. He showed no mercy. According to later Jewish sources, "They kept slaughtering the Jews until a horse sunk into blood up to his nose, and the blood would roll boulders" (Jerusalem Talmud, *Ta'anit* 4.69a). Today, no one believes that Simon was the Messiah that God had promised.

As Simon bar Kokhba's example shows, some Jews believed that the Messiah would accomplish his goals through military means, but other Jews were of a different persuasion. They believed that the ethical and religious qualifications of the Messiah were more important than his military prowess.

The Jewish library known as the Dead Sea Scrolls is famous for the manuscripts containing the books of the Old Testament. These manuscripts are many hundred years older than other known manuscripts, and they provide valuable knowledge about the transmission of the Old Testament writings. But this library also contains many nonbiblical works, and many of these writings show a great interest in Israel's Messiah. This community was apparently expecting both a priestly and a royal Messiah. Neither one of them would be known as a hero of war, however. In one of the Dead Sea Scrolls, the Messiah is also called the Son of God, and he will make peace, not war. "His kingdom will be an eternal kingdom, and all his paths in truth.

He will judge the earth in truth and all will make peace. The sword will cease from the earth, and all the provinces will pay him homage" (4Q246 2.5–7a).[1]

Jewish expectations of the Messiah were quite diverse, much like contemporary Christian expectations of the future. Christians look forward to the day when Jesus will come again, but they cannot even agree on how many times he will come. The Jews at the time of Jesus knew that the Messiah would come; Herod's sages even knew in what town he would be born (Matt. 2:4–5). Jews would have agreed that the Messiah was going to bring God's rule to Israel. He would eliminate all the problems in society and bring peace and prosperity to the land. If you asked a Jew how the Messiah would accomplish these things, the answers would vary greatly. Some would think of a military victory over the Roman oppressors; others would envision a religious awakening among the people of Israel. Their expectations may be compared to the expectations people have of political leaders today. The right leader will bring a good society. That is what everyone expects. When the question concerns the means to make it happen, opinions differ.

In one respect, there was agreement among most Jews, however. Like most people today who are looking for politicians to make great changes, Jews were looking for a human ruler who would lead them into a better world. In the Old Testament, the Messiah is given names that are only appropriate for God himself. He is "Wonderful Counselor, Mighty God, Everlasting Father, Prince of Peace" (Isa. 9:6). But all available evidence shows that the Jewish people did not expect a divine Messiah. The Messiah they were waiting for was a human. He was not God. In a Jewish book known as *Fourth Ezra*, from around 100 CE, the reign of the Messiah is said to last for four hundred years. When his time is complete, the Messiah will die, and the end of the world will come (*4 Ezra* [= 2 Esdras] 7:28–29).

Greater Than a Messiah

When Jesus came, many Jews were wondering if he might be the Messiah. In some ways he conformed to their expectations, but in other ways he did not. Jesus himself affirmed that he was the Messiah (Mark 14:61–62; John 4:25–26), but he also wanted his followers to know that he was more than the Messiah they were waiting for.

1. Florentino García Martínez and Eibert J. C. Tigchelaar, eds., *The Dead Sea Scrolls: Study Edition*, 2 vols. (Leiden: Brill, 1997–98), 1:495.

The Messiah was the king of Israel, and the messianic kingdom was the Israelite kingdom. But Jesus brought something greater. He brought the kingdom of God, the universal kingdom in which God would rule, not only over Israel, not only over all the earth, but over heaven as well. He would defeat not only his people's earthly enemies but their spiritual enemies too. When he came to earth, he demonstrated his complete triumph in the way he dealt with the evil spirits and made them flee. When Jesus came, the power of evil was broken.

When he cast out the demons, people were puzzled by Jesus's overwhelming power. His detractors tried to claim that Jesus was in cahoots with the devil himself. "By Beelzebul, the prince of demons, he is driving out demons," they said (Luke 11:15). It was a desperate attempt to discredit him. How could Satan be driving out Satan? In response, Jesus explains the true nature of his power: "If I drive out demons by the finger of God, then the kingdom of God has come upon you" (11:20). With Jesus's presence and ministry, the kingdom of God has already arrived. It is already present. And the proof of its presence is that the demons have to flee.

The reason why Jesus has the power to bring the kingdom of God is that he is driving out the demons by the finger of God. By saying this, Jesus has implicitly identified his own work with the work of God. When he casts out the demons, it is God who is casting them out. Jesus is not acting on God's behalf; he is doing God's work himself because he himself is God. He is not only a human Messiah. He is a ruler who has come with the power and authority of God himself.

This truth was very difficult for the Jewish people to understand, as it is for us today. The Bible teaches that there is only one God (Deut. 6:4), and he is known as God the Father in heaven. Jesus was not himself the Father; he prayed to the Father and made it clear that he was the Son of the Father. But he was the Son in such a way that he shared all power and authority with the Father (John 5:19–27) and was equal to him (5:18). Because of that, Jesus also shares the name of God (1:1, 18; 20:28; 1 John 5:20).

Jesus spoke with the same authority as God. For ordinary humans, it would be blasphemous to add something and expand on the word of God. When God speaks, we listen and obey; we don't try to improve on what he said. When Jesus quoted from the Old Testament, he made clear that his own words were more important than the text he was quoting. "You have heard that it was said to the people long ago," he says, and then he quotes from the law of Moses: "'You shall not murder, and anyone who murders will be subject to judgment.'" Crucially, however, he continues, "But I tell you that anyone who is angry with a brother or sister, will be subject to judgment"

(Matt. 5:21–22). Only Jesus quotes Scripture and proceeds to say, "But I tell you." His own words take precedence over the divine words of the Old Testament; he develops the commandment of God and takes it to a new level. A mere human cannot do that without blaspheming. But when Jesus speaks, it is God himself who speaks.

Jesus not only talked the talk but walked the walk. He did things that only God can do. When he and his disciples were in a little fishing boat on Lake Galilee, the storms threatened to sink the boat and let all of them perish. Jesus silenced the sea and waves merely by talking to them, controlling weather phenomena with divine power (Mark 4:35–41).

He told people to sell all their possessions, give the money to the poor, and follow him (Mark 10:21). He insisted that he was more important than people's families, even their father and mother, spouse and children (Luke 14:26). He would not accept that people had any priorities that took precedence over their duties toward him. What he was demanding was that people love him with all their heart and all their soul and all their mind and all their strength. In other words, they would fulfill the commandment to love God (Deut. 6:5) by loving him. He wanted to be their God.

Most Jews found Jesus's claims to be unacceptable. They did not believe that he was God's Son, and they did not accept his authority to do the things that only God can do, such as to forgive sins and to judge the living and the dead. When Jesus explained that he was able to do these things, he was accused of blasphemy because he implicitly said that he was equal to God (Mark 2:7; 14:64; John 10:33).

Like political leaders today, Jesus divided opinion. Some believed what he said, and they believed that he was the one who brought the kingly rule of God, the new world order that would ensure peace, harmony, and happiness for all. Others thought he was a fraud, a man who talked big and made promises he could never keep.

The reasons why people were divided about Jesus had nothing to do with political ideology, however. Jesus did not come with a controversial message that some people embraced and others rejected. Jesus's message was his own person. He did not come to teach a new philosophy, a new way of life, or a new religion. He made a much more outrageous claim. He maintained that he was God and had come to establish God's rule on earth. He had come to provide the ultimate solution to the problem of evil and usher in a new age of pure bliss. Jesus came with promises that not even the most audacious politician would dare to offer. He came to make the dream of utopia a reality. He came to bring an entirely new creation, an age of salvation, the kingly rule of God.

Why Jesus Had to Come

Politicians always end up being a disappointment. They are never able to keep all their promises. But they are also put in an impossible position. What people expect of them is more than anyone can deliver. One of America's leading intellectuals, Noam Chomsky, holds political views that most Americans do not share, but he understands some fundamental issues very well. His explanation for the failure of the political process is as profound as it is simple. In the movie *Requiem for the American Dream* (2015), he states it succinctly: "I don't think we're smart enough to design in any detail what a perfectly just and free society would be like."[2] What we hope to accomplish is simply beyond our reach. We are unable to realize our dreams for a good society. As humans, we don't have it in us.

God's promise of the Messiah was given to King David. David's throne would be established forever, and his offspring would have an eternal kingdom (2 Sam. 7:12–16). In light of these promises, the expectations of David's son Solomon could hardly have been greater. His early reign showed some exciting potential, but in the end Solomon proved to be a failure. His oppressive policies eventually led to the dissolution of the Israelite kingdom.

Of the kings who followed in David's line, some were good and some were bad. Kings like Hezekiah and Josiah instituted some promising reforms, but the positive developments did not last. In the sixth century BCE, Judah was conquered by the reigning superpower, the Babylonian Empire. David's offspring had failed to deliver, and God's promise seemed to have come to nothing.

The kings of Israel had enjoyed the best preconditions for success. They ruled a nation that had been chosen by God. The nation's constitution had been written by God himself. Their laws were perfect since they were of divine origin. God had promised to be with them and protect these kings, yet the kings still turned out to be failures. A just society was beyond their reach, as it has been for every political leader who has tried to institute it.

For the promise to be fulfilled, God had to take matters into his own hands. He had to intervene personally. It was not enough for political leaders to have God's backing. It was not enough for them to have his help. To establish God's rule was not something humans could do, no matter what God did to empower them.

This is why the political process will never be ultimately successful. Humans are not capable of accomplishing the goal of a just society, no matter

---

2. In 2017, Chomsky published a book by the same title with Seven Stories Press.

what tools they are given or have at their disposal. Humans cannot usher in utopia. They cannot establish a genuinely good rule, the rule of God. They cannot bring salvation to earth.

God's Messiah had to be more than a Messiah of David's lineage. While he came as a human and a descendant of David, he also had to be more than a human, more than David's son. He had to be God's Son, God's equal. That was the only way in which God's rule could be reestablished on earth. God had to take care of it himself. No human had the resources necessary to defeat the evil forces. God had to do it on his own.

God's sending his Son to the world is the ultimate condemnation of all human attempts at accomplishing what is good. They have failed irredeemably, and it could never be different. People cannot save themselves. Not even help from heaven can change that. "I know that good itself does not dwell in me, that is, in my sinful nature," the apostle Paul confesses (Rom. 7:18). This insight is driving him toward despair: "What a wretched man I am! Who will rescue me from this body that is subject to death?" (7:24).

God's sending his Son into the world is the only reason why there is hope in the midst of this despair. "For what the law was powerless to do because it was weakened by the flesh, God did by sending his own Son in the likeness of sinful flesh to be a sin offering" (Rom. 8:3). The law that Paul is talking about is the good and spiritual law of God (7:14). But even with the help of this excellent law, humans were unable to accomplish that which is good. God had to send his own Son to make things right. Human sin had made it impossible for us to see God's good will being realized. But God's Son dealt with the problem of human sin once and for all. "And so he condemned sin in the flesh, in order that the righteous requirement of the law might be fully met in us, who do not live according to the flesh but according to the Spirit" (Rom. 8:3–4). Now the rule of God could be carried out; now God's good will, as revealed in his perfect law, could be fulfilled by his people.

When Jesus came as the Messiah and the Son of God, he didn't come as a human leader who would institute a superior political system that would bring a just society. He didn't teach a new ideology that would finally solve our social ills. He did something altogether different.

In Matthew's Gospel, Jesus often teaches about the "kingdom of heaven" rather than the "kingdom of God." The two terms refer to the same reality, as we can understand when we compare the parallel accounts in Matthew and Mark. Where Mark refers to the "kingdom of God" (10:23), Matthew refers to the "kingdom of heaven" (19:23). Matthew also uses the two terms interchangeably (compare 19:23 and 19:24). What is the purpose of using the term "kingdom of heaven," then, if it does not have a different meaning than "kingdom of God"? Matthew is the only evangelist who uses this language, and since Matthew is the most Jewish of all the Gospels, many interpreters have found this terminology to reflect his Jewishness. Jews often avoid direct references to God. They never pronounce the divine name, and they often refer to God indirectly with terms like "the Blessed One." Many scholars think that Matthew preferred the term "kingdom of heaven" in order to avoid direct references to God. However, this explanation is not compelling. Matthew has no problem referring to God directly; he does it frequently, and he also uses the term "kingdom of God" many times. A better explanation is therefore that Matthew wants to emphasize the well-known contrast between heaven and earth. When he refers to the "kingdom of heaven," he stresses the fact that this kingdom stands in contrast to the kingdoms on earth. It is much greater than they are and of a completely different nature. Whereas earthly kingdoms will pass away, this kingdom will last forever. Jesus brought a kingdom that was entirely different from all the kingdoms on earth. He brought a heavenly kingdom, a divine and eternal kingdom.

This divine kingdom had to be brought by none other than God himself. No mere human could do it. When Jesus came as ruler of his kingdom, he came as God. His work was the work of the finger of God. And he did what God does. Jesus created something new out of nothing. Where there was death, he brought life. Where there was sickness, he brought health. Where there was sorrow, he brought joy. Where there was hatred, he brought reconciliation. Where there was enmity, he brought peace. Where evil reigned, he brought the rule of God.

The Nature of Divine Power

The reason why Jesus could bring the rule of God was that he came with a completely different kind of power than the power of humans. On one occasion he explained to his disciples the nature of his divine power. It was an explanation they would not be able to understand until much later. Jesus and his disciples were preparing to go up to Jerusalem. The twelve disciples were full of expectation. They had heard Jesus talk about the kingdom of God, and they probably thought that this kingdom now would come with power. Jerusalem was the city that God had chosen, and it was the city from which his Messiah would rule the world. When Jesus soon would enter the Holy City, he would certainly establish the full kingly rule of God. The Twelve had followed Jesus from the beginning. Surely Jesus would not forget this now that he was going to establish his kingdom. When he was going to appoint his government, he would have to turn to them first. The disciples were excited.

James and John, known for their quick temper, decided that they were going to be proactive and talk to Jesus ahead of time. When he reached Jerusalem and his kingdom appeared, all his indecisive, half-hearted supporters would no doubt crawl out of the woodwork and compete for Jesus's attention. James and John realized that they had better act now, when they could enjoy their privileged access to Jesus without interruption. So they approached him with their request: "Let one of us sit at your right and the other at your left in your glory" (Mark 10:37). They thought Jesus was just about to appear in the glory of his kingdom, and they wanted to submit their request before it was too late.

James and John did not understand what they were asking, for they did not understand the nature of Jesus's power. They thought he would have the kind of power that earthly rulers have, but nothing could be further from the truth. Jesus showed his power through his death. He exercised his might by suffering, by being humiliated, and by appearing to suffer the ultimate defeat: the shameful death of crucifixion at the hands of the arrogant and brutal Roman army.

Jesus had to explain the difference between his power and the power of this world:

> You know that those who are regarded as rulers of the Gentiles lord it over them, and their high officials exercise authority over them. Not so with you. Instead, whoever wants to become great among you must be your servant, and whoever wants to be first must be slave of all. For even the Son of Man did not come to be served, but to serve, and to give his life as a ransom for many. (Mark 10:42–45)

Powerful people in this world rise to the top by always taking care to display strength. Anything that might give the appearance of weakness is vigilantly kept hidden. In the criminal world, power is projected through brutality. When drug lords eliminate their rivals, they are not content just to kill them; they make an example of their competitors. They provide elaborate displays of sadism so that other potential rivals will be paralyzed by fear that something similar might happen to them. The ones who rise to the top in that world are the ones who excel in violence.

In politics, things work in a similar way, but usually more subtly. Those who aspire to power need to project strength. They cannot afford to be seen as weak. When they are facing challenges, they need to divert attention. Few things work better than to highlight the perceived weaknesses of their opponents, as every negative election campaign amply demonstrates. In a crisis situation, swift and decisive action is necessary: find someone to blame and make an example of them.

An even more ruthless strategy is to attack weak and marginal groups. Hitler blamed the Jews for all the ills of society, and many a politician has borrowed from his playbook. They have nourished people's fears of minorities that do not fit into mainstream society. Picking on the weak always works as a way to give the appearance of strength, all the way from the playground to the political arena.

Even church leaders follow a similar strategy. They hide their sins carefully and present a public persona characterized by piety, hard work in service of the church, a happy family life, and excellent mental health. In their sermons, pastors may mention that they know temptations to sin, and occasionally they may even have fallen, but their sins are of the kind that everyone commits every day—certainly not anything egregious, such as sexual immorality. Pastors portray themselves as not having psychological problems and their families as textbook examples of harmony and happiness.

Every once in a while these illusions are shattered, and we hear about church leaders who have led a secret life. They have embezzled funds from the church or had an extramarital affair. Their secrets may have been hidden for many years, and they may have been very successful in their ministry. As long as they had been able to conceal the truth and maintain their perfect facade, they had been able to rise to the top in the church.

The ways of the world, and too often the ways of the church, are epitomized well by Jesus: "Those who are regarded as rulers of the Gentiles lord it over them, and their high officials exercise authority over them." But Jesus shows us a different way: "Not so with you. Instead, whoever wants to become great among you must be your servant, and whoever wants to be first must be slave of all. For even the Son of Man did not come to be served, but to serve, and to give his life as a ransom for many."

Jesus himself provided the ultimate example of this different kind of power. He appeared in this world with divine strength, the power that could bring salvation and do what no human would ever be capable of doing. His power functions in exactly the opposite way from the powers of this world. Jesus showed his strength in weakness. He triumphed by dying. He accomplished his purpose by giving his life as a ransom for many. His death brought freedom to his followers; it set them free from sin and death.

Divine power is not more of the kind of power we already know from this world. It is the opposite. It is the power of service, the power of humiliating oneself, lowering oneself, and taking the place of a slave. In his relationship with his disciples, Jesus honored them as a slave would treat a master. On the night before his death, Jesus "got up from the meal, took off his outer clothing, and wrapped a towel around his waist. After that, he poured water into a basin and began to wash his disciples' feet, drying them with the towel that was wrapped around him" (John 13:4–5). Jesus did the degrading work of a slave, washing the dirty feet of his disciples. He showed his power, not by elevating himself above others, but by debasing himself and by serving them.

Jesus's power is the power that truly transforms the world. It is the power that brings the new creation, the kingly rule of God, because it is the power that brings the rule of love, not the rule of coercion. Jesus triumphs over evil by thwarting its power. One does not defeat violence by escalating it. One does not put an end to violence by exacting vengeance. All that vengeance can do is to perpetuate the cycle of violence. But the cycle of violence is broken when someone has the audacity to forgive instead of taking revenge.

In the small African country of Rwanda, the Belgian colonial power had arbitrarily divided the population into two groups, the Tutsi and the Hutu. The Tutsi were designated to be the rulers, and the Hutu were given a subservient role. In the 1990s the country was ravaged by civil war between these two groups, a war that resulted in the Rwandan genocide of 1994. Between half a million and a million Tutsi and moderate Hutu were massacred in carefully planned attacks.

Since the genocide, the country has gone through a period of reconciliation. Tutsi survivors of the atrocities and family members of those killed confront the Hutu perpetrators, and the perpetrators confess and take responsibility for their crimes. Then the victims grant them forgiveness.

During the genocide, Godefroid Mudaheranwa had attacked and tried to kill Evasta Mukanyandi and her children, but he was unsuccessful, which he now attributes to God's protection. Years later, he approached Evasta and asked for her forgiveness. "I used to hate him," Evasta testifies. "When he came to my house and knelt down before me and asked for forgiveness, I was moved by his sincerity. Now, if I cry for help, he comes to rescue me. When I face any issue, I call him."

François Ntambara killed the son of Epiphanie Mukamusoni. Afterward he decided to ask her for forgiveness. She granted it to him, and the two are now reconciled. "We share in everything," François says. "If she needs some water to drink, I fetch some for her. There is no suspicion between us, whether under sunlight or during the night. I used to have nightmares recalling the sad events I have been through, but now I can sleep peacefully. And when we are together, we are like brother and sister, no suspicion between us."[3]

3. Susan Dominus, "Portraits of Reconciliation," New York Times Magazine, https://www.nytimes.com/interactive/2014/04/06/magazine/06-pieter-hugo-rwanda-portraits.html.

The power of forgiveness breaks the cycle of violence and brings reconciliation where there was hatred. This is the power of Jesus. He defeats the power of violence, not only on the individual level but also on the cosmic level, by taking all the sins of the world on himself. He dies for them and offers forgiveness for them. That is the nature of divine power. This kind of power transformed the nation of Rwanda, and this is the power with which Jesus establishes his kingdom. With this power, he gathers a people for his kingdom, a people that will know the benefits of having such a mighty king.

Further Reading

Many New Testament scholars believe that Jesus did not claim to be divine in the way the church has later understood him to be. In his book *Jesus the Jew: A Historian's Reading of the Gospels* (London: Collins, 1973), the Hungarian Jew **Géza Vermès** argues that Jesus was a charismatic miracle worker within Judaism.

E. P. Sanders, who wrote *Jesus and Judaism* (Philadelphia: Fortress, 1985), thinks that Jesus's conflict with the establishment was caused by his attack on the temple. As a prophet who believed God was about to fulfill his promises for the restoration of Israel, he announced the destruction and replacement of the temple and the reconstitution of Israel centered around the twelve disciples. He probably saw himself as king in the new kingdom and differed from his contemporaries in accepting sinners without requiring repentance.

In *The Historical Jesus: The Life of a Mediterranean Jewish Peasant* (New York: HarperCollins, 1991), a famous member of the Jesus Seminar,[4] **John Dominic Crossan**, sees Jesus as a peasant Jewish Cynic and a magician. Valuing practice above theory, Jesus used his combination of free healing and common eating to protest against the economic and social elite. Thereby he announced the egalitarian and unmediated kingdom of God.

According to **James Dunn** in *Jesus Remembered*, vol. 1 of *Christianity in the Making* (Grand Rapids: Eerdmans, 2003), Jesus was God's final spokesperson, who proclaimed the kingdom of God. This mission was more important than any titles Jesus may have claimed.

In contrast to these scholars, **I. Howard Marshall** argues in *The Origins of New Testament Christology* (Downers Grove, IL: InterVarsity, 1990) that the church's confession of Jesus as the Son of God was based on the claims that Jesus had been making for himself.

---

4. The Jesus Seminar was a collection of scholars who met periodically during the 1980s and '90s to evaluate the historicity of the Gospel accounts concerning Jesus's words and actions. They were generally skeptical about the historical reliability of most of the Gospel content.

In his work *Jesus and the Victory of God*, vol. 2 of *Christian Origins and the Question of God* (Minneapolis: Fortress, 1996), **N. T. Wright** maintains that the coming of Jesus represents the coming of Israel's God to Zion.

The argument presented above is what I have developed in more detail and through interaction with other scholars in **Sigurd Grindheim**, *God's Equal: What Can We Know about Jesus' Self-Understanding?*, Library of New Testament Studies 446 (London: T&T Clark, 2011). There I maintain that Jesus through his words and deeds implicitly claimed to be God's equal.

In his book *Christ Is King: Paul's Royal Ideology* (Minneapolis: Fortress, 2015), **Joshua W. Jipp** argues that the New Testament portrait of Jesus as king is based on descriptions of the ideal king in the Old Testament, Judaism, and Greco-Roman sources.

In *Heaven and Earth in the Gospel of Matthew*, Novum Testamentum Supplements 126 (Leiden: Brill, 2007), **Jonathan Pennington** argues that Matthew uses the language "kingdom of heaven" to emphasize that this kingdom stands in contrast and opposition to earthly kingdoms and that this kingdom will replace the other kingdoms in the end.[5]

---

5. See also further reading at the end of chapter 2.

4

A Different Border Control

Entrance into the Kingdom

The kingdom of God is clearly not for everyone. "Children, how hard it is to enter the kingdom of God!" Jesus warned his disciples. "It is easier for a camel to go through the eye of a needle than for someone who is rich to enter the kingdom of God" (Mark 10:24–25). Not only is it hard to enter; it is easy to be kicked out too. On another occasion, Jesus told his followers that "the subjects of the kingdom will be thrown outside, into the darkness, where there will be weeping and gnashing of teeth" (Matt. 8:12).

The kingly rule of God can only be a reality when God has a people to govern. When Jesus came to earth to establish this rule, he also formed a new community, a people to enter the kingdom and belong to it. And as this king defies all expectations regarding his rule, so does he overthrow all conventions when he gathers his people.

Jesus's people are the same people God chose in Old Testament times, the people of Israel, which he brought to fulfillment. Jesus gathered twelve disciples around himself and told them that they would sit on twelve thrones and judge the twelve tribes of Israel (Luke 22:30 par.). In this way, he made it clear that God continued his rule over his people Israel and that he would be exercising it through these twelve men.

On the night of his betrayal, Jesus ate the Passover meal with his disciples. This meal had been observed through the centuries in memory of God's deliverance of Israel from Egypt. When the angel of death went through the land

and killed the firstborn in every family, he passed over the people of Israel. All that the people had to do was to eat the Passover lamb and have the blood of the lamb on their doorframes. This divine act of deliverance constituted the birth of Israel as a nation. When Jesus celebrated this nation-defining meal with his disciples, he reconstituted it and made it about himself. He identified the bread with his body and the cup with his blood, which he gave for the people's sins (1 Cor. 11:23–26). The community of God's people was now the community of those who enjoyed the benefits of Jesus's sacrifice.

Partying with Jesus

It is fitting that Jesus would center his community around a meal. Throughout Jesus's ministry, his meals had drawn much attention. Jesus was a man of hospitality and conviviality. His detractors found his practices inappropriate for a pious man. "Here is a glutton and a drunkard," they said (Luke 7:34 par.). Jesus knew how to have a good time, and he shared his joy generously. He surrounded himself with all kinds of people and freely shared meals with them.

Jesus liked to talk about parties and festivities too. Some of his best-known parables are about banquets and festive meals. He likened his return to the arrival of a bridegroom and the celebrations that would follow (Matt. 25:1–11). Jesus insisted that the time of his presence was the time of joy because it was the time when the bridegroom was here (Mark 2:19 parr.). In the famous parable of the prodigal son, Jesus compared salvation to a big party with an abundance of food and merriment (Luke 15:23, 25). The parable of the lost sheep ends on a note of festivity, when the sheep owner celebrated by calling his friends and neighbors together (Luke 15:6).

Jesus's way of sharing a meal must have been one of his most striking characteristics. When they first met him after his resurrection, his disciples did not know it was Jesus. But when he sat down to share a meal with them, everything clicked. Two of his disciples had been accompanied by Jesus for the better part of a seven-mile hike from Jerusalem to Emmaus, but they did not realize who he was. Finally, "when he was at the table with them, he took bread, gave thanks, broke it and began to give it to them. Then their eyes were opened and they recognized him" (Luke 24:30–31).

Thus Jesus was known by his social practices. One of the reasons was that he did not follow the accepted conventions. When people invite guests to their events, they usually pick those who could be useful to them, those who might be able to reciprocate, those with whom they have something in common, and those who may be their friends.

But Jesus did the opposite. When he threw a party, he invited characters that others would normally avoid. He had a knack for attracting individuals with a bad reputation, the kind of people in whose company you would never want to be seen. People known for their shady and unethical business practices couldn't get enough of Jesus. The sick and demon-possessed, lepers and beggars—such folks came flocking to Jesus. And he made them feel right at home. The kind of people who counted for something in the community took notice and criticized him for it. People lost their respect for Jesus when they saw what kind of company he kept: "Here is . . . a friend of tax collectors and sinners," they contemptuously observed (Luke 7:34 par.).

Jesus's social practices demonstrated the characteristics of his kingdom. In his teaching, he likened the kingdom of heaven to a wedding banquet. This illustration was taken from the Old Testament. The prophets would often describe the end-time salvation as a wedding. A wedding was the happiest event they could imagine. It was an occasion to celebrate the love of a young man and a young woman, and the whole community would join in. There would be all kinds of merriment, the food would be superb and plentiful, and the wine would flow freely. The mere thought of it had the prophet Isaiah licking his lips: "On this mountain the LORD Almighty will prepare a feast of rich food for all peoples, a banquet of aged wine—the best of meats and the finest of wines" (Isa. 25:6).

Yet Jesus didn't just talk about it. He made it happen. The apostle John tells us that his first sign took place at a wedding. They had been partying for three days, having so much fun that they had run out of wine. The couple's family was not rich, and they had overextended themselves when they planned the wedding. Responsible people would have told them they got what was coming to them when they were trying to be so extravagant.

Here Jesus took the opportunity to show why he had come to earth: to fulfill the prophecies regarding the fabulous feast that God was preparing, to let people experience the joy of salvation, to bring the glory of the new creation. He asked the servants to take the stone water jars that were used for ceremonial washing and fill them with water. They filled them to the brim, and then Jesus turned the water into wine. Together the six water jars would have held between 120 and 180 gallons of wine, enough to keep the party going. When the master of the banquet tasted it, he concluded, "Everyone brings out the choice wine first and then the cheaper wine after the guests have had too much to drink; but you have saved the best till now" (John 2:10).

Jesus's first sign could have been to feed the hungry or heal the sick. People who despise frivolity and are concerned to be ethical and responsible no doubt would have told him that's what he should have done. But how fitting it was that his first sign was to make sure simple people could have the best party of their lives. Nothing could have summed up better what he came to do. He came to give joy, joy in abundance, the kind of joy that characterizes God's new creation. And he brought it to ordinary people, people who had done nothing special to put them in this position.

Who's Invited?

In one of his parables, Jesus explains how people get invited to the feast in the kingdom of God:

> A man was giving a large banquet and invited many. At the time of the banquet, he sent his servant to tell those who were invited, "Come, because everything is now ready." But without exception they all began to make excuses. The first one said to him, "I have bought a field, and I must go out and see it. I ask you to excuse me." Another said, "I have bought five yoke of oxen, and I'm going to try them out. I ask you to excuse me." And another said, "I just got married, and therefore I'm unable to come." So the servant came back and reported these things to his master. Then in anger, the master of the house told his servant, "Go out quickly into the streets and alleys of the city, and bring in here the poor, maimed, blind, and lame." "Master," the servant said, "what you ordered has been done, and there's still room." Then the master told the servant, "Go out into the highways and hedges and make them come in, so that my house may be filled. For I tell you, not one of those people who were invited will enjoy my banquet." (Luke 14:16–24 CSB)

Those who first received the invitation seemed to think they had better things to do. It is both surprising and deeply tragic that there are people who have been invited to enjoy all the gifts of God's kingdom yet do not value these gifts very highly. They think their work or their family is more important. The main point of Jesus's parable lies elsewhere, however. The invitation now goes out to people you wouldn't normally find at this kind of banquet: the poor, the maimed, the blind, and the lame. The people now invited are those who would never be able to do anything in return, who can never reciprocate. These people have never been in a position to earn the host's attention and have their names included on the guest list. They have always been and always will be totally dependent on their benefactors.

The Gospel of Luke describes things in very concrete ways. Luke makes us see what is happening: the maimed, the blind, and the lame are coming to the banquet. Not only would these people normally have missed out on the invitation to attend such a lavish party; they also would have had no way of even getting there. The maimed and the lame would not be able to walk to the banquet hall, and the blind would not have been able to find it. These individuals would have had to rely on someone else from beginning to end. The fact that they were invited was an act of grace. Their helplessness is what sets them apart from the people who ended up being excluded from the banquet, excluded not because they were not invited but because they chose not to go, thinking they had more important things to do. The maimed, the blind, and the lame didn't have anything else to do. Nothing else was competing for their attention—or at least nothing that could tempt them to forgo the invitation.

What Luke portrays in such concrete images, Matthew tends to explain with more spiritual categories. In Matthew's version of the same parable, we read how the servants were sent out: "Go to the street corners and invite to the banquet anyone you find" (Matt. 22:9). Once again, it is evident that those who ended up attending were those who were not preoccupied with more pressing matters; they were idling on street corners. Then Matthew adds: "So the servants went out into the streets and gathered all the people they could find, the bad as well as the good, and the wedding hall was filled with guests" (v. 10). In this way, he makes clear that the invitation had nothing to do with whether they were good or bad people. The invitees were not chosen based on what they had done, whether good or bad. God has not reserved his kingdom for people of a superior ethical or religious standard. His servants were sent to invite anyone they could find, regardless of who they were, their social status, how good they were, how godly they were, or how well they were perceived to fit in with the other guests.

This is the great news of the kingdom of heaven: the gates to the kingdom are wide open, and everyone is invited. No credentials are necessary. There is nothing they need to do; no qualifications are required. The invitation goes out to everyone, and the door is open to all. No matter what they have done, no matter how many and how great their sins are, no matter if everyone else has written them off as hopeless, they are granted privileged access to the kingdom of God.

Moreover, God compels them to enter. There are countless people who feel that they are utterly unworthy of being in God's presence. It may be because they have done something that makes them feel so guilty that they can never forgive themselves. It may be because they have experienced so much abuse that they have come to think of themselves as unworthy of anyone's love. They may be so full of self-loathing that they can't even stand their own company, and they can't make themselves believe that anyone, let alone God, will ever genuinely care for them. The kingdom is for them, and Jesus cannot say it strongly enough. His servants are told to bring in anyone they can find. According to Luke, the host's servant must compel people to come in. That's how much our Lord wants us to join him. Not only is the door open; he is also urging us to enter—the good and the bad, the maimed, the blind, and the lame, those who cannot even find their way on their own. "The good news of the kingdom of God has been proclaimed, and everyone is urgently invited to enter it" (Luke 16:16 CSB). Jesus is urging us. That's how much he wants us to be there.

Entrance into the kingdom is offered as a free gift. There are no bouncers outside the door to check the credentials of those who want to come in. The kingdom is free for the taking. That is why Jesus says we have to become like children to enter (Matt. 18:3). Children know what it means to receive gifts. They don't question whether they have deserved the gifts or whether they are worthy of them. They just take what is handed to them.

Impossible Requirements

At the same time, Jesus made it crystal clear that it was not just difficult to enter the kingdom of heaven; it was humanly impossible. A rich young ruler once approached him to ask what he had to "do to get eternal life" (Matt. 19:16). Jesus directed him to the commandments in the books of Moses: "'You shall not murder, you shall not commit adultery, you shall not steal, you shall not give false testimony, honor your father and mother,' and 'love your neighbor as yourself'" (19:18–19). The inquirer claimed to have kept all these commandments, but he sensed that there was something that was still missing. "Jesus answered, 'If you want to be perfect, go, sell your possessions and give to the poor, and you will have treasure in heaven. Then come, follow me.' When the young man heard this, he went away sad, because he had great wealth" (19:21–22).

Jesus then explained to his disciples: "Truly I tell you, it is hard for someone who is rich to enter the kingdom of heaven. Again I tell you, it is easier for a camel to go through the eye of a needle than for someone who is rich to enter the kingdom of God" (19:23–24). In popular interpretation, this is one of the most misunderstood sayings of the Bible. We are often told that "the eye of a needle" refers not to a literal eye of a needle but to a gate in the wall encircling Jerusalem. Inside the main gate, there was a smaller gate that could be used by pedestrians during the night, when the main gate was closed. This gate would not be used for the main traffic or for camels that were loaded with products to be brought to the city. The idea of a camel entering through this gate was outright comical but not impossible. There might be a possibility that a camel could squeeze through this smaller gate, provided that it was stripped of its load and was forced to crawl through on its knees. The meaning of Jesus's saying would then be that a rich man might enter the kingdom of God but only with great difficulty. He would have to give up his love for the wealth of this world and humble himself. He would have to come naked and on his knees, metaphorically speaking. There are two fatal problems with this interpretation: (1) there is no historical evidence that the Jerusalem wall had a smaller gate that was known as "the needle's eye" before the tenth century CE, and (2) the interpretation runs directly against the context of the passage.

Jesus elaborates on the meaning of his saying when the disciples ask him. They are understandably shocked by Jesus's words. In the first century, the general assumption would be that rich people were favored by God. Their wealth had presumably come as a result of God's blessing. If it was so difficult, even for those who were uniquely blessed by God, to enter the kingdom of God, how could an average Joe have any hope of entering? "'Who can then be saved?' Jesus looked at them and said, "With man this is impossible, but with God all things are possible" (Matt. 19:25–26). When Jesus is asked for a clarification, he explains that it is not merely difficult for the rich to enter the kingdom; it is impossible—not only for them but for anyone. What is impossible for humans, however, is possible for God. The point of Jesus's words is not that one has to humble oneself in order to enter the kingdom. His point is that no one can do it, no matter how much they humble themselves; it is only possible through a miracle of God, who can do things that are impossible for humans.

The Jewish council member Nicodemus was also schooled by Jesus about the difficulty of entering the kingdom of God. "Very truly I tell you, no one can see the kingdom of God unless they are born again," Jesus told him (John 3:3). Nicodemus was understandably puzzled. "'How can someone be born when they are old?' Nicodemus asked. 'Surely they cannot enter a second time into their mother's womb to be born!'" (3:4). He totally misunderstood what Jesus was talking about. Jesus was teaching him about spiritual birth, but he was thinking of biology. He got one thing right, however. People cannot make themselves be born, and that was the point of what Jesus was telling him. Entrance into God's kingdom depends on a new birth, something no one can do for oneself. Only God can do it, as the evangelist explains in his prologue: "to all who did receive him, to those who believed in his name, he gave the right to become children of God—children born not of natural descent, nor of human decision or a husband's will, but born of God" (1:12–13). To be born again, to be born as children of God, is not a matter of human decision; it is God's work.

Jesus explains to Nicodemus how it happens: "Just as Moses lifted up the snake in the wilderness, so the Son of Man must be lifted up, that everyone who believes may have eternal life in him" (John 3:14–15). During the wilderness wanderings, when Israel rebelled against their God, the Lord sent poisonous snakes into the camp of the Israelites. They bit the people, and many of them died. When the people repented of their sins, Moses prayed to God on their behalf. The Lord told Moses, "Make a snake and put it up on a pole; anyone who is bitten can look at it and live" (Num. 21:8). Moses did so, and whenever anyone was bitten, they would look at the bronze snake and live.

Jesus uses this incident as an illustration of what it means to be born again and receive new life. It is the work of God, but it also involves a human response. The Israelites who were bitten could not give life to themselves. They were left for dead. But God could save them, and he decided to use Moses's bronze snake to do it. The bitten Israelites had to look at the snake to live. They had to trust the promise of God and take a chance that looking at the bronze snake would save them.

I imagine some of them were not entirely convinced. Maybe some were thinking: "What can looking at a bronze snake do for me? The poison is in my body; I can feel it inside me. My strength is waning, and I am about to die. Looking at bronze snakes has never done any good for anybody. If only Moses would give me some kind of antidote, some disgusting medicine that I could swallow, something that could enter my body and fight the poison that is already inside me. Maybe that would work. But looking at a bronze snake—what a joke!"

Others perhaps kept thinking: "If I am just lying here, I will almost certainly die. It couldn't hurt just to tilt my head a little so that I can take a look at this bronze snake." Then as soon as they turned their head, that was it. They would live!

This story of the bronze snake is a beautiful illustration of what it means to believe in Jesus. It is not about how well you understand the finer points of theology, about how firmly you believe, or about the power of your conviction. It is about what you rely on. The Israelites in the wilderness had to rely on the bronze snake to give them life. Nicodemus had to rely on Jesus to give him new birth and new life. Like the bronze snake, so would Jesus be lifted up. He would be lifted up on a cross so that he could give salvation and life to those who rely on him.

The Israelites would rely on the bronze snake only when they were bitten by the poisonous snakes and knew they were going to die. When they were healthy, they had no reason to turn toward the bronze snake. It works in a very similar way today. Those who do not see their need for new life are not going to turn to Jesus. They will rely on their own resources instead. They will trust in themselves and believe that they can create for themselves the life they want. People only turn to Jesus when all other options are exhausted, when they are desperate and know that they have no other hope but to surrender and look to Jesus. The great news is that when they do, they have life. They are born again, by the miraculous power of God. "For God so loved the world that he gave his one and only Son, that whoever believes in him shall not perish but have eternal life" (John 3:16).

The Citizens of the Kingdom

Entrance into the kingdom is a free gift; yet it demands everything of those who enter. One of the most challenging things Jesus has to say about entering the kingdom is found in the Sermon on the Mount. At the beginning of his sermon, he lets his disciples know about the stakes: "For I tell you that unless your righteousness surpasses that of the Pharisees and the teachers of the law, you will certainly not enter the kingdom of heaven" (Matt. 5:20). Some Christians think Jesus is here talking about righteousness as a gift that God gives to believers, in the way Paul describes it in Romans 4:5: "To the one who does not work but trusts God who justifies the ungodly, their faith is credited as righteousness." But this is not how Jesus talks about righteousness in the Sermon on the Mount.

In Matthew's Gospel, the term "righteousness" is more or less synonymous with the term "works of righteousness," as we understand from the way the term is used in Matthew 6:1: "Be careful not to practice your righteousness in front of others to be seen by them." In this verse, we learn that righteousness is something to be practiced. When it comes to righteous practice, Jesus teaches that those who wish to enter the kingdom have to outdo the Pharisees and the teachers of the law. That is a tall order. The Pharisees were the strictest party in Judaism when it came to law observance. Referring to his former life as a Pharisee, the apostle Paul said that with respect to "righteousness based on the law," he had been faultless (Phil. 3:6). Who can top that? Those who wish to enter the kingdom had better make sure they do.

Toward the end of Matthew's Gospel, Jesus once again impresses on us that a certain kind of righteousness is required in order to enter the kingdom. He teaches about his coming in glory, when he will come to judge the living and the dead. All the people of the universe will be gathered before him, and he will divide them into two groups based on the works they have done. His words are found in Matthew 25:31–46 (CSB):

When the Son of Man comes in his glory, and all the angels with him, then he will sit on his glorious throne. All the nations will be gathered before him, and he will separate them one from another, just as a shepherd separates the sheep from the goats. He will put the sheep on his right and the goats on the left. Then the King will say to those on his right, "Come, you who are blessed by my Father; inherit the kingdom prepared for you from the foundation of the world. For I was hungry and you gave me something to eat; I was thirsty and you gave me something to drink; I was a stranger and you took me in; I was naked and you clothed me; I was sick and you took care of me; I was in prison and you visited me."

Then the righteous will answer him, "Lord, when did we see you hungry and feed you, or thirsty and give you something to drink? When did we see you a stranger and take you in, or without clothes and clothe you? When did we see you sick, or in prison, and visit you?"

And the King will answer them, "Truly I tell you, whatever you did for one of the least of these brothers and sisters of mine, you did for me."

Then he will also say to those on the left, "Depart from me, you who are cursed, into the eternal fire prepared for the devil and his angels! For I was hungry and you gave me nothing to eat; I was thirsty and you gave me nothing to drink; I was a stranger and you didn't take me in; I was naked and you didn't clothe me, sick and in prison and you didn't take care of me."

Then they too will answer, "Lord, when did we see you hungry, or thirsty, or a stranger, or without clothes, or sick, or in prison, and not help you?"

Then he will answer them, "I tell you, whatever you did not do for one of the least of these, you did not do for me."

And they will go away into eternal punishment, but the righteous into eternal life.

Those who inherit the kingdom are those who have done good deeds. These deeds are similar to the works of Jesus himself. Jesus spent his time among those who were in miserable life situations, people with debilitating diseases, panhandlers, and social rejects. He had brought God's kingly rule by showing the love of God to the weak, the poor, and the unpopular. They were set free from the oppression of sickness, evil forces, and sin. Jesus inaugurated the kingly rule of God and called people to follow him and participate in his rule.

Those who belong in his kingdom are those who follow him and thereby let him be the one who rules their lives. They show their love to the weak, the poor, and the unpopular. They feed the hungry, receive strangers, give clothes to the needy, look after the sick, and visit those who are in prison.

Those who belong in the kingdom have done good deeds, but that is also true about those Jesus is going to turn away. That much he makes clear toward the end of the Sermon on the Mount, when he is warning his disciples of self-deception: "Not everyone who says to me, 'Lord, Lord,' will enter the kingdom of heaven, but only the one who does the will of my Father who is in heaven. Many will say to me on that day, 'Lord, Lord, did we not prophesy in your name and in your name drive out demons and in your name perform many miracles?' Then I will tell them plainly, 'I never knew you. Away from me, you evildoers!'" (Matt. 7:21–23). At the final judgment, there will be many people who believed they were followers of Jesus, people who have the works to back up their claim, but who will be turned down. They have been active for the cause of the kingdom, and they have done mighty works in Jesus's name. They have been professing Christians—and not only professing but practicing too. No doubt, many of the people that Jesus is talking about have been counted among the leaders of the church.

There is a difference between the kinds of works that had been done by the genuine disciples and the false disciples. The false disciples had done many impressive works, the kinds of works that people would notice, deeds that would cause people to talk about them. Basically they were works that would make the false disciples look good—impressive feats of spiritual strength, such as prophecy, exorcism, and miracles.

The genuine disciples had not been noticed by anyone. Their good works were done to those who could not repay them, those who could not return the favor by giving them access to their network of powerful friends. Strangers, prisoners, and people who are starving don't have networks, and their friends are not powerful. The powerful people they do know are not their friends. That's why they're starving.

The genuine disciples had not focused on doing works that would make them look good; they were focused on following their master, Jesus Christ. Just as he had given priority to people who were unimportant and of no consequence in society, so did his followers do acts of mercy to people that everyone else had forgotten. In this way, God's kingly rule was carried out.

For the false disciples, even their "good works" were ultimately aimed at accomplishing something for themselves. In contrast, Jesus's real disciples genuinely did their acts of mercy to benefit other people. Their orientation was quite different; they were focused on others, not on themselves.

When they faced the ultimate judgment, this difference between the true and the false disciples was on display once again. The false disciples relied on themselves, and they faced Jesus's judgment with self-confidence. When Jesus told them that they were going away to eternal punishment because they had failed to show him the acts of mercy that he was looking for, they objected: "Lord, when did we see you hungry, or thirsty, or a stranger, or without clothes, or sick, or in prison, and not help you?" They came to the judgment with a claim; they were confident that they were righteous. The same attitude is on display in the way Jesus describes them in the Sermon on the Mount: "Lord, Lord, did we not prophesy in your name and in your name drive out demons and in your name perform many miracles?"

Jesus's portrayal of this self-confident attitude has a lot in common with accounts of the last judgment in the ancient Near East, both within Judaism and within other religions. One such account is found in a Jewish commentary on Psalm 118. This commentary also bears a striking resemblance to Jesus's description of the last judgment in Matthew 25:31–46. The relevant passage reads as follows:

> Open to me the gates of righteousness (Ps. 118:19). When a man is asked in the world-to-come: "What was thy work?" and he answers: "I fed the hungry," it will be said to him: "*This is the gate of the Lord* (Ps. 118:20). Enter into it, O thou that didst feed the hungry."
>
> When a man answers: "I gave drink to the thirsty," it will be said to him: "*This is the gate of the Lord.* Enter into it, O thou that didst give a drink to the thirsty."
>
> When a man answers: "I clothed the naked," it will be said to him: "*This is the gate of the Lord.* Enter into it, O thou that didst clothe the naked."
>
> This will also be said to him that brought up the fatherless, and to them that gave alms or performed deeds of lovingkindness.
>
> And David said: I have done all these things. Therefore let all the gates be opened for me. Hence it is said *Open to me the gates of righteousness; I will enter into them, I will give thanks unto the Lord* (Ps. 118:19).[1]

Both in Jesus's account and in this portrayal, the scene is the final judgment, entrance into salvation is determined on the basis of the works that someone has done, and most of the works in question are the same: feeding the hungry, giving drink to the thirsty, and clothing the naked.

This Jewish text is much younger than the New Testament, and there is no reason to believe that Jesus had this text in mind when he offered his picture of the final judgment. But this text is only one of many similar examples. These examples reflect an idea that was widespread and well-established in the ancient Near East long before the time of Jesus: in the last judgment, each

---

1. *The Midrash on Psalms*, trans. W. G. Braude, Yale Judaica Series 13 (New Haven: Yale University Press, 1959), 2:243.

person had to refer to the works they had done, and the judge would decide on that basis whether they could enter into salvation.

This is where these accounts differ so markedly from the picture of judgment that Jesus offered. In Matthew 25:31–46, no one told the judge, Jesus, what they had done. In a strange reversal of roles, the defendants were not asked to provide the evidence for their acquittal. The judge did it for them! Jesus himself explains why they are saved. He recounts the works they have done. What is equally striking is that those who are saved are caught completely by surprise by what Jesus has told them. They were apparently totally unaware that they had performed the works that were required in order to stand in this judgment. "Lord, when did we see you hungry and feed you, or thirsty and give you something to drink? When did we see you a stranger and take you in, or without clothes and clothe you? When did we see you sick, or in prison, and visit you?"

In contrast to those who were condemned, these individuals did not appear before the judge with a claim, thinking that they deserved to enter into salvation. In this way, they also contrast with the man in the Jewish commentary on God's judgment quoted above. According to this commentary, David, who stands as an example of a righteous person, came to God's judgment well prepared. He knew what he had done, and he was ready to talk about it. He reminded the judge that he had fed the hungry, given drink to the thirsty, clothed the naked, brought up orphans, given to charity, and performed acts of kindness. This Jewish picture of a righteous person has much in common with how Jesus pictures the condemned: they came to the judge ready to argue their case. They were confident that they belonged in the kingdom of heaven.

Not so with the followers of Jesus. They had not performed their acts of kindness in order to store up credit that could be used on the day of judgment. They were oblivious of what they had done, much like Jesus had taught them: "When you give to the needy, do not let your left hand know what your right hand is doing, so that your giving may be in secret. Then your Father, who sees what is done in secret, will reward you" (Matt. 6:3–4).

Poverty in Spirit

Those who entered the kingdom did not come before the judge with a claim. They came in the way that Jesus had described in the first of the Beatitudes: "Blessed are the poor in spirit, for theirs is the kingdom of heaven" (Matt. 5:3). In Greek, there are two different words that may be translated "poor." One of them refers to someone who is so poor that they have to work for a living. The second means to be so poor that one has to beg. It is the second word that is used in this Beatitude. Those who are blessed are those who are beggars in spirit, those who relate to God as beggars. To come as a beggar is the opposite of coming with a claim. A beggar comes with nothing but an open hand and stretches it out toward those who might give them something. They are utterly dependent on the grace of their benefactor. A beggar can offer nothing in return for the gifts they receive. They can only appeal to the mercy of the giver.

The Gospel of Matthew provides two excellent examples of what it means to come to Jesus in this way. There are only two characters in this Gospel who are told that their faith is great: the Roman centurion who asked Jesus to heal his servant (8:5–13) and the Canaanite woman who prayed for her demon-possessed daughter (15:21–28). Both of them are gentiles, which is one of the many ways in which Matthew shows that Jesus brings salvation to all kinds of people, not only to the Jews. But they have other things in common as well. Both of them had an acute awareness of their own unworthiness in their encounter with Jesus.

When Jesus was in the gentile region of Tyre and Sidon, to the north of Israel's land, a Canaanite woman came to him and cried out, "Lord, Son of David, have mercy on me! My daughter is demon-possessed and suffering terribly" (Matt. 15:22). Jesus's response is surprising to us since we are so accustomed to seeing the picture of a merciful Jesus who cares for everyone. Jesus did not even dignify the woman with an answer. He completely ignored her. At this point, the disciples decided to intervene, not because they cared for the poor woman but because the situation was awkward and embarrassing. This woman was crying out to Jesus, and she was relentless. So they asked Jesus to deal with her, just so that she would stop. The woman's strategy reminds me of what I have seen many times while visiting areas of the world with desperate beggars. If you don't give them any money, they will become so persistent that most people end up giving them something just to make them go away.

But Jesus was not so easily swayed. "I was sent only to the lost sheep of Israel," he replied (15:24). He didn't even address the woman; he kept ignoring her and was just talking about her, in a conversation with his disciples. Jesus's words constitute nothing less than what we would call ethnocentrism, if not racism. Jesus was able to heal, but he was not going to do it. Not for this woman. She was from the wrong people. She was a Canaanite, not a Jew. Jesus seemed not to care for those people. But the woman still didn't give up. She came, knelt before him, and said, "Lord, help me!" (v. 25). Jesus finally had to acknowledge her existence and say something in response: "It is not right to take the children's bread and toss it to the dogs" (v. 26). Now the cruelty is spelled out. Jesus is not going to help her because she is not worth it; she is nothing but a dog. Calling someone a dog was one of the worst insults you could hurl at them. It was to say that they were not human. They were so despicable that they didn't count as humans. They were to be regarded as filthy animals.

I have often wondered why the woman didn't rebuke Jesus for his abusive behavior. It was so unlike him, and it went directly against what he was teaching his disciples. Wasn't Jesus the one who taught them that "anyone who says, 'You fool!' will be in danger of the fire of hell" (Matt. 5:22)? Scholars usually point out that this was a stage in salvation history when God's salvation was not yet fully including the gentiles. That time would come after Jesus's resurrection and the outpouring of the Holy Spirit, but while Jesus was still involved in his earthly ministry, he was still focused on the Jewish people. That may be the case, but it had not stopped Jesus from helping gentiles on other occasions, and it does not explain his use of such abusive language. We can't always know the full reason why Jesus acts in the way he does; Jesus does things we don't always understand. But we do know how the Canaanite woman reacted. We might have expected her to object, to protest that she is not a dog and that Jesus has no right to talk to her in that way. But she didn't. She agreed with him. "Yes, Lord," she said, "yet even the dogs eat the crumbs that fall from their masters' table" (Matt. 15:27 NRSV). She accepted that Jesus had called her a dog, and she was content to come to him as a dog, begging for the crumbs that would fall from the table. She came to him as a beggar in spirit. To this request, Jesus said to her: "Woman, you have great faith! Your request is granted" (15:28). With her approach, she exemplified Jesus's own words in the Beatitudes: "Blessed are the poor in spirit, for theirs is the kingdom of heaven" (Matt. 5:3).

Those who are poor in spirit come to Jesus knowing they have no right to come to him. They are not worthy of his attention. They know that they are sinners who do not belong in his company. But they refuse to turn away. Without concern for their own pride and dignity, they cry out for his mercy. Like a hungry baby clinging to its mother, they are clinging to Jesus, craving to hear his words of grace.

A Roman centurion offers a similar example. He asked Jesus for healing on behalf of his servant, who was paralyzed. Jesus offered to come to his house and heal the servant, but the centurion demurred: "Lord, I do not deserve to have you come under my roof" (Matt. 8:8). He had much of the same attitude as the Canaanite woman. He did not think he was worthy of Jesus's presence, but he had great faith in what Jesus could do. "But just say the word, and my servant will be healed," he added (v. 8). He also came to Jesus as a beggar, hanging on the words that Jesus would say. That was enough for him. He also got to hear the amazing words from Jesus as his request was granted: "Truly I tell you, I have not found anyone in Israel with such great faith" (v. 10).

Jesus has two things to say about those who enter the kingdom. Their righteousness is far greater than that of the scribes and the Pharisees, and they are spiritual beggars, who have nothing to show for themselves. It is now clear how these two characteristics belong together: the latter is the necessary precondition for the former. They came to Jesus with an open hand, as beggars, and they would cling to whatever he would give them. Their relationship with Jesus was about what he could give them, not about what they might have to show him, for they knew they had nothing. As a consequence, their relationship with other people was about what they might give to them, not about what they might receive. They did not do their good works so that their good works might somehow bring them some benefits in the end. They didn't need that. They didn't need any good works that they could show to Jesus. They came to Jesus as beggars, and they were fully content with that. In his presence, they preferred to come empty-handed so that he could shower them with his gifts. Jesus will do so in the last judgment as well, when he will tell them what their good works are, works they don't even know about. And then he will tell them, "Come, you who are blessed by my Father; take your inheritance, the kingdom prepared for you since the creation of the world" (Matt. 25:34). With their works, they have showed themselves to be citizens of the kingdom, but their possession of the kingdom was a gift all along, an inheritance prepared not by them but for them since the creation of the world (cf. Luke 12:32). With these citizens, Jesus forms a new community. In this community, God rules as king, and his gifts are flowing freely. This is a community unlike any other.

Further Reading

Following the work of Gustaf Dalman, most scholars correctly understand the term "kingdom of God" to mean "kingly rule of God" (as discussed in chaps. 1 and 2 above). However, building on the studies of Sverre Aalen and Hans Kvalbein, **Dale Allison** shows in *Constructing Jesus: Memory and Imagination* (Grand Rapids: Baker Academic, 2009) that Jesus also envisions the kingdom as a territory and that he describes salvation as entering into this kingdom.

According to the interpretation of **Petri Luomanen** in *Entering the Kingdom of Heaven: A Study on the Structure of Matthew's View of Salvation*, Wissenschaftliche

Untersuchungen zum Neuen Testament 2/101 (Tübingen: Mohr Siebeck, 1998), Matthew teaches that obedience, confession of Jesus as Lord, and following him are the requirements for entrance into the kingdom.

In contrast, **Roger Mohrlang** points out in his work *Matthew and Paul: A Comparison of Ethical Perspectives*, Society for New Testament Studies Monograph Series 48 (Cambridge: Cambridge University Press, 1984) that grace is the foundation for obedience in Matthew's Gospel.

Similarly, **Charles Talbert** argues in an essay, "Indicative and Imperative in Matthean Soteriology," *Biblica* 82 (2001): 515–38, that our understanding of Jesus's teaching on judgment and good works must be balanced by Matthew's narrative. His narrative shows that God has broken into our world and empowers the disciples to show obedience.

In **Sigurd Grindheim**, "Ignorance Is Bliss: Attitudinal Aspects of the Judgment according to Works in Matthew 25:31–46," *Novum Testamentum* 50 (2008): 313–31 (http://www.sigurdgrindheim.com/), I provide more background for the topic of this chapter, arguing that Matthew's view of genuine discipleship contrasts with the self-righteousness of the false disciples and that Matthew emphasizes dependence on the grace of Christ.

In his book *Salvation by Allegiance Alone: Rethinking Faith, Works, and the Gospel of Jesus the King* (Grand Rapids: Baker Academic, 2017), **Matthew Bates** maintains that salvation is not a matter of intellectual assent but of showing fidelity to the king.

In *A New Testament Biblical Theology: The Unfolding of the Old Testament in the New* (Grand Rapids: Baker Academic, 2011), 469–555, **G. K. Beale** treats the New Testament teaching on justification and reconciliation as a manifestation of the new creation that has been inaugurated through Christ's crucifixion and especially his resurrection.

Udo Schnelle argues in *Theology of the New Testament*, trans. M. Eugene Boring (Grand Rapids: Baker Academic, 2009), 101–10, that "the hidden beginning of the kingdom of God happens in the form of the overpowering, unrestrained love of God for human beings" (105).

In *New Testament Theology: Magnifying God in Christ* (Grand Rapids: Baker Academic, 2008), 546–58, **Thomas R. Schreiner** emphasizes that entrance into the kingdom is by faith in the salvation that comes from God. This faith results in a new obedience.

George Eldon Ladd points out in *A Theology of the New Testament*, ed. Donald A. Hagner (Grand Rapids: Eerdmans, 1993) that the righteousness of the kingdom is a free gift (131–32) and describes justification as "one of the blessings of the new age that have come to us in Christ" (478–98, here 480).

5

A Different Community

The People of the Kingdom

If Jesus brought the kingly rule of God, what happened to this rule when Jesus ascended into heaven? What became of the new creation and the age of salvation? Many Christians think that we will enter the kingdom of heaven when Jesus comes again. In the meantime, while Jesus is in heaven, we have to wait for him to come back so that we can receive the gift of salvation. When Jesus was walking around in the land of Israel, people were experiencing his gifts in a way that differs from what we can expect to do today. We have to focus on what Jesus will do for us in the future, they say, not on what he is doing for us now.

If Jesus established his kingly rule when he came to earth, did he cease to rule when he was lifted up to heaven? Did he go on vacation and leave the devil in peace for a while longer, until he was going to return and resume the fight? No, Jesus has not abdicated his rule. To the contrary, the Bible teaches that his resurrection and ascension were the time when he was enthroned as king. Christ's entering into heaven is the fulfillment of what is written in Psalm 110:1: "The Lord says to my lord: 'Sit at my right hand until I make your enemies a footstool for your feet'" (cf. Acts 2:33–35). The apostle Paul prays to God who "raised Christ from the dead and seated him at his right hand in the heavenly realms, far above all rule and authority, power and dominion, and every name that is invoked, not only in the present age but also in the one to come" (Eph. 1:20–21). Jesus's resurrection and ascension mean that he has been seated on his throne and has taken his place in power. Far from pausing from his work of defeating evil, Jesus continues to rule, and he is subduing all the powers that stand against him. Paul explains that "he must reign until he has put all his enemies under his feet" (1 Cor. 15:25).

Delegated Rule

As Israel was called to rule on God's behalf (Exod. 19:6), so Jesus delegated his rule to his twelve disciples, who formed the nucleus of the reconstituted people of God (Luke 22:30). Just before Jesus sent out the Twelve, Luke tells us: "When Jesus had called the Twelve together, he gave them power and authority to drive out all demons and to cure diseases, and he sent them out to proclaim the kingdom of God and to heal the sick" (9:1–2). The disciples were sent to do the same works that Jesus had been doing: to drive out all demons and to cure diseases. They were to go with the same authority as Jesus had, and to do the same works he did. Jesus even told his disciples that those who believe in him "will do the works I have been doing, and they will do even greater things than these, because I am going to the Father" (John 14:12). Through the disciples, the kingly rule of God would continue to be made known. The power of evil was banished, and the new creation was present.

Jesus comes as king, but he is not a tyrannical, authoritarian king. He involves his followers in the tasks of government. How could he possibly imagine that they would be qualified for such tasks? After all, God himself has now come to the world, and he is in the process of reestablishing his perfect rule of the universe. If he wanted to delegate some of the responsibility, one would think he would call on some of the most exalted angels, creatures who would be competent to rule on his behalf. But that is not what he is doing. He is calling on humans, people with serious character flaws, who are slow to understand what he is teaching them, who are temperamental and prone to argument and quarrel, and who are arrogant and think themselves invincible but run away like cowards when they are put to the test. He could have found some who were much better, but he chose to share his authority with these disciples. He even told the Twelve: "I confer on you a kingdom, just as my Father conferred one on me, so that you may eat and drink at my table in my kingdom and sit on thrones, judging the twelve tribes of Israel" (Luke 22:29–30).

Jesus came to this world to defeat evil and to establish his rule in this world so that evil would be thwarted forever. And he shares this rule with his disciples so that we will rule with him and triumph over evil with him. We need to be precise about this point: the battle against evil was a battle that Jesus fought alone. He faced the devil by himself, and he bore our sins alone. No one helped him, and no one was called on to do so. In the Bible, the establishment of God's kingly rule is often described as a military victory. God is the almighty warrior who defeats his enemies and emerges as the unchallenged king. Jesus is this triumphant warrior, and he goes to battle alone. But his victory over sin, death, and evil has reestablished God's kingly rule, and we are called to participate in this rule. We are called to exercise authority over evil.

Forgiveness

The disciples were called to exercise Christ's authority over evil spirits and drive them out, and they were also given the authority to bring the gifts of the new creation and to heal diseases. They were even called to exercise Jesus's authority to forgive sins. In Matthew 18:15–18, Jesus teaches the disciples how to deal with a fellow Christian who commits a sin:

> If your brother or sister sins, go and point out their fault, just between the two of you. If they listen to you, you have won them over. But if they will not listen, take one or two others along, so that "every matter may be established by the testimony of two or three witnesses." If they still refuse to listen, tell it to the church; and if they refuse to listen even to the church, treat them as you would a pagan or a tax collector.
>
> Truly I tell you, whatever you bind on earth will be bound in heaven, and whatever you loose on earth will be loosed in heaven.

Jesus gives his disciples a heavenly authority. He promises them that there will be perfect correspondence between what happens in heaven and what happens on earth. "Whatever you bind on earth will be bound in heaven, and whatever you loose on earth will be loosed in heaven." When it comes to the forgiveness of sins and the withholding of forgiveness, Jesus has called the church to put the heavenly reality into practice here on earth. The forgiveness of God, the forgiveness of heaven, is becoming a tangible reality in the church. This promise is not a license for church ministers to abuse their power and dispense forgiveness to the people they like and withhold it from people they don't like. It is a call to put the heavenly judgment into visible reality.

In the cross of Jesus Christ, the judgment of God has been carried out. The cross of Christ is God's judgment on the sins of all the world, and the cross of Christ means that every sinner who turns to Christ is set free in the final judgment of God. God has passed his verdict: Jesus dies and the sinner goes free. Every sinner who seeks forgiveness in Jesus Christ is cleared in God's last judgment. And every human who refuses to turn to Jesus in repentance is condemned.

Jesus calls on us, his community on earth, to execute this sentence. This does not mean that we are to hit sinners with the wrath of God; church discipline means to communicate in word and in deed that an unrepentant sinner is outside the community of God. The aim of church discipline, as Jesus makes clear in verse 15, is that the sinner may receive forgiveness: "If they listen to you, you have won them over."

When a sinner repents, the church exercises the kingly rule of God. The community of God's people serves as a manifestation of a heavenly reality. We experience the kingdom of heaven right here on earth. The heavenly forgiveness of God is communicated here by his people. The divine presence of the Son of God is in their midst: "For where two or three gather in my name, there am I with them" (Matt. 18:20).

When God spoke to Moses on Mount Sinai, he came down to earth and covered the mountain with smoke, and "the whole mountain trembled violently" (Exod. 19:18). But that terrifying display of divine power pales in comparison with what happens every day, when the people of God gather in Jesus's name. This is because when they do, heaven moves right down to earth, and the final judgment of God is executed in their midst. The heavenly forgiveness—won by the sacrifice of the only begotten Son of God, by the shedding of the blood of our Savior Jesus—is turned into practical experience right there, where two or three are gathered in Jesus's name.

I have experienced God's kingly rule here on earth many times, when the people of God have demonstrated it to me. One of the most powerful experiences happened when I had just returned to Ethiopia on a mission trip. One evening right after I had arrived in Addis Ababa, I was chatting with someone at home via email. The quality of the internet connection made it impossible to use anything sophisticated like video calls, so we were restricted to emailing back and forth. While we were doing this, I received an email from my supervisor in my mission organization. The content of the email offended me deeply, for reasons that turned out to be completely petty and so selfish that I am not going to detail them here. I am too embarrassed. I forwarded this email and equipped it with a commentary about how offended I had been by it. A few days later, I realized that I had made a mistake when I forwarded the email. I had in fact not forwarded it; I had clicked the reply button instead of the forward button. I had been bad-mouthing my supervisor in a disrespectful tone, for no good reason at all, thinking that I was talking to my confidant, and I had sent the email straight back to my supervisor himself. I was devastated. I had been caught with my pants down, metaphorically speaking. There was no way out of the situation. I could not tell my supervisor that he misheard me, that he didn't have the whole context, or that I didn't really mean what I had said. He had gotten it in writing. I had meant to say it to someone I trusted completely. I had spoken freely. I had meant every word of it. And I had had no reason to bad-mouth him. The only real problem was that in my heart I had been insisting on harboring negative thoughts and misinterpreting innocent things in the worst possible way. I had to make a special trip through the city and find my supervisor in his office. I can still remember walking up the stairs and knocking on his door. I felt rotten. There was nothing I could say to him other than this: "You have gotten a glimpse of my sinful heart. You have seen the evil that dwells inside me."

The first words that came out of his mouth were these: "Let's forget that it even happened. We are all sinners. Let's just put it behind us."

The forgiveness of God. Brought to me in Ethiopia. By my brother in Christ. The kingly rule of God. Reestablished on earth. Salvation brought near.

Forgiveness and Conflict Resolution

When they forgive each other their sins, the people of God exercise the kingly rule of God, and they fulfill the commandment that Jesus gave to his disciples the night before he died: "As I have loved you, so you must love one another" (John 13:34). Above all, Jesus has loved us by taking away our sins, and he calls on us to do the same. On one occasion, the apostle Peter asked Jesus how many times he should forgive his brother or sister. He made sure to hint at the fact that he had already forgiven seven times, no doubt thinking that his master would be impressed with such a magnanimous display of mercy. Jesus's answer must have floored him: "I tell you, not seven times, but seventy-seven times" (Matt. 18:22). Jesus himself is the one who has offered unlimited forgiveness, and he calls his disciples to follow in his footsteps also in this regard—especially in this regard.

The power of forgiveness gives the church a unique ability to deal with conflicts in its midst. The people of God do not need to gloss over their differences and pretend that nothing is wrong. The fellowship of the church is not based on feigned friendship; it is not the polite coexistence of people who exchange niceties and proceed to tell the truth behind each other's backs. The family of God owes its very existence to the forgiveness of God, and it lives together as a community on the same basis. God's forgiveness is the sustenance on which the people of God depend every day. They offer it to one another, and they receive it from one another. Conflicts are resolved in the same manner: through confession, repentance, and forgiveness.

For the church that proclaims the kingly rule of God, all sin is a violation of his rule. It is an act of defiance against Christ's kingship, and it destroys the harmony of the new community, the order of the new creation. It is an infection that threatens the health of the community. When the church is threatened by the disease of sin, the remedy is to seek and provide healing, to ensure that sin is forgiven.

When the Bible discusses the topic of church discipline, the purpose of discipline is always restoration and redemption. When Jesus gave his instructions about what to do when a church member sins against another (quoted from Matt. 18:15–20 above), he included these instructions in a sermon about forgiveness and restoration. When a church member needs to confront another, the purpose is not for the offended party to achieve vindication and to be proved right. The purpose is to be able to offer forgiveness. Jesus tells his disciples to try to solve any conflict in private, if possible. Only when such an approach proves impossible should the matter be taken further. Even then, as few people as possible should be involved. Jesus says to bring one or two others along for a second confrontation. Only when these options are exhausted should the matter be brought before the whole church. The purpose throughout is that there be repentance and forgiveness.

Even in the cases when a sinner does not repent, the goal of discipline is that the sinner may eventually have a change of heart and be saved. When Paul advised the Corinthian congregation to excommunicate the man who lived with his father's wife, the judgment was intended to serve a greater purpose: "Hand this man over to Satan for the destruction of the flesh, so that his spirit may be saved on the day of the Lord" (1 Cor. 5:5). This punishment sounds harsh. We cannot be sure exactly what Paul had in mind when he wanted the man to be handed over to Satan; at least exclusion from the Christian community had to be in view. Perhaps Paul also envisioned that he would experience some form of punishment that affected his physical health, inflicted not by the church but by Satan, as a result of his sinful lifestyle. In any case, even this severe punishment would serve the man's salvation. The intention was for the punishment to lead the man to repent and in that way to receive forgiveness for his sins.

More specifically, Jesus explains how to approach an erring brother or sister in the Sermon on the Mount: "Why do you see the speck in your neighbor's eye, but do not notice the log in your own eye? Or how can you say to your neighbor, 'Let me take the speck out of your eye,' while the log is in your own eye? You hypocrite, first take the log out of your own eye, and then you will see clearly to remove the speck out of your neighbor's eye" (Matt. 7:3–5 NRSV).

This passage is often quoted to make the point that we should not criticize one another, but that is not what the passage says. Jesus says that there is a way for us to remove the speck from our neighbor's eye: when we have removed the log from our own eye. Jesus is warning us against correcting the errors of others without demonstrating any awareness of our own sins. Unfortunately, this is often how Christians try to correct others; this is often how church discipline is practiced. Christians behave in a spirit of self-righteousness, pointing out the sins of other people and condemning them, all the while doing everything they can to make sure their own sins are kept secret. Such a person should not expect to be able to help others. A judgmental Christian is not likely to bring others to genuine awareness of their sins, much less repentance. A person who speaks to another from a position of superiority will just make the other person resentful and spiteful: "Who are you to talk to me like that? Get off your high horse and clean up your own mess before you try to tell me what to do!"

Christians who genuinely want to help others must begin by being aware of the log in their own eye; they have to understand that their own sins are much greater than the little error they have discovered in someone else. They are lost sinners and owe everything they have to God. In Matthew 18, where Jesus talks about correcting other church members, he continues by telling the parable of the unmerciful servant. This servant owed his master ten thousand talents. One talent was roughly the equivalent of twenty times a worker's salary for a whole year, so ten thousand talents in today's currency would correspond to the total gross domestic product of a small country—an unpayable debt. The master forgave the debt, but as the servant went on his merry way, he ran into a fellow servant who owed him one hundred denarii. That was a considerable amount of money—the pay for one hundred days of work—but compared to the amount the servant had been forgiven, it was nothing. Nonetheless, the servant attacked his debtor and demanded to have his money back. He had not learned the lesson of forgiveness. As a result, his master withdrew his forgiveness and had him thrown into jail (18:21–35).

Every Christian should know that they are the servant who has been forgiven ten thousand talents. They should consider this fact when they are wronged by other people. They should remember that however seriously they have been offended, the offense is nothing compared to the sins they have been forgiven by God. It is like one hundred denarii compared to ten thousand talents. Nothing we may need to forgive will ever compare to what

God has had to forgive us. Because of that, our forgiveness should be given freely and generously.

When we must correct other people for their sins, we should do it in the same spirit: I am the greatest sinner. I am in no position to correct others in an attitude of superiority. If I wish to talk to someone else about their sins, I need to come in a spirit of humility, knowing full well who the greatest sinner is. Then I can come alongside other sinners in my community, not as someone taking the higher ground but as someone who speaks with transparency about my own sinfulness. Then I can walk together with my fellow Christians on the same way that we all need to be on: the way of confession, repentance, and forgiveness. I can no longer keep my distance and direct others to that road; I need to be on it myself.

This is what Paul is talking about when he tells the Galatians: "Brothers and sisters, if someone is caught in a sin, you who live by the Spirit should restore that person gently. But watch yourselves, or you also may be tempted. Carry each other's burdens, and in this way you will fulfill the law of Christ" (Gal. 6:1–2). Christians carry each other's burdens. They have learned from Christ, who bore our sins and took them away when he died for them on the cross. In a similar way, his followers bear each other's sins by forgiving them. When Christians love one another in this way, "love covers a multitude of sins" (1 Pet. 4:8 NRSV).

Reconciliation

By forgiving one another and sharing the love of Christ, the people of God enjoy the greatest benefit of the kingly rule of God: the gift of reconciliation. The rule of God brings peace. It puts an end to hostility and enmity. Paul paints a beautiful picture in his Letter to the Ephesians. He begins by describing the bleak situation of the gentiles, "without hope and without God in the world" (Eph. 2:12). But Christ has changed everything.

> So then, remember that at one time you were Gentiles in the flesh—called "the uncircumcised" by those called "the circumcised," which is done in the flesh by human hands. At that time you were without Christ, excluded from the citizenship of Israel, and foreigners to the covenants of promise, without hope and without God in the world. But now in Christ Jesus, you who were far away have been brought near by the blood of Christ. For he is our peace, who made both groups one and tore down the dividing wall of hostility. In his flesh, he made of no effect the law consisting of commands and expressed in regulations, so that he might create in himself one new man from the two, resulting in peace. He did

this so that he might reconcile both to God in one body through the cross by which he put the hostility to death. He came and proclaimed the good news of peace to you who were far away and peace to those who were near. For through him we both have access in one spirit to the Father. So then you are no longer foreigners and strangers, but fellow citizens with the saints, and members of God's household, built on the foundation of the apostles and prophets, with Christ Jesus himself as the cornerstone. In him the whole building, being put together, grows into a holy temple in the Lord. In him you are also being built together for God's dwelling in the Spirit. (Eph. 2:11–22 CSB)

Christ has brought reconciliation. First and foremost, this is reconciliation between us and God. Because of our sin and rebellion against God, we were God's enemies, but Christ took the enmity away when he died on the cross. He doesn't just *bring* peace; he *is* our peace. In him, through our fellowship and community with him, we have peace.

In Ephesians, however, Paul's focus is not primarily on our restored relationship with God; it is on the new relationship that has been made possible between Jews and gentiles. There was little fellowship between these two groups but a lot of enmity. The Jews had suffered under the oppression of one gentile nation after another, and they knew more than anyone would want to know about the sinfulness of the gentiles. As God's holy nation, Israel was called to separate itself from the gentiles and their sinful ways. And most of the Jews did. They lived their life dedicated to God, not mingling with the gentiles. Among the gentiles, hatred of the Jews was widespread; anti-Semitism has its roots in antiquity.

The work of Christ changes all of that. He has brought the gentiles near to God and thereby brought them together with the Jews. The two groups that were previously divided by hostility are now united because they have both been reconciled to God. Christ has brought them so near that they are now one new humanity. And this is the point that Paul is impressing on the Ephesians: their new relationship with God changes their relationship with each other. Their new status before God changes their status vis-à-vis one another.

Previously, the gentiles did not know God and were alienated and estranged from him. They did not have a share in the citizenship of Israel. But now they have something far greater than what the Jewish people could ever experience under the old covenant. They have become fellow citizens with God's people and members of God's household. They are not only welcome in God's kingdom; they also belong to his house and are members of his family. And Paul does not stop there: the gentiles are now "a dwelling in which God lives

by his Spirit." They have come so near to God that God has made his permanent address in their midst. In the Old Testament, God had promised that he
would dwell in the tabernacle and later in the temple. To the people of Israel,
God was both near and distant at the same time. They had his house right
in their own neighborhood, on Mount Zion. All Israelites were required to
make pilgrimage to the Holy City three times a year, and then they could all
see the house in which God lived. But it was as though God was a recluse; no
one could enter into his presence except the high priest, and he was allowed
to do so only once a year. His audience with God was a dangerous affair. If
he was not rightly prepared, God might strike him dead (Exod. 28:35, 43;
Lev. 16:13).

Paul describes a situation that is fundamentally different: God now dwells
in his people. The church, consisting of both Jews and gentiles, is now God's
house. "You who once were far away have been brought near by the blood of
Christ," Paul says. Indeed!

As a consequence of this new state of affairs, there is no longer any basis
for the hostility between Jews and gentiles. They have both become members
of God's family; they have both been brought near. The gentiles are no longer
far away, and the Jews do not need to look at them as sinners who are banned
from the presence of God, people whom Jews had better keep at a distance.
God has accepted them and brought them into the household. The Jews and
gentiles are now one new humanity in Christ.

Since the time of the apostle Paul, the challenges posed by ethnic conflicts
have not diminished. In Africa, country after country is going through constant conflict because of the differences between various ethnic groups. For
painful historical reasons, these groups often distrust each other. Such distrust
makes any political cooperation across ethnic lines next to impossible, and
allegiances are based on ethnic identity. New conflicts inevitably arise when
one ethnic group gains more power than others.

In Europe and North America, ethnic tensions have become more and
more significant. The increasing presence of ethnic groups from different
parts of the world has been met with suspicion by many of those who claim
long-standing historical ties to their country. How to respond to the influx
of new immigrants and refugees is one of the most hotly debated political
questions of our time. Some believe that we live in an era of new mass mi-
grations and that the profound cultural changes are just beginning to be felt.
Ethnic tensions continue to be one of the most serious threats to peace and
stability all over the world.

Jesus Christ changes all of that. He is our peace. He eliminates ethnic
conflict by his work of reconciliation. He draws people of all ethnicities near

to God and makes them members of God's family. Together they become the very dwelling in which God lives. In himself he has created one new humanity.

In 1993 I had the privilege of attending a mission conference in the Netherlands. This was during the war in Yugoslavia, the war that defined the term "ethnic cleansing" in the modern era. Serbs were systematically trying to eradicate the Croats from the territories they claimed as their own. They pillaged their villages, killed the men, and raped the women. In the areas where the Croats had the upper hand, they were not much better, systematically killing Serbs and burning their churches.

At the conference I attended, there were Christians from all over Europe, including some from Yugoslavia. Some of them were Croats, and some of them were Serbs, but all of them met together for a prayer meeting. I had the opportunity to join them, and I could see people from Serbia and Croatia bowing their heads together in prayer to the same Lord in heaven. Then I met personally with two of the young men in attendance, one Serb and one Croat. I asked them how they could meet peacefully like this, and they responded by throwing their arms around each other. One of them said: "Back home in Yugoslavia, our two peoples are trying to kill each other and destroy each other, but in Jesus Christ, we are brothers." Christ was their peace. He had made the two to be one and brought them into the same family, the family of God. They were now both God's children, and they treated each other as brothers.

The church is the demonstration that Christ's work of reconciliation was effective. The reconciliation of Jews and gentiles and all ethnic groups in the church is the visible proof that Christ has brought peace to the world. In Ephesians 3, Paul continues to talk about the new unity that exists between Jews and gentiles in the church. He sees this unity as a revelation of divine wisdom. God's "intent was that now, through the church, the manifold wisdom of God should be made known to the rulers and authorities in the heavenly realms, according to his eternal purpose that he accomplished in Christ Jesus our Lord" (vv. 10–11). The church announces the wisdom of God when it demonstrates that God has brought Jews and gentiles together as one new humanity.

This is why the unity of the church is so important to the apostle. The unity of the church serves as a living testimony to what God has done in Jesus Christ. He has brought reconciliation between the world and himself, and he has brought reconciliation between humans that used to be enemies. The existence of the church is a testimony to these truths.

One cannot help but reflect on the poor witness the church bears when it fails to demonstrate reconciliation. Perhaps the most damning indictment of the church I have ever read is found in the essay "England Your England," by

George Orwell. Orwell points out "the overwhelming strength of patriotism, national loyalty." He observes that "as a positive force there is nothing to set beside it. Christianity and international Socialism are as weak as straw in comparison with it."[1] Anyone who knows history will have a hard time proving Orwell wrong. When Christians allow their ethnic identity to be more important than their identity as the family of God, they fail as witnesses of what Christ has done. When the church is divided, especially along ethnic lines, it cannot be true to its mission. Churches that are effectively segregated according to ethnic background and racial identity do not serve as a living testimony of the reconciliation in Christ. Instead of being a witness to the truth of the gospel, the church then becomes a witness that testifies against the word of God.

The gospel proclaims that God has brought reconciliation, but the church is in effect saying, "It is not true; God did not bring reconciliation. There is no reconciliation among his people here; there are conflicts and tension." The gospel proclaims that believers are one, but the church is testifying, "We are not one; we are still divided; we live in factions and disunity." The gospel proclaims that our identity as God's children is more important than everything else, but the testimony of the church says that ethnic identity is more important than the gospel and what Christ has done for us. As God's people, we need to repent of our sins and our failure to take God's word seriously. For a church that belongs to God, racial reconciliation, ethnic diversity, and integration of minorities are not optional. These are essential characteristics of the church if it is to be true to its call from God.

On the night before his death, in his high-priestly prayer, Jesus prayed to his Father, "I have given them the glory that you gave me, that they may be one as we are one—I in them and you in me—so that they may be brought to complete unity. Then the world will know that you sent me and have loved them even as you have loved me" (John 17:22–23).

Jesus here ties the effectiveness of his disciples' testimony directly to their unity. He has the most beautiful vision for the unity of his disciples: he prays that they will be one, just as he and the Father are one. The same level of fellowship and intimacy, the same degree of unity in purpose, and the same kind of harmony in thought and mind that exist between Jesus and the Father are what Jesus intends for his disciples as well. A church that demonstrates that kind of unity is a church in which God truly rules. A church like that is

---

1. George Orwell, "England Your England," in *The Lion and the Unicorn: Socialism and the English Genius*, Searchlight Books 1, ed. T. R. Fyvel and George Orwell (London: Secker & Warburg, 1941).

a church that bears an effective witness. "Then the world will know that you sent me and have loved them even as you have loved me." Perhaps the two most common objections against the Christian faith are that Jesus cannot really be God's Son and that God cannot really be a loving God. These objections would be silenced if the disciples of Christ showed unity. By showing the world the gift they have received, the gift of reconciliation, the disciples of Christ proclaim the kingly rule of God. Through this proclamation, all people in the world are invited to enter the kingdom, to experience God's kingly rule and enjoy his gifts.

The Kingdom and the Church

The relationship between the kingdom of God and the church is often misunderstood. Many Christians think that the two are more or less identical. To be engaged in the activities or mission of the church is to "build" or "extend" the kingdom of God. To bring people into the church is to bring them into the kingdom. When the church grows, the kingdom grows.

However, the church is not the kingdom of God. No church is. Not even the most biblical, most loving, most Spirit-filled local church community is identical with the kingdom of God. The kingdom of God is the active rule of God in the world and the presence of his gift of salvation. The church is a community. To compare the church and the kingdom of God is like comparing the US Congress or the UK Parliament with the rule of law. No political body is identical with the rule of law. These are two different categories. They are related, but they are not the same. A political body is responsible to ensure the rule of law. It is intended to practice it and abide by it. It may or may not succeed, but even when it succeeds, it cannot be confused with the rule of law itself.

The church is not the kingly rule of God. It represents the kingly rule of God. It shows what his reign looks like and serves as a living testimony to God's rule. The benefits of God's rule are experienced in the community of the church, and the members of the church make God's rule visible as they live their lives in obedience to his will.

In living under God's rule and kingdom, the church demonstrates that it belongs to a different nation than the nations of this world. The church and its members do not pledge their primary allegiance to their nation. Their allegiance is to the kingdom of God. Their "citizenship is in heaven" (Phil. 3:20). Their Lord has imposed on them a loyalty that takes precedence over all other allegiances. "If anyone comes to me and does not hate father and mother, wife and children, brothers and sisters—yes, even their own life—such a person cannot be my disciple," Jesus said (Luke 14:26). When he calls on his followers to hate their family, this is not to be taken literally; Jesus upholds the commandment to honor one's parents (Mark 7:10 parr.; 10:19 parr.). Rather, his words are a strong way of saying that nothing or no one can be a higher priority in one's life than the call to follow Jesus.

The church therefore lives by a different set of laws and a different set of values than this world; they live by the laws and values of the kingdom of God. That does not mean that they are free to disobey the laws of the land in which they live, or that they are called to rebel against these laws. The apostle Paul makes clear that believers are to submit to their earthly authorities (Rom. 13:1).

The point is that the followers of Christ march to a different drum and organize their lives according to different principles than the people of this world. Money, success, popularity, and self-actualization will not be the guiding principles of their lives. Their lives are determined by their identity as citizens of the kingdom of God. They heed the exhortation of the apostle Paul: "Do not conform to the pattern of this world, but be transformed by the renewing of your mind. Then you will be able to test and approve what God's will is—his good, pleasing and perfect will" (Rom. 12:2).

One of the earliest known Christian writings, the *Letter to Diognetus* (ca. 150–225), describes this most unusual people:

> They live on earth, but their citizenship is in heaven. They obey the established laws; indeed in their private lives they transcend the laws. They love everyone, and by everyone they are persecuted. They are unknown, yet they are condemned; they are put to death, yet they are brought to life. They are poor, yet they make many rich; they are in need of everything, yet they abound in everything. They are dishonored, yet they are glorified in their dishonor; they are slandered, yet they are vindicated. They are cursed, yet they bless; they are insulted, yet they offer respect. When they do good, they are punished as evildoers; when they are punished, they rejoice as though brought to life. (5.9–16)[2]

Proclaim, Don't Build

We may get a better grasp of the distinction between the church and the kingdom of God by taking a closer look at the language the New Testament

2. *The Apostolic Fathers: Greek Texts and English Translations*, ed and trans. Michael W. Holmes, 3rd ed. (Grand Rapids: Baker Academic, 2007), 703.

authors use when they speak about the disciples' role in the kingdom. The New Testament does not say that believers extend or build the kingdom of God. Instead, believers enter, receive, possess, inherit, and proclaim the kingdom. Their possession of the kingdom is a gift. Jesus encourages his followers: "Do not be afraid, little flock, for your Father has been pleased to give you the kingdom" (Luke 12:32). In the famous Beatitudes, he promises the poor, "Yours is the kingdom of God" (Luke 6:20).

To be the church, to be the people of the kingdom, means above all to receive the gift of the kingdom. The preeminent task of the church is to accept the grace that God gives: he freely gives us forgiveness of sins, his unconditional acceptance, and loving inclusion in his family. The first responsibility of the church is to accept this gift, like little children who run toward their father to receive his loving embrace. Indeed, everyone who wants to enter the kingdom must come like a little child. Jesus says that children are the role models for all his followers: "Let the little children come to me, and do not hinder them, for the kingdom of God belongs to such as these" (Luke 18:16).

The disciples of Jesus make this kingdom known, show others how to enter into it, and serve as the very manifestation of its presence. But they do not establish it, build it, make it grow, or extend it. They proclaim it. After Jesus gave the twelve disciples "power and authority, . . . he sent them out to proclaim the kingdom of God and to heal" (Luke 9:1–2). The disciples invite others to enjoy the gift they have been given by God. They have no gifts of their own. They have no kingdom of their own. They have the kingdom of God. They live under the kingly rule of God, and by making this rule seen, they allow others to enter into this kingdom and enjoy the benefits of God's rule.

The church has the most wonderful gift to share with the world, a gift that is not their own. The gift they have is the gift that God has already given to them. They are recipients of God's kingdom, and they are sharing with others what they have received.

When Peter and John encountered a beggar outside the temple in Jerusalem, Peter told him plainly that he had no money to give him. "Silver or gold I do not have, but what I do have I give you. In the name of Jesus Christ of Nazareth, walk" (Acts 3:6). Peter could not give him anything of his own, but he gave him the gift that he had been given. He shared Christ with him.

When Paul wrote to the Corinthians, he made clear to them that his ministry was not based on his own expertise, skills, or abilities. He said, "I came to you in weakness with great fear and trembling. My message and my preaching were not with wise and persuasive words, but with a demonstration of the Spirit's power, so that your faith might not rest on human wisdom, but on God's power" (1 Cor. 2:3–5). Paul was not interested in sharing any of his own greatness; he was among the Corinthians as someone who didn't have any great abilities of his own. Instead, he showed them that he owed everything he had to the grace of God; he depended on the grace of God every day. He did not have any strength of his own; he could only rely on the power of God. He had no wisdom of his own; he could only rely on what God gave him.

In his Second Letter to the Corinthians, he told them about one of his many humiliating experiences:

> We do not want you to be uninformed, brothers and sisters, about the troubles we experienced in the province of Asia. We were under great pressure, far beyond our ability to endure, so that we despaired of life itself. Indeed, we felt we had received the sentence of death. But this happened that we might not rely on ourselves but on God, who raises the dead. He has delivered us from such a deadly peril, and he will deliver us again. On him we have set our hopes that he will continue to deliver us. (2 Cor. 1:8–10)

In the Corinthian culture, someone who held a leadership position, like Paul, was always supposed to display unassailable strength. Any hint of weakness would be carefully covered up. A near-death experience, like what Paul was telling the Corinthians about, would be seen as deeply humiliating, as something to be guarded as a tightly held secret. If anyone were to hear about it, it would shatter the image that a leader had carefully cultivated.

For a man who claimed to speak for God, as Paul did, it would be important to let other people know that God had blessed him and looked after him. If Paul were a messenger of God, one would expect God to protect his spokesman and keep him from danger. He should be above the problems and challenges that face ordinary people. If Paul cared about his reputation as a holy man, he would not talk about his weakness.

Paul's strategy for his ministry was of the exact opposite nature. He did not want to present a carefully manicured facade, to give the impression that he did not know weakness, that God had made him invincible. Instead, he was fully open and transparent about his vulnerability. He told the Corinthians candidly about his humiliating experiences. His ministry was not about sharing his own excellent qualities with the believers. He was not a model of self-improvement that they were invited to imitate.

Paul bared his soul for the Corinthians. He allowed them to get an unobstructed view of his personal failures. He let them understand that he was a man familiar with weakness, fear, anxiety, humiliation, and temptation. By allowing them to see all of that, he could share what God had given to him. God had met him in the midst of his weakness, fear, anxiety, humiliation, and temptation. If Paul had shared his strength with the Corinthians, there would have been no room for God's grace. But by sharing his weakness with them, Paul was able to share God's grace with them, for he could show them how God's grace had worked in his life, messy, pathetic, and unimpressive as it was.

The disciples of Christ cannot offer people the grace of God by showing others how admirable they are, how sinless they are, and how great they are in every way. Christ's followers are a witness of God's grace by being transparent about their own sins and their own brokenness. Only in the context of their own failure can they share the good news: God has taken our failures away, he has seen us in our misery and given us healing, he has transformed our darkness into his wonderful light, and he has redeemed us from our sins.

My favorite definition of the church is that it is the community of sinners who have been forgiven. But too often, I am afraid, the church appears as anything but a community of forgiven sinners. It emerges as a community of those who successfully cover up their mistakes and their wrongdoing. The church is seen as a fellowship of people who take care to show that they are above reproach in every way. The biblical picture of the church is very different. It is a community where people can be honest about their sins and their shortcomings. It is a community where people don't have to perform. It is a community where they can receive the forgiveness of God. Because the church is where they receive God's forgiveness, the church is also the community in which believers can show that they depend on his forgiveness. Without it, they would be lost. In practice, however, it often appears that God's forgiveness makes little difference to the members of the church. Very few of them seem to have any serious need of it. Too often we forget that Jesus came "to call not the righteous but sinners" (Mark 2:17 NRSV). To be a witness to Christ is to be a witness to the gift he has given us, not to be a witness to the fact that we don't need his gift.

The Parable of the Talents

The mission of Christ's disciples is to make use of the gift they have been given, as Jesus's parable of the talents makes clear. Jesus compares the kingdom of God to a man who entrusts his financial assets to three of his servants. One of them was given five talents, another was entrusted with two, and the last received one talent. The first two invested the money and doubled their amount, but the last servant hid the money in the ground. On his return, the master commended the servants who had made a profit and gave them even greater responsibilities. But he condemned the third servant, had his money taken away from him, and cast him outside (Matt. 25:14–30).

The main point of the parable is clear: the disciples have been entrusted with the gift of the kingdom, and it is their responsibility to put the powers of this kingdom to work. Those who do will receive their reward, and those who don't will be punished. The issue is not the capabilities of the servants, as we understand from the fact that although the first servant made five talents and the second made two, they both doubled their money. Their success was relative not to their cleverness but to the amount of money they had been given initially. Even though the first servant made much more money than the second, they both received an identical reward. To each of them the master says, "I will put you in charge of many things" (25:21, 23). It was the entrusted money that was decisive for their success, not their own skills or efforts. The gift with which they had been entrusted was not something they could keep to themselves and keep hidden; it had to be put to use.

The nature of the gift of the kingdom is such that it cannot be kept to ourselves. It has to be used, and it has to be shared. The gift of God's kingdom consists above all in the gift of forgiveness. By its very nature forgiveness involves more than one person. One person has to forgive someone else. Forgiveness creates community. The gift of the kingdom of God creates a new community that is founded on the reconciliation brought by Christ. Reconciliation cannot be enjoyed in isolation; then it would cease to exist. Reconciliation involves more than one party. It is enjoyed when people come together and exchange their enmity for friendship. The gift of the kingdom is not a purely spiritual and immaterial gift but a gift that has concrete manifestations. While it results in feelings of joy and exultation, the gift of Christ is not the gift of enjoying a new feeling, as if it were a hallucinatory drug. Christ's gifts are experienced and enjoyed in real life, and they can only be enjoyed in community.

The third servant did not understand the nature of the gift, and he revealed the reason why when he replied to his master, "Master, I know you. You're a harsh man, reaping where you haven't sown and gathering where you haven't scattered seed. So I was afraid and went off and hid your talent in the ground. See, you have what is yours" (Matt. 25:24–25 CSB). He had acted out of fear, and he had not dared to invest the money because he knew his master to be a hard man.

Those who hear and read the parable understand that the master represents Christ himself, and the servants represent his disciples; the first two are genuine disciples, and the last one is a false disciple. They also realize that the third servant has a flawed understanding of his master, an understanding that is ultimately inadequate. Christ may be a hard man when he comes in judgment, but his disciples know that he is above all "gentle and humble" (Matt. 11:29). While he may show his wrath, he is in fact slow to wrath, and he delights in showing mercy. The psalmist praises the Lord, "for his anger lasts only a moment, but his favor lasts a lifetime" (Ps. 30:5). The third servant, who did not know his master's mercy, did not have any genuine knowledge of him.

The false disciples do not genuinely know Christ because they only know him as someone who teaches us how God wants us to live. They know him as the one who comes and demands everything of us, demands that we leave everything in order to follow him, that we need a righteousness surpassing that of the Pharisees in order to enter the kingdom of heaven. To them, Jesus is a hard man. From their personal experience with him, they do not know that he is the one who blesses the poor in spirit and grants them the kingdom of heaven as a gift. They do not know that he is the one who forgives all their sins and asks them what they want him to do for them. They do not know his mercy and grace. As a result, they are unable to put his gifts to the right use; they don't know the nature of these gifts. They may have heard that Christ is merciful, but they have not experienced his forgiveness; they have not experienced his grace. No one can share Christ's grace if they have not received it themselves—if they have not experienced the love that Christ shows to the sinner who comes to him and begs for mercy.

Many readers of this parable have been shocked by the concluding note of judgment. The master commanded: "So take the talent from him and give it to the one who has ten talents. For to everyone who has, more will be given, and he will have more than enough. But from the one who does not have, even what he has will be taken away from him. And throw this good-for-nothing servant into the outer darkness, where there will be weeping and gnashing of teeth" (Matt. 25:28–30 CSB). It seems cruel when Jesus says that "from the one who does not have, even what he has will be taken away from him." Applied to the parable, it appears downright unjust that the third servant should be judged and punished merely because he had been given a smaller amount of money to begin with. But as we have seen, he was not judged because of his initial limitations. He was judged because of his failure to make use of the gift he was given.

In the end, Jesus's words are illustrative when we pay attention to precisely what he is saying. He does not say that "from the one who has little, even what he has will be taken away from him." He says that "from the one who does not have, even what he has will be taken away from him." In the parable we see that the third servant didn't really have anything, even though he had been given a whole talent. When the money was taken away from him, he didn't really lose anything, because he had not made any use of it while it was in his possession. He had kept it buried in the ground.

The judgment described in this parable does not involve taking anything away from those who are condemned; they didn't receive the gift of the kingdom in the first place. It had never become theirs. They might have heard about the kingdom, and they might even have believed it was theirs, but they never internalized the gift of the kingdom so that it had become a part of who they were. The gift of forgiveness and reconciliation had not genuinely become their own, they had no use for it, and they were not putting the gift to use in their lives.

They resemble the servant who had been forgiven ten thousand talents and proceeded to brutalize his fellow servant to make him pay a debt of one hundred denarii (Matt. 18:22–35). He had not internalized the gift of forgiveness. Ultimately these characters are closely related to the people who are condemned throughout Matthew's Gospel: the self-righteous, those who have no genuine need for the gift of Christ. As Jesus explains: "It is not the healthy who need a doctor, but the sick. But go and learn what this means: 'I desire mercy, not sacrifice.' For I have not come to call the righteous, but sinners" (Matt. 9:12–13). Those who think they are righteous never think they have any real need for the forgiveness that Jesus gives, and they remain on the outside of his kingdom, even when they profess to be his followers.

Fellowship

The church exists because it has received the gift of Christ, and its mission is to share the gift it has received. God's people have been the beneficiaries of God's generosity, and they live to show the same generosity.

When Jesus was taken up to heaven, he sent the Holy Spirit to continue his kingly rule. The book of Acts gives an account of the Holy Spirit's work through the disciples. Acts is framed by references to the proclamation of God's kingdom (1:3; 28:31), and the whole book may be read as the story of this proclamation. Through the power of the Holy Spirit, the disciples proclaim the kingdom to different ethnic groups all over the world (1:8). During this time, the church went through explosive growth and experienced God's kingly rule in a most powerful way. Acts shows us a beautiful picture of this community.

They devoted themselves to the apostles' teaching and to fellowship, to the breaking of bread and to prayer. Everyone was filled with awe at the many

wonders and signs performed by the apostles. All the believers were together
and had everything in common. They sold property and possessions to give
to anyone who had need. Every day they continued to meet together in the
temple courts. They broke bread in their homes and ate together with glad and
sincere hearts, praising God and enjoying the favor of all the people. And the
Lord added to their number daily those who were being saved. (Acts 2:42–47)

Luke's description of a community that lived together in perfect harmony
and shared everything would sound familiar to his audience. They had heard
of similar societies before, when Greek and Roman philosophers were waxing
poetic about their dreams of utopia. In such a society, no one would suffer
need, humans would live in genuine fellowship with one another, they would
freely share all their possessions, and peace and harmony would rule. Such
dreams could be quite popular, but everyone knew it was nothing but a dream.
It could never be reality.

Luke's point is as clear as it is provocative. Through the gift of the Holy Spirit,
in the community of Jesus's disciples, utopia is no longer a dream. It is reality.
The kingly rule of God has been established on earth. The blissful life that we
will experience when God comes to earth, overpowers evil, and reestablishes his
kingly rule—the people of God are living this life now! The political and military
authority structures of the Roman Empire did nothing to establish it. Far from
it. But the outpouring of the Holy Spirit has made it a reality. By the Holy Spirit,
God rules his people from within their hearts. And where this rule is exercised,
utopia is a present reality. People come together and have everything in common.
They sell their property to give to anyone in need. No one claims anything as
their exclusive possession, but they share everything with the community.

What Luke describes may sound like communism, but the early church
was something entirely different. Under communism, equality and economic
fellowship are enforced by the state. Efforts at establishing such a society not
only result in inevitable failure but also tend to bring unspeakable human suffering. Humans are not able to do what only God can do; they are incapable
of establishing this kind of society. When they try, equality proves elusive. The
only tools at their disposal are the coercive powers of government. When the
government is tasked with creating a society of equals, certain individuals
will need to be entrusted with the power to enforce it. The ideal of equality
must be abandoned at the very outset. In the novel *Animal Farm*, an allegory
about the Soviet Union, George Orwell sums up the Communist experience
well: "All animals are equal, but some animals are more equal than others."[3]

3. George Orwell, *Animal Farm: A Fairy Story* (London: Secker & Warburg, 1945), chap. 10.

The early church did not rely on external force to ensure equality. It relied on the Holy Spirit. The Holy Spirit was poured out into the hearts of believers and motivated them to share their possessions voluntarily. No coercion was involved in the economic fellowship of the early church. The account of Ananias and Sapphira shows very clearly that the apostolic church did not eliminate private ownership. Ananias and Sapphira sold their property and brought the money to the apostles, but they lied about the amount and kept some of the money to themselves. Peter discerned the nature of their sin and confronted each of them individually. Both of them declared that they had given all the money to the apostles, demonstrating that they had planned their sin together. When they persisted in their sin, God struck both of them dead and punished them for their wickedness. The sin was not that they had kept some money for themselves but that they had lied to God. Peter explained it clearly to Ananias: "Ananias, how is it that Satan has so filled your heart that you have lied to the Holy Spirit and have kept for yourself some of the money you received for the land? Didn't it belong to you before it was sold? And after it was sold, wasn't the money at your disposal? What made you think of doing such a thing? You have not lied just to human beings but to God" (Acts 5:3–4). The land belonged to Ananias, not to the church, and after it was sold, the money was his own. He was free to do with it whatever he pleased.

The Holy Spirit did a miracle in the early church: he made the believers want to give away their possessions and share everything with those in need. Their economic fellowship was a result of the spiritual fellowship that existed among them. God had given them a new life and a new identity. They all belonged to him now, and they were fully united with one another.

> All the believers were one in heart and mind. No one claimed that any of their possessions was their own, but they shared everything they had. With great power the apostles continued to testify to the resurrection of the Lord Jesus. And God's grace was so powerfully at work in them all that there were no needy persons among them. For from time to time those who owned land or houses sold them, brought the money from the sales and put it at the apostles' feet, and it was distributed to anyone who had need. (Acts 4:32–35)

The believers had received the grace of God, and this grace was not a passive gift that they could keep to themselves. God's grace was powerfully at work. The nature of the church was to share what it had received. God had been gracious and generous to them; they were gracious and generous to each other.

Love of Strangers

The account in Acts shows us that the generous spirit of the early church was key to its phenomenal growth. Luke reports that "they broke bread in their homes and ate together with glad and sincere hearts, praising God and enjoying the favor of all the people" (2:46–47). The last phrase is difficult to translate because the Greek is ambiguous. It could mean that the church was "enjoying the favor of all the people." However, another meaning is equally possible: "They were showing favor toward all the people."[4] If the latter translation is correct, the point is not that the church was well-liked but that the church reached out to all people in a spirit of generosity. They did not have a reclusive or reactionary stance toward their community; they interacted with others with an attitude of trust and openness. In any case, the early chapters of Acts show us a church that had a positive impact on its surroundings, a church that was eager to share the gifts that God had given to them. The rumor of the church soon spread outside Jerusalem, so that people from the surrounding towns brought "their sick and those tormented by impure spirits, and all of them were healed" (5:16).

The disciples eventually learned to share God's gifts with everyone, even those who would be considered unqualified for the kingdom of God, the gentiles. But this level of inclusiveness did not come naturally to them; God had to intervene very decisively for Peter to understand that gentiles now belonged in the people of God. Three times he had a vision of unclean food that God told him to eat. Then he was called to the house of the Roman officer Cornelius, and as he was proclaiming the gospel, he witnessed the Holy Spirit fall on all those present. At that point, he finally realized that the good news about the kingdom of God was for the gentiles too (10:9–48).

Peter had to learn that God was now reaching out to those who had not previously been eligible for inclusion among God's people. Such was the nature of God's grace: to come to those who were far away from him. Christ died for us while we were still God's enemies (Rom. 5:8, 10). When we had done nothing to make ourselves likable, he had mercy on us and came down to our world to save us. Even though we had turned against him, disobeyed him, and rebelled against him, he looked on us with compassion.

Christ's work of salvation was the ultimate act of crossing boundaries and reaching out to those who were far away. The nature of the church is to share what we have been given by Christ and to imitate him in embracing those who

4. The Common English Bible renders this verse, "They praised God and demonstrated God's goodness to everyone."

are different from us. The nature of Christ's love is to love strangers, and he calls on his followers to do the same.

When Jesus gave his life, he died not only for his friends; he died for his enemies, for those who had turned their backs on him. When he was hanging on the cross, he was abandoned by even his own disciples. He was surrounded by people who hated him, who celebrated watching his slow and agonizing death. His reaction was to pray, "Father, forgive them, for they do not know what they are doing" (Luke 23:34). As he was dying, he sought the forgiveness of his executioners.

Jesus's practice of love for strangers knew no limitations. The parable of the good Samaritan (Luke 10:25–37) is a story of the kind of love Jesus taught us. An expert in the law wanted to know what Jesus thought about a knotty problem of biblical interpretation. The law of Moses commands us to "love your neighbor as yourself" (Lev. 19:18). There was a long-standing discussion about this commandment among the Jewish people. How do you define "neighbor"? Who is it, exactly, that God commands us to love? A common interpretation held that the "neighbor" could only mean a fellow Jew, someone who belonged to the Jewish nation and followed the Jewish religion. It could not refer to people from other nations and other faiths. Some Jewish groups even taught their followers to hate those who did not belong to their particular brand of Judaism. (We may wonder how different modern-day Christian practice is, even if a hostile attitude toward people of other convictions is rarely that clearly stated.)

Jesus responded with the parable of the good Samaritan. Jews and Samaritans had a long history of bitter hostility. They both hailed from the twelve tribes of Israel. The Samaritans traced their ancestry to the ten northern tribes who had been conquered by the Assyrians in the eighth century BCE. In the aftermath, they had been subjected to forced migration and ended up intermarrying with the gentiles. As a result, the Jews did not view them as pure Israelites. Jews and Samaritans were also bitterly divided about their religion. The Samaritans had always rejected the idea that God had chosen David and his seed to be the king of Israel, as well as the choice of Jerusalem as the place of worship. The Jews and the Samaritans were closely related, but they hated each other with the kind of hatred that is reserved for people of one's own kin.

When Jesus told the parable of the good Samaritan, it would have been as provocative as a flag burning. A man had been attacked by robbers and left for dead. A priest and a Levite, representatives of Jewish piety, passed by but failed to do anything to help the victim. Then a Samaritan appeared, the proverbial villain, like the rider in a black hat in classical Western movies or the Middle Eastern Muslim extremist in more recent thrillers. But the bad guy turns out to be the hero in Jesus's story. The Samaritan emerges as the role model that we all should imitate. The parable shows us what it means to love our neighbor; it is to throw aside everything we think we know about who our enemies are, embrace them, and love them with no concern for our own safety. It is to reach out to those with whom we have nothing in common, even to our perceived enemies—just as Jesus did.

In a challenging twist, Jesus also turned around the question he had initially been asked, "Who is my neighbor?" (Luke 10:29). Jesus asked, "Which of these three . . . was a neighbor?" (10:36). The expert in the law wanted to define his neighbor; he wanted to define the object of his love—how far should his love extend? Jesus did not answer that question. Instead, he told the legal expert to define the subject of love: define yourself as a loving person. When you do, the question of whom to love will answer itself. A loving person shows love. Their love is not motivated by who the recipient is. Their love is welling up from within their heart.

We can't make ourselves love like this. "We love because he first loved us," the apostle John says (1 John 4:19). Christ's disciples can only love the way they do because they are sharing the love that Christ has showed them. The apostle Paul constantly returns to this theme when he is giving exhortations to his churches. Their new behavior comes as a result of what Christ has done in their lives. He has given them a new identity. "There is neither Jew nor Gentile, neither slave nor free, nor is there male and female, for you are all one in Christ Jesus" (Gal. 3:28). Jesus Christ has made us all children of God. We have become new people with a new status; we belong to Christ. All our conventional ways of defining ourselves have become irrelevant in comparison to our new identity in Christ.

In this world, people claim their loyalty to their family, their hometown, their ethnic group, and their nation. In our postmodern era, when all people can find like-minded souls on the internet, it has become increasingly common to identify with others who have the same interests, the same tastes, the same ideology, or the same political convictions, however extreme and obscure they may be. The gospel does not eliminate these individual characteristics, but their significance fades in light of the one identity that truly matters: we belong to Christ, and we are children of God. No matter what our differences may be, they do not change the fact that we belong together as one. Our unity has one reason only: we belong to Christ; he has cleansed us from our sins and made us God's beloved children, his holy people.

A local church that genuinely proclaims the kingly rule of God will therefore always be a community of people from a conglomerate of various backgrounds.

In such a community we find people of different skin color and ethnic background, people from the upper class of society and people from the lower class, wealthy and poor, educated and uneducated, people with a diversity of political and ideological views, people who seem to have little in common, and people who do not naturally seem to get along. They are united not because of who they are and because of natural characteristics that bring them together but because of what Jesus has done for them.

As a missionary in Ethiopia, I have often met Christians with whom I have so little in common that I have found it very difficult to carry on a conversation. The language barrier is one thing, but even if I could overcome it, I don't know what experiences we share that we could talk about. Their life is so different from mine that I don't know how to relate to it. On one occasion, one of my students told me that he was moving into a new apartment. He did not have a car, but he knew I did, so he asked me if I would help him. I was not happy, because I had made other plans, and I assumed that moving a whole family would take the better part of the day. But I did not want to be the selfish guy who was unwilling to help other people, so I put my plans aside to go and help my student. Things did not go as I had anticipated. It took the two of us five minutes to load all his family's belongings into my car, and that included the leftovers from their dinner the day before. The whole moving job was completed in less than an hour, and I could return to the comforts of my home, quite ashamed of how ignorant I was about the life of my own students. It is difficult for me to relate to people whose situation is so different from my own.

As different as our lives are, however, I have shared some of the happiest moments of my life with my Ethiopian friends. They have showed me that there is indeed a bond that is stronger than anything else: the bond that binds us together in the family of God. When someone with whom I have nothing in common treats me like a brother, I know what it means to be a child of God. When I can worship the same Lord as people with whom I am unable to have a conversation, I know what it means that Christ has made us one.

The church in Rome consisted of both Jewish and gentile believers. The differences between them could make it difficult for them to live together as one congregation. Some of them were vegetarians, and some were omnivores. Their different diets were a matter not of personal choice but of deep religious conviction. The vegetarians abstained from food they believed God prohibited them from eating. Those who ate everything belittled the vegetarians for their immature faith. Did they not know that Christ had "declared all foods clean" (Mark 7:19)? Similar differences existed among them concerning the drinking of wine and what holidays to observe as well.

In terms of conviction, Paul agreed with those who emphasized a Christian's freedom in Christ, but his concern lay elsewhere. He did not want the Roman Christians to be divided over these matters. Instead, Paul instructed them, "Accept one another, . . . just as Christ accepted you, in order to bring praise to God" (Rom. 15:7).

In the church, believers may have different opinions about many things. Some may be right, and some may be wrong. But in the family of God, there is something that is more important than for everyone to agree about everything, and there is something that is more important than to be right. What matters is to demonstrate the same kind of acceptance of others that Christ has showed us. He has forgiven us all our sins and accepted us despite the most damning flaws. If he had asked how much he liked the things we do and the attitudes and opinions we have, he would have condemned us to eternal damnation. Instead, he accepted us in his mercy. And he calls us to show the same attitude toward one another: to accept one another as he has accepted us.

Too often, local congregations consist of people who have found other things to bond over, things that are unrelated or tangential to the bond that binds all Christians together: their faith in Christ and the gift of God's Holy Spirit. They have formed a community of people with the same background, interests, opinions, and tastes in music. Some churches are tailored to specific subsets of the general population, churches for the wealthy, churches for the middle class, churches for the working class, churches for young professionals, churches for college students, churches for retirees, churches for immigrants, churches for Norwegians, and churches for Koreans. These churches deprive themselves of one of their most significant opportunities to proclaim the kingly rule of God: to demonstrate that Christ accepts us despite all our differences.

In our social activities, we tend to look for people who can do something for us, who can help us become more popular or connect us to a community of higher social standing. Knowing that, as the saying goes, If you tell me with whom you associate, I will tell you who you are, we like to count admirable people among our friends. Jesus picked his friends based on very different principles. He was known for keeping bad company, and he wants his followers to do the same. His followers should be known as people with friends in low places. Jesus was comfortable among "deplorables," and his disciples should be no different.

In my own church experiences, I have often wondered why there are so many annoying people in church. Some churches just seem to be jerk magnets. It has caused me frequent frustrations. But as I turn to the Bible, I think that is exactly how Jesus wanted it to be. Jesus loves annoying people. He loves them to death. He came to die, not just for awesome and wonderful people, but even more so for disgusting people, for sinners, real-life sinners. When he chose his twelve closest friends, he picked Judas Iscariot, a thief who was full of judgment against other people. Judas resented the woman who spent all her perfume on Jesus, and he self-righteously and hypocritically asked why she hadn't spent her money on the poor instead (John 12:5–6). Later he betrayed his master for a monetary reward. Jesus picked Peter as his closest friend, someone who never engaged his brain before he said anything. How could the all-knowing and all-wise Creator put up with him? He chose John and James, who were so arrogant they thought they deserved the places of honor in Christ's kingdom (Mark 10:35–37). None of them ever seemed to understand the most basic things that Jesus was teaching them. Jesus was such a genius that he had the nation's best scholars spellbound when he was at the tender age of twelve. How could he bear to hang out with these bozos? The simple answer is that he loved them. Jesus loves the unlovable.

That is why I think one of the best measures of the Christlikeness of a church is that annoying people feel at home in it. A church that is modeled after Christ loves the unlovable and welcomes them. The loud, the grouchy, the socially awkward, the needy—the church is their hangout. That's how the manager wants it. The church is where they are accepted, and the church is where they find healing.

The Great Commission

Christ's love knows no limits. His kingdom is universal; it encompasses the entire planet. The proclamation of the kingly rule of God must therefore reach every nation and every ethnic group in the world. It is never enough for the church to proclaim God's kingly rule to its immediate surroundings. The church must reach out to other parts of the world, where God's kingly rule is not yet recognized and honored.

In his last words before he was taken to heaven, Jesus gave his disciples the Great Commission. They should be single-mindedly occupied with this mission until his return: "All authority in heaven and on earth has been given to me. Therefore go and make disciples of all nations, baptizing them in the name of the Father and of the Son and of the Holy Spirit, and teaching them to obey everything I have commanded you. And surely I am with you always, to the very end of the age" (Matt. 28:18–20).

Jesus speaks as the one who rules as king, as the one who has all author-ity in heaven and on earth. Precisely because he has this authority, he sends his disciples to every corner of the planet. Because he is king everywhere, in heaven and on earth, his kingly rule must be proclaimed everywhere, to every nation under heaven. They all need to know that God's kingdom is here, that the forces of evil have been handed their ultimate defeat, that Christ now rules as the divine king, that the kingdom of God is here to be entered. They have to be made disciples, to be turned into citizens of this kingdom, to be made subjects of the eternal king.

Because Christ's rule and authority extends everywhere, the church cannot be a witness of his kingdom in only their own geographical location. They must go out. They must go to those who have not yet heard of this kingdom. The church is therefore a sending community. It is always sending missionaries to areas of the world where God's kingdom is unknown and his kingly rule is not upheld. The church must claim every patch of the earth for their Lord.

In today's world, most ethnic groups of the world are represented in many different nations. It is now possible for many local churches to engage in world mission without traveling outside their hometown. The world's population is coming to them. Their ministries can reach other ethnic groups by serving immigrants and refugees, showing them hospitality, and demonstrating the love of Christ to them. These migrants often stay in close contact with their family members back home, and they often provide for them financially. When they accept Christ, they are in a better position than anyone else to bring the gospel to their home country. A church that is intentional about showing hospitality to strangers may therefore have a more far-reaching ministry than they are able to imagine. When they are proclaiming the kingly rule of God at home, they may see ripple effects all over the world.

But those with the least resources will never be able to become immigrants in another country. In many cases, they will not even be able to make it to another country as refugees. They are stuck in poverty and starvation, experiencing high infant mortality, frequent untimely deaths, and endless suffering where they are.

God sent his Son to the world to bring salvation to those who were far away. And as the Father sent him, so does Jesus send his disciples (John 20:21). The disciples go to those who are far away, to the weakest of the weak and the poorest of the poor. They can only do this when they relocate to countries that are far away, learn languages that are difficult to learn, and become a part of cultures that are difficult to understand, sometimes cultures that are inhospitable and downright hostile. Jesus's disciples have to go because their king has sent them. They go to proclaim the kingly rule of the one who has all authority in heaven and on earth, and they go with the assurance that the all-powerful one will be with them always, to the very end of the age.

Acts of Mercy

When the disciples proclaim the kingdom of God, they share the mercy they
have received from Christ. Their proclamation takes place both in word and
in deed. Jesus calls his followers, "Be merciful, just as your Father is merciful"
(Luke 6:36). In the mighty judgment scene in Matthew 25:31–46, Jesus shows
us how his disciples follow in his footsteps. Those who enter into eternal life at
the last judgment are the ones who took care of the least of Christ's brothers
and sisters, those who did not have anyone else to look after them, those who
were alone and without any resources in this world. Just as Christ saved those
who had no means by which to save themselves, so do his disciples provide
for those who have no means of their own. They reach out to those who are
hungry and give them something to eat. They find the thirsty and give them
something to drink. They notice strangers and invite them in. They see those
who need clothes and provide for their need. They take care of the sick and
look after them. They show mercy to those who are in prison and come to
visit them. Jesus tells them, "Whatever you did for one of the least of these
brothers and sisters of mine, you did for me" (25:40).

In the history of Christian mission, there has been a constant debate about
the relationship between acts of mercy and the proclamation of the gospel.
In practice, the proclamation of the gospel has usually been accompanied by
development aid, including health care and education projects. Historically,
such acts of service have often been viewed as secondary to what mission
ultimately is about: proclamation.

In the 1970s, the Evangelical Ethiopian Church Mekane Yesus (EECMY)
was faced with the opposite problem. They experienced that many international organizations were more than happy to help with development projects,
but it was difficult to receive funding for the church's evangelistic programs. In
response, they issued a statement, "On the Interrelation between Proclamation
of the Gospel and Human Development," which is a brilliant affirmation of
holistic Christian ministry. The Ethiopian church leaders boldly emphasized
that they "see development of the inner man as a prerequisite for a healthy
and lasting development of our society. Unless our people are helped to the
spiritual freedom and maturity which enables them responsibly to handle
material development, we are afraid that what was intended to be a means
of enhancing the well-being of man can have the opposite effect and create
new forms of evil to destroy him."

At the same time, they hoped "that the present artificial division between
spiritual and physical needs would be done away with and provision would be
made for an integral development of man in order to enable him to play his

role as an agent in the development process."[5] These church leaders saw clearly that the proclamation of the Word of God is the foundation for everything that is genuinely good in human society. Only the gospel of Jesus Christ has the power to transform humans and their communities. People can only know the good life, in the real sense, when they know Jesus Christ as their Lord.

However, the Ethiopian leaders, who were familiar with the curse of poverty, refused to accept a gospel that offered nothing in terms of delivering people from that curse. They knew what James had written to his church: "Suppose a brother or a sister is without clothes and daily food. If one of you says to them, 'Go in peace; keep warm and well fed,' but does nothing about their physical needs, what good is it?" (James 2:15–16). A gospel that does nothing to address people's most immediate needs is no good. God's concern is for people as complete humans. His salvation is a salvation that embraces the whole person, not merely a part.

Healing

Jesus's own activity is the best example of holistic ministry. He did not merely bring a message of spiritual salvation or offer a hope of future bliss when he met people in need. Jesus addressed their needs at every level. When he met a blind man, he did not tell him that he might have spiritual sight, which was more valuable than physical sight. "Jesus asked him, 'What do you want me to do for you?'" (Luke 18:40–41). The man wanted to be able to see, and Jesus gave him what he asked for.

Jesus sent his disciples out with the same mission. "He gave them power and authority to drive out all demons and to cure diseases, and he sent them out to proclaim the kingdom of God and to heal the sick" (Luke 9:1–2). There are many accounts in the New Testament about the disciples providing physical healing like Jesus did. When Peter met a paralyzed man outside the temple, he spoke to him in Jesus's name, and the man "jumped to his feet and began to walk" (Acts 3:8). We hear of many people who were healed of sickness and evil spirits (5:15–16). In Lydda, Peter told another paralyzed man, Aeneas, that Jesus healed him (9:32–35), and in Joppa he raised Tabitha from the dead (9:36–43). Paul saw a paralyzed man begin to walk when he was proclaiming the gospel in Lystra (14:8–10), and in Philippi he cast out an evil spirit from a female slave (16:16–18). In Ephesus, "God did extraordinary miracles

5. Øyvind M. Eide, *Revolution and Religion in Ethiopia: The Growth and Persecution of the Mekane Yesus Church, 1974–85*, with a foreword by Carl Fr. Hallencreutz, Eastern African Studies (Oxford: James Currey, 2000), 264–65.

through Paul, so that even handkerchiefs and aprons that had touched him were taken to the sick, and their illnesses were cured and the evil spirits left them" (19:11–12). A young man named Eutychus was raised from the dead when Paul was in Troas (20:9–12). On Malta, Paul healed the chief official Publius's father from fever and dysentery, as well as many others who were sick (28:7–10).

Such miracles are not limited to New Testament times. Craig Keener, a leading biblical scholar, points out that hundreds of millions of Christians claim to have witnessed miracles in our time. Most of these claims are difficult to verify, and we should not necessarily believe every miracle account we are told. But Christians all over the world experience God performing miracles today. Keener has carefully collected numerous eyewitness accounts of Christians who have been healed of serious diseases. He documents several reports of blind and paralyzed people being healed and even dead people being brought back to life. In many cases the healings have been confirmed by physicians and independent witnesses.[6] When his people pray to him, God continues to do miracles in our time. These miracles are not usually advertised and made widely known, but many people experience the healing intervention of God every day. These healings show that God continues to exercise his kingly rule through the church and that the new creation is present.

Holistic Healing

When Christ healed people, he did not provide only physical healing. He also cared for the whole person. Jesus did not cure only people's physical ailments; he brought restoration on the emotional and social levels as well. A student of the Gospels will be struck by the many references to Jesus's touching the people he healed. For those who were seriously ill, such as the lepers, Jesus's hand must have genuinely felt like a touch from heaven. In accordance with the law of Moses, the lepers in Israel were proclaimed unclean, and they were not allowed to live with the other Israelites. They had to wear torn clothes and let their hair be unkempt so that they were easily identified as unclean. Whenever someone approached them, they had to cry out, "Unclean! Unclean!" (Lev. 13:45). No one was supposed to come within an arm's length of them, so that they would not become infected. For those who were diagnosed with such a disease, their life as they knew it was over. They lost their job,

6. Craig S. Keener, *Miracles: The Credibility of the New Testament Accounts*, 2 vols. (Grand Rapids: Baker Academic, 2011).

their family, their house, everything. They were doomed to live the rest of their life in isolation. The loneliness must have been unbearable. When they met other people, thus experiencing a temporary respite from the misery that was their life, lepers were obligated to scare them away as soon as they came within shouting distance.

When a leper approached Jesus, the first thing Jesus did was touch him (Mark 1:41). Before he even talked to the man, and before he cured him of his physical disease, he gave him what he must have longed for more than anything else: Jesus showed him a physical manifestation of his love. He touched him. He allowed him back into the fellowship of another human who cared for him, accepted him, and not only could stand his company but actually wanted to be near him and to touch him.

Like Jesus, so does the church offer holistic healing. More often than we know, God gives physical healing through the prayers of believers. The disciples also provide holistic healing when they follow in the footsteps of their master. They welcome into their community those who have been written off by everyone else—people who are not viewed as productive members of society, people no one wants because they are seen as a burden to everyone. Jesus wants them, and his church puts his will into action.

The Lord's Supper

The most tangible experience of the heavenly reality here on earth is the celebration of the Lord's Supper. When Jesus instituted this meal, he told his disciples, "Truly I tell you, I will not drink again from the fruit of the vine until that day when I drink it new in the kingdom of God" (Mark 14:25 parr.). It is easy to miss the significance of what Jesus is saying in this verse. He anticipates that he will again drink with them from the fruit of the vine. The drink that the disciples share with their Lord is a drink they will share with him again, in the future kingdom of God. The same drink that the disciples are drinking now is a drink they will drink in their future salvation. When Jesus's followers come together to celebrate the Lord's Supper, they are participating in a meal that will continue in the new creation. In other words, if someone wants to enjoy a foretaste of our heavenly salvation, they may participate in the Lord's Supper. The Lord's Supper is a meal that bridges the gap between our world and the heavenly world. The Lord's Supper is a heavenly meal that we can enjoy right now.

When I was preparing to go to Ethiopia as a missionary for the first time, I had never visited the country before, and I was curious about what it would be like to live there. At the time, my home was in Chicago, where there are many Ethiopians and many good Ethiopian restaurants. In order to get a foretaste of Ethiopia, I went to one of these restaurants, and I got my first exposure to the delicious Ethiopian cuisine. It was a wonderful taste of a country to which I had never been but which was soon to become my home.

We now have an opportunity to patronize a heavenly restaurant right in our own neighborhood. Whenever the church comes together to celebrate communion, a meal is served by a restaurant from heaven. A heavenly supper is provided, and we may have a foretaste of the heavenly banquet. The meal that Jesus says will continue in the heavenly world, the supper he instituted, is available right now.

It should come as a surprise to no one that Jesus intended for this meal to be continued in his heavenly kingdom. Jesus was both beloved and infamous for his meal practices. Could there be a better way for the church to make his rule known than by sharing a meal together? Perhaps more than anything else, Jesus's meals demonstrated his grace and inclusive attitude. He welcomed everyone and shared freely with them.

Today the Lord's Supper is the church's opportunity to demonstrate how the grace of Christ is shared. The gifts are provided free of cost, and there are no distinctions of status, class, ethnicity, gender, or any other kind of discrimination when the church comes together for this heavenly meal. All come to the same table, as sinners who are forgiven, and all receive the same gifts: the body and blood of Christ. He gave his body and blood to atone for our sins so that he could forgive them, and he grants his forgiveness when we receive his gifts at his table. It is a wonderful picture of Christ's way of accepting everyone.

This is why the apostle Paul got so upset about the Corinthians and their way of observing the Lord's Supper. He was so indignant that he bluntly told them it was not the Lord's Supper they were eating (1 Cor. 11:20). They were using the Lord's Supper to demonstrate the disunity that existed among them. In contrast to how communion is often observed today, the church met in a private home and shared a real meal. In accordance with secular practice, it would appear that the host in the Corinthian church gave the wealthy church members the nice seats inside the house, whereas the less privileged were served outside. The wealthy guests also received the best food and drink, and the others were left with the scraps. The meal was not being shared, and Paul accused them: "When you are eating, some of you go ahead with your own private suppers. As a result, one person remains hungry and another gets drunk" (11:21). When they came together, the rich had plenty, but the poor had nothing. Those of limited means were being shamed in front of the wealthier members of the church. Paul was incensed: "Do you despise the church of God by humiliating those who have nothing?" (11:22). The Lord's Supper is the church's meal of unity. To use it as a demonstration of disunity and to humiliate the poor is a terrible sin. Paul goes so far as to tell the Corinthians that "those who eat and drink without discerning the body of Christ eat and drink judgment on themselves" (11:29). What he has in mind is the Corinthians' divisive practices. The church is the body of Christ, but they are not discerning this body, and they are sinning against Christ's own body when they are sinning against the weaker members of the church.

The Lord's Supper was intended to be something very different: a foretaste of the heavenly meal, a demonstration of the grace of Jesus Christ, the grace that extends to the greatest of sinners and that knows no distinctions between persons, the grace that shows that we are all one in Jesus Christ. This grace is tangibly manifested in the meal that the church has the opportunity to celebrate every time they come together.

The Lord's Supper is a foretaste of our heavenly meal because it takes place in remembrance of Jesus. When Jesus instituted it, he told his disciples, "Do this in remembrance of me" (1 Cor. 11:24). This means more than to remember Jesus. (The disciples would presumably always remember him, not only when they were eating this meal.) To eat the meal in remembrance of Christ is to see his presence in it. Through the sharing of this meal, the benefits of Jesus's self-sacrifice, his gracious inclusion of sinners into his fellowship, and his generous distribution of the heavenly gifts are present once again.

Unfortunately, many Christians have not been trained to taste the sweetness of this meal. Churches often surround communion with a solemn atmosphere, and most of those who participate look like they are going to a funeral. Unbiblical teaching about the need to examine oneself has even made many Christians reluctant to partake of the meal, fearing that they will "eat and drink judgment on themselves" if they are not rightly prepared (1 Cor. 11:29). However, Paul's warning about judgment has nothing to do with being worthy of the meal or of having prepared oneself by doing the right kind of self-examination. He was talking to the Corinthians who misused the Lord's Supper to humiliate the poor. To eat the bread or drink the cup "in an unworthy manner" (11:27) is to use the meal to demonstrate disunity. Paul's warning is against those who intimidate other Christians from fully participating in the fellowship constituted by this meal. When these words are used to tell believers that they cannot take part in the meal unless they are well-prepared, then weak Christians are once again being intimidated and are deterred from participating. Those who interpret Paul's words in this way have changed their meaning to the exact opposite of what Paul intended. Paul was against intimidating the weak, but this interpretation introduces a new way of intimidating them. The meal is a fellowship meal, but this interpretation destroys the fellowship.

The Lord's Supper is for sinners like the disciples—traitors, bad-tempered, fickle, and unreliable—who need forgiveness. This meal is for those who need a savior, someone who gave his body and blood for their sins, a redeemer who sacrificed himself in their place. The Lord's Supper is the occasion when he gives himself to us so that we can feel it and taste it.

The Lord's Supper is the time for the most joyful celebration. It is the event when the grace of Christ flows freely. In the parable of the prodigal son, the loving father throws the most lavish party, and he tells his older son, "We had to celebrate and be glad, because this brother of yours was dead and is alive again; he was lost and is found" (Luke 15:32). The Lord's Supper is our opportunity to have a genuine foretaste of that banquet. It is the time when sinners come home to eat and drink the gifts of our heavenly Lord.

A Paradoxical Reality

When I reflect on what the Bible says about the church, I am deeply challenged. I have had many depressing experiences in church. I often despair about the whole idea. The Bible teaches that the church is the manifestation of God's kingly rule on earth, but I rarely see it. I have seen it, and at times I do see it. The people of God have showed me the love of God in so many wonderful ways; I can't deny the divine touch that is there. But a lot of the time, I see something else. I see a church that is divided, church members who are judgmental, and Christian communities so closed that it is impossible for outsiders to penetrate. Sometimes I feel more accepted by non-Christian friends than by members of the church. And I hate to admit it, but I am afraid many people have experienced the church in the same negative way that I have, precisely because they have met me there. Is the biblical vision for the church just a dream after all? Is it impossible to believe that we can experience it on this side of eternity?

The French New Testament scholar Alfred Loisy famously quipped, "Jesus came proclaiming the kingdom, and what arrived was the church." Was the whole project of organized Christian religion a mistake from the beginning? Was it the invention of power-hungry religious charlatans who betrayed the beautiful vision of their master and turned it into an instrument of oppression? Many people have thought so. Other Christians usually do not go that far, but in practice they entertain ideas that are quite similar to Loisy's. They do not see the church as a genuine manifestation of the kingdom. Instead, they view the church more as a preparation for the kingdom. Their understanding of the world may be compared to a ship that is sinking in the ocean. The church is a lifeboat that picks up as many people as it can. Those who are rescued are kept safe in the lifeboat until their salvation arrives. The church does not provide the ultimate gift of salvation but makes it possible to receive salvation sometime in the future.

The New Testament clearly teaches that the people of God have their minds set on the future. The book of Revelation concludes with this plea: "Come, Lord Jesus" (Rev. 22:20). Paul expresses the same prayer at the end of his First Letter to the Corinthians: "Come, Lord!" (1 Cor. 16:22). To be a Christian is to wait for the Lord.

But Christians have their mind set on the present as well. Jesus didn't think that his followers had to wait to experience the reality of God's kingly rule. He delegated his authority to the disciples and told them to continue his own ministry. The one who is the light of the world also told his followers, "You are the light of the world" (Matt. 5:14). He affirmed that his own salvific power would be at work through those who believed in him. He gave them the same mission that his Father had given him. "As the Father has sent me, I am sending you," he said when he had been resurrected and gave the disciples his Holy Spirit (John 20:21).

If we do not believe that the full power and presence of the kingdom and kingly rule of God are present in the church, we do not believe the New Testament, and we do not believe the words of Jesus himself. This is why most of the Jewish people rejected Jesus, and this is why most of them continue to reject him, because they cannot accept that he has delivered on the promise to make God's kingly rule a reality.

One thing that distinguishes Christians from Jews is the Christian belief that Jesus came and established the kingly rule of God. It is a reality here and now. What distinguishes the Christian faith from the old heresy known as gnosticism is the belief that the kingly rule of God is not merely a spiritual reality but comes to expression through the Christian community. It can be experienced here and now; it is embodied in the church.

Christians are characterized by the belief that God created the physical universe and called it good, that we expect a bodily resurrection, and that God himself has become a human like us. It follows from these beliefs that the gift of God is experienced through our physical and material existence. God's salvation can be experienced and not just believed in this world. It is fundamental to the Christian understanding of salvation that salvation is embodied. It is felt, seen, and heard. Just as the first believers could touch, see, and hear their Savior (1 John 1:1), so can our salvation be touched, seen, and heard today. It is experienced through the body of Christ, his church. The people of God demonstrate the love of God and the gift of God by giving themselves in acts of love and mercy, by giving themselves in the act of forgiveness.

As Jesus's glory was hidden under an appearance of weakness, so is the glory of the church hidden under the church's many weaknesses as well. Jesus came to the world with the power of God, but his power appeared to the world as weakness. He brought victory, but it looked like defeat. The same pattern applies to the church. It brings the new, heavenly reality that Jesus gives, but this reality is hidden under the guise of failure.

In the parable of the sower (Matt. 13:3–23 parr.), Jesus likens the proclamation of the kingdom to the sowing of seed. Some of it fell along the path, some on rocky places, and some among the thorns. None of these seeds bore fruit, and Jesus compares them to people who hear the message about the kingdom but ultimately fail to benefit from it. In the case of the seed along the path, the evil one snatches it away so that it is not even understood by those who hear it. The seed on rocky places corresponds to those who accept the message but do not persevere in times of hardship and persecution. Finally, the seed among the thorns is likened to those cases when "the worries of this life and the deceitfulness of wealth choke the word" (v. 22). With all these examples, Jesus shows that the kingdom of God does not advance as if its progress were automatic. The kingdom does not force itself on its subjects; it presupposes their willing participation, as in the case of the seed that fell on good soil and bore fruit. That seed "refers to someone who hears the word and understands it" (v. 23).

In another agricultural parable, Jesus explains that "the kingdom of heaven is like a mustard seed, which a man took and planted in his field. Though it is the smallest of all seeds, yet when it grows, it is the largest of garden plants and becomes a tree, so that the birds come and perch in its branches" (Matt. 13:31–32). The point of the parable is not that the kingdom will grow until it has taken over the whole world, as some interpreters have suggested. It is rather to show the contrast between the appearance of insignificance, as in the case of the minuscule mustard seed, and the power inherent within it. The kingdom of heaven does not emerge in greatness. To the untrained eye, it seems to be so small as to be virtually nonexistent, something that can safely be ignored. But the full power of the kingdom is found within this almost invisible seed. In its appearance in this world, the power of the kingdom seems to be entirely negligible, but the power of God's complete victory over evil is at work within it.

When Paul writes to the church in Corinth, he addresses them as "the church of God in Corinth, . . . those sanctified in Christ Jesus and called to be his holy people" (1 Cor. 1:2), but anyone who reads his letters can see that their holiness is very well hidden indeed. The Corinthians are quarreling with each other, they fail to proclaim the truth to one of their members who is living with his father's wife, members are engaged in lawsuits against one another, some are consorting with prostitutes, some are participating in idolatrous practices, they are misusing the Lord's Supper to the point that Paul says it is not even the Lord's Supper they are observing, they are using spiritual gifts for their own self-aggrandizement, and some of them have denied the Christian belief in the resurrection. Yet Paul insists that they are holy, that they are sanctified in Christ.

God's kingly rule was present in Corinth, but it would have been hard to notice it. Plenty of people would not have been able to see it. Plenty of people were unable to see the kingly rule of God when it came in the person of Jesus as well. When Jesus came to earth, he won his ultimate triumph against the forces of evil. He triumphed over them on the cross. It was a triumph that looked very much like defeat. The kingly rule of God is present in his church today, but it looks very much like something else. That is not to say that it cannot be seen. It is as visible as anything in this world. When the church comes together to eat the Lord's Supper, the gifts of the kingdom are on visible display. But they don't look like much, and plenty of people don't take notice. When the members of the church offer each other forgiveness in the name of the Lord, the kingly rule of God is exercised. When enemies are reconciled and people who have been at war with each other become friends, God's victory over the devil is manifested. When a local congregation accepts outsiders and shows the hospitality of Christ, God's kingdom is a visible reality. When the prayers of the believers bring healing to the sick, the power of the new creation is present. The kingdom of God can be seen and observed every day, and yet it is hidden in plain sight. It is hidden because it coexists with so many obvious manifestations of evil, even among the members of the church themselves. In this world, the kingdom of God does not appear in its full visible glory. It is hidden under the form of the cross.

As the church lives in this tension between their own sinfulness and the new reality that God gives, they are constantly crying out to God that he will bring the full manifestation of his kingly rule. The prayer that Jesus taught his disciples to pray is a prayer for the church as a community (Matt. 6:9–13 par.). It is not a prayer to *my* Father but to *our* Father. It is a prayer that the disciples are called to pray together. The prayer begins with three petitions that focus on God and his purposes in the world. We pray that God will make his true nature evident in the world, that he will make his name to be seen as holy. And we pray that he will bring his kingly rule and that his will would be done. Even though Jesus taught his disciples that this rule is already here, it was also necessary to be constantly praying for it to come. Because disciples live in the tension between the present experience of this kingly rule and the utter sense of despair that his kingly rule is nowhere to be found, the church prays, "Your kingdom come!"

Further Reading

In his book *The Gospel of the Kingdom: Scriptural Studies in the Kingdom of God* (Grand Rapids: Eerdmans, 1959), **George Eldon Ladd** shows that the power of the kingdom is at work even if it appears insignificant in this world.

In **Sigurd Grindheim**, "What the OT Prophets Did Not Know: The Mystery of the Church in Ephesians 3,2–13," *Biblica* 84 (2003): 531–53 (http://www.sigurdgrind heim.com/), I argue that the unity of the church, consisting of Jews and gentiles, is at the very heart of Paul's gospel.

The influential work by **Lesslie Newbigin**, *The Open Secret: An Introduction to the Theology of Mission*, rev. ed. (Grand Rapids: Eerdmans, 1995), and that of **David J. Bosch**, *Transforming Mission: Paradigm Shifts in Theology of Mission*, American Society of Missiology 16 (Maryknoll, NY: Orbis Books, 1998), emphasize that mission is not primarily an activity of the church but the work of God and that the church is sent by him into the world (*missio Dei*).

The book edited by **Darrell L. Guder**, *Missional Church: A Vision for the Sending of the Church in North America* (Grand Rapids: Eerdmans, 1998), maintains that mission is not a special activity reserved for select individuals within the church but defines the very nature of the church itself.

In their book *What Is the Mission of the Church? Making Sense of Social Justice, Shalom, and the Great Commission* (Wheaton: Crossway, 2011), **Kevin DeYoung** and **Greg Gilbert** argue against an overly broad definition of the mission of the church. They maintain that proclamation of the gospel is the essence of the church's call and that social change follows as a consequence.

In his book *Kingdom Conspiracy: Returning to the Radical Mission of the Local Church* (Grand Rapids: Baker Academic, 2014), **Scot McKnight** takes a more ho-listic approach. McKnight deviates from the common definition of the kingdom as kingly rule and argues that the kingdom of God refers to the people of God. There can therefore be no kingdom outside the church, the community that is called to embody the law of Christ in lives that are truly countercultural.

The book that more than any other has taught me that God's heavenly gifts are ex-perienced in the church is *The Church in the New Testament*, trans. W. J. O'Hara

(London: Burns & Oates, 1974) by **Rudolf Schnackenburg,** who writes from a Roman Catholic perspective.

In the book *The Church of Christ: A Biblical Ecclesiology for Today* (Grand Rapids: Eerdmans, 1996), **Everett Ferguson** provides a thorough overview of the New Testament teaching on the church. He writes from within the tradition of the Churches of Christ and emphasizes that the nature of the church is defined by its relation to Christ.

In *A New Testament Biblical Theology: The Unfolding of the Old Testament in the New* (Grand Rapids: Baker Academic, 2011), 592–613, **G. K. Beale** develops the New Testament idea of the church as the new temple, established through the outpouring of the Holy Spirit on the day of Pentecost. He emphasizes that Christ is the true Israel and that those who believe in him are therefore also included in the true Israel (651–749). In fulfillment of Old Testament models, the church shows itself to be a new-creational community through its observation of the Sabbath (although the church observes it on Sunday), baptism, and the Lord's Supper, as well as through the institution of elders (775–823).

George Eldon Ladd, in *A Theology of the New Testament*, ed. Donald A. Hagner (Grand Rapids: Eerdmans, 1993), 103–17, 576–94, explains that the church is not to be identified with the kingdom but is the people who "enter it, live under, and are governed by it" (109). The church is created by the kingdom and serves as a witness to it. Through the authority given to the disciples, the church is also the instrument of the kingdom. Entrance into or exclusion from the kingdom takes place through the ministry of the church. While it is looking forward to inheriting the kingdom, the church has already been given a taste of the kingdom and is therefore meant to let the world see the nature of this reality.

Thomas R. Schreiner, in *New Testament Theology: Magnifying God in Christ* (Grand Rapids: Baker Academic, 2008), 675–754, emphasizes that the New Testament church represents the fulfillment of God's promise to Abraham. This church is defined by its faith in Jesus Christ and is described as the people of God, the body of Christ, the true Israel, the temple of God, and God's assembly, among other terms.

6

A Different Government

The Role of Christ's Disciples in the Kingdom

In 1964, Nelson Mandela was condemned to life in prison. He was found guilty of sabotage and conspiracy to overthrow the government in South Africa. He ended up being imprisoned for twenty-seven years. In 1990, it was no longer possible to sustain the oppression of black South Africans, and Mandela was set free. Four years later, he was elected president in the first fully democratic election in his country. His life had taken him from the prison cell to the presidential residence, and he became the leader of his nation as they went through the reconciliation process after apartheid. Similarly, Christ has brought an entirely new rule into this world. As a result, the gates of prison are sprung open; the inmates are set free and are taking their seats as rulers in the new kingdom. "Do you not know that the Lord's people will judge the world?" Paul asks the Corinthians (1 Cor. 6:2).

God's plan from creation was to delegate his rule of the earth. He created humans in his image so that they could rule on his behalf. Humans did not live up to their call, and God sent his Son, the one who best represents the image of God (2 Cor. 4:4; Col. 1:15). He sets people free from sin and gives them a new life. When they are united with him, humans become like him and realize their true purpose.

The apostle Paul does not teach about the kingdom of God as much as Jesus does. Many biblical scholars have thought that Paul did not know Jesus's teaching very well and that he developed his theology in a way that was very different from the message of Jesus himself. But when we look more closely, we can see that Paul was very familiar with the words of Jesus, even if he has his own way of saying things.

God's kingly rule is an important idea to Paul. He knows that Christ was enthroned as ruler of the universe after he had defeated the evil powers. Paul reminds the Ephesians that God "raised Christ from the dead and seated him at his right hand in the heavenly realms, far above all rule and authority, power and dominion, and every name that is invoked, not only in the present age but also in the one to come" (Eph. 1:20–21).

Christ does not reserve this power and might for himself. He shares it with his people. When people believe in him, they are transformed, and they reflect his image, the image of him who is the image of God. "And we all, who with unveiled faces contemplate the Lord's glory, are being transformed into his image with ever-increasing glory, which comes from the Lord, who is the Spirit" (2 Cor. 3:18).

Christians Rule

As the image of God, believers will rule on God's behalf. Through their union with Christ, they are empowered to rule with him. Paul elaborates on this theme in his Letter to the Romans. It all begins with the victory of Christ, the victory he has won in our place. As he outlines the similarities and differences between Adam and Christ, Paul explains: "Just as one trespass resulted in condemnation for all people, so also one righteous act resulted in justification and life for all people. For just as through the disobedience of the one man the many were made sinners, so also through the obedience of the one man the many will be made righteous" (5:18–19). Paul is clear on the different roles of Christ and his people. The victory was won by Jesus alone. The whole purpose of the comparison between Adam and Christ is to explain that the acts of one person had consequences for all those who would follow. Adam brought sin, death, and destruction into the world. Christ put things right again. And he did it alone. Paul's point is to emphasize the "one righteous act" and "the obedience of the one man." Christ won the victory. All by himself.

Christ's victory means that he has established his rule, and that is where his people enter into the picture. They are the ones who enjoy the benefits of his victory. "If, by the trespass of the one man, death reigned through that one man, how much more will those who receive God's abundant provision of grace and of the gift of righteousness reign in life through the one man, Jesus Christ!" (5:17). Those who receive the grace of Christ will also rule with him.

Christ does not call us to participate in the one righteous act that brought us justification and life, but he makes us participants in the new rule that he has established. We will "reign in life through the one man, Jesus Christ!"

At first, Paul uses the future tense when he refers to this rule because he is looking forward to the consummation of God's kingdom. But Paul also knows that Christ has already been seated on the throne, his rule has already been established, and his people may enjoy their part in his rulership right away. In Romans 6:11–14 (CSB) he explains how:

> So, you too consider yourselves dead to sin and alive to God in Christ Jesus.
> Therefore do not let sin reign in your mortal body, so that you obey its desires. And do not offer any parts of it to sin as weapons for unrighteousness. But as those who are alive from the dead, offer yourselves to God, and all the parts of yourselves to God as weapons for righteousness. For sin will not rule over you, because you are not under the law but under grace.

Here Paul brings a new dimension to our understanding of God's kingly rule. He shows us that the enemy opposing this rule resides deep within ourselves. Paul knows that our ultimate foe is not outside us but inside. When we examined the kingly rule of God in the Old Testament, we saw that the enemies needing to be defeated were the rulers of this world, those who defied God's good rule and refused to submit to his will, those who caused injustice and suffering. When we turned to the teaching of Jesus, we saw that the enemies were spiritual forces that oppressed humans. Jesus defeated these forces and set humans free. Paul most clearly teaches that the spiritual enemies that stand against God's rule are not forces that threaten us from the outside. The enemy is on the inside. The enemy has infiltrated us to such a degree that he has turned us into instruments of his will, as if we had a Manchurian candidate inside us.[1]

This is why God cannot reestablish his rule simply by changing the circumstances around us. This is why there can never be a political solution to the trouble that our world is in. It will not do to introduce a more perfect government, establish a new and more just world order, and elect a better leader. Such a solution can never neutralize the real enemy, which is inside us. The enemy is not in the system, in the structures of our society. It is not in the people who surround us. The enemy is our own sin. The rebellion against the kingly rule of God is the rebellion that we all commit every day: when we choose to think of ourselves before we think of the will of God, when

---

1. In the novel *The Manchurian Candidate*, by Richard Condon (New York: Signet, 1959), a brainwashed former US prisoner of war becomes the unwitting puppet of an enemy regime.

we place our own needs and those of our own family above those of others, when we do not submit to the will of God.

The gospel is the good news that this enemy has been defeated: not on some day in the future but in the past; not through our own righteous act but through the righteous act of the one who died on the cross for our sins; not just on paper but in reality. Jesus has triumphed over sin.

Sin had held us in its grip so completely that Paul describes our situation as slavery. As humans we like to think that we are free and autonomous, that we are free to do what we decide to do, and that we are the master of our own destiny. This is an illusion. The truth is that we are in bondage to sin. We are not our own master. Our master is sin. We have no choice but to obey sin. We keep putting ourselves first, and we are powerless to do anything else.

Christ has put an end to our slavery and set us free from sin. "For we know that our old self was crucified with him so that the body ruled by sin might be done away with, that we should no longer be slaves to sin—because anyone who has died has been set free from sin" (Rom. 6:6–7). "Anyone who has died" refers to Christians, those who have been united with Christ, who share in his death. "Anyone who has died has been set free from sin." Paul uses the perfect tense, not the future. He says not that believers *will be* set free from sin but that they *have been* set free from sin.

How is this possible? When I read these verses I often think: It doesn't feel like I have been set free from sin. I feel the power of sin in my life every day. I don't feel like I am free from it. Sometimes I feel quite the opposite. But Paul is not talking about a subjective experience. He is talking about an objective fact. We have been set free. We are no longer in slavery. We no longer belong to sin. We belong to Christ. Sin is no longer our master. Christ is our master. This is an objective fact, and in Romans 6 Paul urges us to put this objective fact into practice.

As humans we are used to being slaves to sin, and it is difficult to wrap our heads around the fact that we now have a new identity. Anyone who has been a lifelong slave will find it difficult to begin to live as a free person. Such persons are accustomed to being slaves. They are accustomed to having someone else tell them what to do every minute of the day. They are not accustomed to making decisions because they have never had the freedom to decide. Someone else has always made their decisions for them. When they are set free, it is hard to know what to do. Sometimes they find it impossible to behave like free people, and they keep behaving like slaves instead. Even though they have been set free, they are still slaves in their mind. Their mind-set is still that of a slave, for they are not used to thinking and acting like free people.

Consider the people of Israel. They had been slaves in Egypt for genera-tions. They had been oppressed by cruel masters. But through the powerful intervention of God, they had been set free. They were led out of the land of slavery and into freedom. But even as they were set free, they still had the mind-set of slaves. They were not used to living independently. When they faced difficulties, they longed to return to Egypt. They even turned against Moses, who had led them into freedom. "In the desert the whole community grumbled against Moses and Aaron. The Israelites said to them, 'If only we had died by the LORD's hand in Egypt! There we sat around pots of meat and ate all the food we wanted, but you have brought us out into this desert to starve this entire assembly to death'" (Exod. 16:2–3). Their habit was to live as slaves, and they didn't know any other way to behave. They didn't know how to act as free people and take responsibility for their own situation and do something about it. Instead, they blamed their leaders, and they thought their life was better when they didn't have their freedom, when they didn't have to be responsible for their own life, when someone else took responsi-bility for them.

We who are used to being slaves to sin face a similar situation. We are not used to being free. We are used to being controlled by our old master, sin. Even though we are free, we continue to live as slaves to sin. In Christ we have a new life, a new identity, but we don't know what to do with it, so we continue to do that which comes naturally to us: sin. That is our habit. That is what we know.

Paul is therefore telling us that we must learn to think of ourselves in a new way. We must no longer think of ourselves as slaves. We must learn to think of ourselves as free. We must learn to think of ourselves the way God thinks of us. And God sees us in Christ, sees us as people who have been set free. "Consider yourselves dead to sin and alive to God in Christ Jesus," he says (Rom. 6:11 CSB). He does not tell us that we must die to sin; in Christ, we are already dead. The point is that we can no longer be anyone's slave when we are dead. Slaves would often be slaves for their entire life, but death would put an end to their slavery once and for all. A dead person could no longer be anyone's slave. A dead person could not be forced to do anything for any master. That is what has happened to us. Through the death of Christ, we are dead and therefore no longer slaves. What Paul is teaching is that we must understand who we are. We must understand that we are dead.

Paul is not telling us to fight against sin. That is a fight we cannot win. We are not able to defeat sin. The good news is that Jesus has fought on our behalf, and he has already won. Sin has been defeated, and we are dead to sin. If we try to fight sin, we are giving sin too much due. We are saying that sin still needs to be fought. By fighting with sin, we just get more entangled with it. We become what we hate, it has been said. We become so obsessed with sin that we become like it. Instead of encouraging us to combat it, Paul teaches us that sin has been defeated, and we need to think of ourselves as people who have already been freed from sin. We need to understand who we are. Then we can act accordingly.

When we understand that sin has been defeated by Jesus Christ and that we are no longer slaves to sin, then we can live as free people. "Therefore do not let sin reign in your mortal body, so that you obey its desires" (Rom. 6:12 CSB). We are under a new rule, and we are now called to put this new rule into practice in our lives. We no longer belong to sin. We belong to Christ. And we are now called to show in our life that we belong to him. "Do not offer any parts of it to sin as weapons for unrighteousness. But as those who are alive from the dead, offer yourselves to God, and all the parts of yourselves to God as weapons for righteousness" (6:13 CSB). We shall no longer use our lives in the service of sin; we shall use our lives in the service of Christ.

"For sin will not rule over you, because you are not under the law but under grace" (6:14 CSB). We are under a new domain. We are no longer under the domain of sin and the law. We are under the domain of grace. Christ does not impose anything on us; he does not force us to do anything. Instead, he shows us generosity. He gives us his grace. Freely and through no merit of our own, he gives us everything with him. He does not force us to serve him. He sets us free.

We serve Christ not because we are forced to do so, as if we were slaves. We serve Christ because we want to, because he has showed us his immeasurable grace. We live our lives in service to him out of gratitude for what he has done for us. He has given us our freedom. He has defeated our enemy. He has given us victory over sin. And now he lets us share in his rule. With him, we rule over evil. With him, sin shall no longer rule us. Christ has done this so that "grace might reign through righteousness to bring eternal life through Jesus Christ our Lord" (Rom. 5:21). We now live under the rule of grace.

It may seem like a contradiction to say that grace rules, because we tend to think of rule as being carried out through force and coercion. Grace is the opposite of coercion. Grace does not impose its will on others; it grants pardon to those who have not done what they were required to do. It might seem as though grace equals anarchy, not any form of rule. The truth, however, is that grace is a much more powerful ruler than any kind of coercion. Through coercion, people may be made to do certain things, but they will always do those things reluctantly. It is impossible to force anyone to do something willingly and enthusiastically.

I am speaking from experience. During my military service in Norway, I was required to take part in a three-day exercise in the woods. I had recently pulled my hamstring badly, and my injury could only heal if the muscle was allowed to rest, so I expected to be exempt from the exercise. To my dismay, however, the military physician did not sign off on my request, so I had to participate anyway. I was not happy, but I had no choice, and I went along. On the second day of the exercise, my commanding officers took me aside and told me they had noticed that I had a bad attitude. With thinly veiled threats to give me a bad review unless I complied, they commanded me to be more enthusiastic about the exercise from now on. I decided I had to get them off my back, so I put a fake grin on my face and pretended to be enjoying our mindless activities. Needless to say, my bad attitude did not disappear. I just decided to conceal it better. My superior officers could force me to smile, but all that their threats could accomplish was to make my attitude even worse.

Only the Free Can Be Good

No one can do good works unless they are free. Those who are forced to do something are not doing anything that is good. No one does anything genuinely good if their actions are coerced by the threat of punishment. Slaves threatened with torture and death unless they do exactly what their masters say do not love their masters. Even though their entire lives are spent doing nothing but what pleases their slaveholders, they have not really showed love toward them. If they had the freedom to choose, they would kill their masters rather than listen to any more of their commands. To call a work good presupposes that the one who does it is free, has a choice, and has the freedom not to do it. Only when the good action is freely chosen does it make sense to call it good.

The apostle Paul knows that one must be free from the law in order to obey the law of God. Paul is often accused of being opposed to the law, of being anti-law, or antinomian. Nothing could be further from the truth. Paul's concern is that believers genuinely fulfill the law. "Do we, then, nullify the law by this faith?" he asks. "Not at all! Rather, we uphold the law" (Rom. 3:31). Later, he emphasizes that "the righteous requirement of the law might be fully met in us, who do not live according to the flesh but according to the Spirit" (8:4).

Paul has understood the paradoxical truth about how we may obey God's law: we can only fulfill the law when we are under no form of compulsion from it. In his Letter to the Galatians, he describes a life that is led by the Spirit.

Those who lead such a life bear "the fruit of the Spirit . . . love, joy, peace, forbearance, kindness, goodness, faithfulness, gentleness and self-control. Against such things there is no law," Paul says (Gal. 5:22–23). A life led by the Spirit is a life that does nothing contrary to the law but rather fulfills the law, as "the entire law is fulfilled in keeping this one command: 'Love your neighbor as yourself'" (5:14). The presupposition for such a life is that one is free from the law. "But if you are led by the Spirit, you are not under the law" (5:18). To the Romans, Paul explains the reason why they can be free from sin: "For sin shall no longer be your master, because you are not under the law, but under grace" (6:14).

To fulfill the law is ultimately to live a life that is pleasing to God. It is not about meeting certain requirements; it is not about completing a list of things one should do and avoiding things one should not do. That is a legalistic misunderstanding of what God desires from us. God wants to have a relationship with us. He wants us to live lives that show that we do not disrespect him, that we do not rebel against him, that we do not turn against him and disobey him, but that we honor him, love him, trust him, and worship him. No one can genuinely trust, love, and worship God if they are forced to do so. They may be saying the words and performing the deeds, but it is not love.

As long as we relate to God as slaves, we are not able to genuinely please him. Those who define their relationship to the Lord on the basis of their obedience to his commandments are in reality relating to him as slaves. In Galatians 4:1–7, Paul describes his own life and his fellow Jews' lives under the law of Moses. He compares it to the life of a minor who is under guardians and trustees, explaining, "So also, when we were underage, we were in slavery under the elemental spiritual forces of the world" (4:3). The good news is that he is no longer living in this kind of slavery. "But when the set time had fully come, God sent his Son, born of a woman, born under the law, to redeem those under the law, that we might receive adoption to sonship" (4:4–5). He is no longer a slave but has been adopted to sonship.

A son is free to love and obey his Father, not because he is forced like a slave to do so but because he chooses to do so. Such obedience is the kind of devotion that God wants from his people. Such obedience is what pleases him and what constitutes genuine fulfillment of his law.

As a seminary professor, I sometimes receive emails from students telling me how much they appreciated a class they took with me. Often they will make sure to write to me after their grades have been submitted so that I can know that they no longer have anything to gain from flattering me. They want me to know that their praise is genuine. God wants to receive genuine praise too. He is not interested in the kind of praise that is offered with a view to the reward that might be given to those who worship him. He is not interested in subjects who obey his law because they think they will gain something from it, that their good works will earn them their salvation and good favor with God. God wants people who obey and worship him without any concern for what they might gain or lose, people who worship him because they love him, people who are devoted to him as children are devoted to their father. They need no reason to do what they do because they are his children and he is their Father.

The Paradoxical Victory

Does this mean that a Christian will experience freedom from sin all the time? If we rule with Christ and we rule over sin, do we have victory over sin so that we will never give in to temptations, so that we will never be controlled by our sinful nature and succumb to selfish attitudes?

Paul makes clear that the victory over sin has already been won and that believers may already rule with Christ. At the same time, he keeps instructing believers to exercise the rule that is theirs: "Count yourselves dead to sin but alive to God in Christ Jesus. Therefore do not let sin reign in your mortal body so that you obey its evil desires" (Rom. 6:11–12). The reason he needs to give them these instructions is that it does not happen automatically. Believers have a role to play in not allowing sin to rule. Sometimes they may be more successful than other times.

Until Christ returns, the kingly rule of God is a reality that is hidden under the guise of weakness. Christ has defeated all evil forces, taken his seat on his throne, and established his sovereign rule. When we experience the gifts of God's kingly rule in our life, we can see that this rule is a present reality. When people who have lived a life in sin turn to Christ, they often find victory over the power of sin in their life. They have been given a new life in Christ. The apostle Paul explains to the believers in Rome the significance of their baptism: "We were therefore buried with him through baptism into death in order that, just as Christ was raised from the dead through the glory of the Father, we too may live a new life" (Rom. 6:4). Baptism meant that the followers of Christ died to their old life in this world. Through baptism, which in the early church would have taken place through immersion, they were buried and raised again to a new life with Christ. In his Letter to the Colossians, Paul addresses the believers as those who "have been raised with Christ" (Col. 3:1). Those who belong to Christ already share in Christ's resurrection, and Paul may even speak to them as those who have already been resurrected with him. Their new life, however, is a life that "is now hidden with Christ in God" (3:3). It is not something they can see and observe.

That is why believers often feel that they are not able to see the kingly rule of God in their life, that they do not find any evidence of having victory over sin. The apostle Paul himself was familiar with this ambiguity of the Christian experience. In his Letter to the Romans, he speaks boldly of the Christian's victory over sin (chap. 6). But when he afterward describes his life in light of the law, he has depressing things to say. He talks about the power of sin in his life and refers to himself as being "sold as a slave to sin" (Rom. 7:14). He confesses, "Good itself does not dwell in me, that is, in my sinful nature. For I have the desire to do what is good, but I cannot carry it out" (7:18). In his despair, he concludes: "For in my inner being I delight in God's law; but I see another law at work in me, waging war against the law of my mind and making me a prisoner of the law of sin at work within me" (7:22–23).

Many Christians have concluded that Paul cannot talk about himself as a born-again believer in these verses. He must be referring to the time before he met Christ, or he may be speaking for someone else, using the first person rhetorically. Paul's view of the Christian life comes to expression later in his Letter to the Romans, they maintain, when he speaks about the power of the Holy Spirit (8:1–17).

What these interpreters typically fail to appreciate is that Paul paints two different portraits of the Christian in this section of Romans, and both of these portraits are true, even though they appear to be contradictory. Christians share in Christ's kingly rule, are guided by the Holy Spirit, and therefore have victory over sin. At the same time, Christians experience the reality of their sinful nature as long as they live in this world, and they frequently have occasion to cry out to God, just like Paul: "What a wretched man I am! Who will rescue me from this body that is subject to death?" (Rom. 7:24).

No sooner has Paul expressed this tortured complaint than he breaks out in praise to God: "Thanks be to God, who delivers me through Jesus Christ our Lord!" (7:25). And that is the nature of the Christian life. Just as in the Old Testament psalms, lament and praise go hand in hand. Christians experience the power of evil in this world, including their own inability to defeat sin in their personal life. In the midst of this misery—and precisely in the midst of it—they see Christ at work. While they are living through sin and failure— precisely when they are living through sin and failure—Christ delivers them from all evil. In Christ, they are free. They belong to him, and he belongs to them. Their sin and failure belong to Christ, and Christ's righteousness belongs to them. "Therefore, there is now no condemnation for those who are in Christ Jesus" (8:1).

New Creation

Christians encounter their old and new reality at the same time. They are still in this world, and their sinful nature has not disappeared. They also belong to the kingdom of God, and they enjoy the reality of the new creation; as the apostle Paul says: "If anyone is in Christ, the new creation has come: The old has gone, the new is here!" (2 Cor. 5:17). The reality of the new creation is an object of faith; it is a matter of believing, not seeing. "For we live by faith, not by sight" (5:7). But it is not something believers are unaware of. The presence of the new creation is a tangible experience for the children of God. God has given them a foretaste of the new heavenly reality that already belongs to them but which they will only fully be able to see in the future.

In his Letter to the Romans, Paul speaks of believers' longing for the future glory that belongs to them. All creation longs for the revelation of God's children in glory, so that "the creation itself will be liberated from its bondage to decay and brought into the freedom and glory of the children of God" (Rom. 8:21). God's creation, as we see it now, is in bondage to decay. Humans and animals grow old and die; the powers of death are constantly at work. The earth suffers from unstable weather conditions, drought, floods, excessive rain, and insufficient rain, affecting the fertility of the land and causing natural disasters. In the consummation, when the children of God are revealed in glory, all this will change; creation will be liberated and made new.

Paul uses the metaphor of a harvest to describe this new creation, and he explains that this harvest has already begun. While he is still focused on his eager expectation of the consummation, he makes reference to the firstfruits of the harvest: "We ourselves, who have the firstfruits of the Spirit, groan inwardly as we wait eagerly for our adoption to sonship, the redemption of our bodies" (Rom. 8:23).

The firstfruits represent the beginning of the harvest and serve as an assurance that there will be more fruit to come. The firstfruits are the same kind of fruit as that which is coming later. They can be tasted and eaten, and they will taste and feel the same way as the abundance of fruit that is to follow. The only difference is that there will be much more fruit when the harvest comes. The Holy Spirit is the firstfruits of the new creation, and he provides a fully authentic foretaste of what the new creation will be like. The gift of the Holy Spirit is in itself the presence of the new creation—not the full presence but the beginning of the new creation. It is not merely a promise that the new creation will come, but it brings the very reality of this new creation.

For the believers, this presence of the Holy Spirit is a matter of tangible experience. As Peter was preaching the gospel to Cornelius, the Holy Spirit fell on Cornelius and all those who were present. When the Spirit fell, those who were with Peter noticed it immediately. They were taken completely by surprise because it did not occur to them that the Holy Spirit would be given to gentiles. It was not wishful thinking that made them believe that they recognized the Spirit; they were convinced by what they saw and heard. "For they heard them speaking in tongues and praising God" (Acts 10:46). The presence of the Holy Spirit was plain for everyone to see; it could not be denied.

Peter's encounter with Cornelius was not a onetime event. Paul explains that something very similar happened when he was first preaching the gospel to the Galatians. "I would like to learn just one thing from you," he writes to them. "Did you receive the Spirit by the works of the law, or by believing what you heard? . . . So again I ask, does God give you his Spirit and work miracles among you by the works of the law, or by your believing what you heard?" (Gal. 3:2, 5). He reminds them of something they know well: when he proclaimed the gospel to them, they received the Spirit, and it was something they could easily observe. The gift of the Spirit was accompanied by miracles that they could not ignore.

It does not always work in the same way when the Spirit is given. Not all Christians experience miracles and the gift of speaking in tongues, but they all experience the presence of the Holy Spirit in their lives. The Holy Spirit is the Spirit of Christ, the Spirit of the Son of God. Those who belong to Christ have been given the same Spirit that he has, the Spirit that makes it possible to know God and to know him intimately.

In his First Letter to the Corinthians, Paul compares the Spirit of God to the human spirit: "For who knows a person's thoughts except their own spirit within them? In the same way no one knows the thoughts of God except the Spirit of God" (2:11). His point is that it is impossible to really know what is inside someone else's head. Only the person's own spirit knows that person's thoughts. In the same way, no one can know God's thoughts except God's own Spirit. But then Paul adds: "What we have received is not the spirit of the world, but the Spirit who is from God, so that we may understand what God has freely given us" (2:12). God's own Spirit is the only completely reliable source of knowledge about God's own thoughts. Not only do we have access to that Spirit, not only can we consult the Spirit, but that Spirit has also been given to us. God's own Spirit has now become ours.

The gift of this Spirit makes it possible to know God intimately, and it makes it possible to relate to him in a way that has never been possible before. Paul describes this new relationship with beautiful words in Galatians 4:6: "Because you are his sons, God sent the Spirit of his Son into our hearts, the Spirit who calls out, 'Abba, Father.'" The Spirit of God's Son is now in our hearts, and we can relate to God in the same way that Jesus Christ, his Son, does.

When Jesus prayed to God, he called him "Father." In Aramaic, the word he used was *Abba*. The way in which Jesus spoke to God was so characteristic of him that it made an indelible impression on the disciples. When Peter was telling the stories of Jesus, he probably felt that Jesus's words in prayer were so impactful that he did not want to translate them. According to early church tradition, the evangelist Mark wrote down his Gospel on the basis of Peter's preaching, yet even he chose to preserve some of Jesus's words in Aramaic, even though his gentile audience would not understand them. When he reports Jesus's prayer in Gethsemane, he renders it like this: "'*Abba*, Father,' he said, 'everything is possible for you. Take this cup from me. Yet not what I will, but what you will'" (Mark 14:36). Little children would use the word *Abba* when they spoke to their dad. It is not as informal as the English "daddy," but it is a word used within the family. In the many prayers that have been preserved in the Old Testament, no one speaks to God in this way. Jesus showed his disciples that he had an intimate relationship with God, his Father. He spoke to him as a little child would speak to his father when he was jumping up into his lap.

When Paul explains what it means to have been given the Holy Spirit, he uses the same Aramaic word, *Abba*, echoing the voice of Jesus. When they pray to God, believers speak like Jesus spoke. They relate to the Father as Jesus did. They approach God as confidently as Jesus did. They speak to him as trustingly as Jesus did. Because they have the Spirit of God's Son, they have an entirely new relationship to God, a relationship they can experience every day. They have the firstfruits of the new creation. They experience the gifts of the kingdom of God.

Elsewhere, Paul refers to the gift of the Holy Spirit as a down payment: "He has also put his seal on us and given us the Spirit in our hearts as a down payment" (2 Cor. 1:22 CSB). A down payment serves to seal a business transaction. When a down payment is made on a house, the house cannot be sold to anyone else. The down payment serves as security that the buyer will eventually pay the full amount in order not to forfeit the initial payment. The Holy Spirit is God's down payment, Paul explains. The Spirit is the initial provision that God makes, a provision that serves as a guarantee that the full provision will also be made. The children of God have received this down payment, and it serves as their assurance. They know the purposes of God. They know that God will give them all his gifts and that the fullness of his salvation and new creation belongs to them. They have already received the down payment, the Holy Spirit.

This down payment ensures that the believers will experience the fullness of the new creation. It ensures that they will enjoy all the benefits of Christ's victory over evil. Everything that happens in this world is therefore forced into service for the children of God. They really are the kings of the world, and all the powers of the world must therefore ultimately contribute to their well-being. Paul explains that "in all things God works for the good of those who love him, who have been called according to his purpose" (Rom. 8:28). Christ has won his victory over all evil forces so that these forces can no longer do any ultimate harm to his followers. This does not mean that Christians will be free from suffering in this world. Paul often makes it clear that suffering is what Christ's followers should expect. If believers do not suffer with Christ, the reason is probably that they do not follow him as they should. Suffering is normal for Christ's followers, sometimes even terrible agony and suffering that leads to death. But in the midst of all such suffering, believers share in Christ's victory, and "in all these things we are more than conquerors through him who loved us" (Rom. 8:37). Whatever happens to believers, therefore, will ultimately work out for their good. In the words of Martin Luther, "There is nothing so good and nothing so evil but that it shall work together for good to me, if only I believe."[2] Christ has made his followers participants in his rule. They rule over sin and death, and their rulership is felt throughout the universe. Human society will never be the same.

Further Reading

A. J. M. Wedderburn thinks there is little continuity between the Jesus tradition and the theology of Paul. In his article "Paul and Jesus: The Problem of Continuity," in *Paul and Jesus: Collected Essays*, Journal for the Study of the New Testament Supplement Series 37 (Sheffield: JSOT Press, 1989), 99–115, he suggests that the words of Jesus were being used by Christians who held a theology different from Paul (more legalistic) and that Paul therefore developed his theology without clear references to the teaching of Jesus. Taking his cue from Rudolf Bultmann, Wedderburn maintains that Paul has substituted the concept of God's righteousness for that of the kingdom of God.

In contrast, the important study of kingdom language in Paul by Karl Paul Donfried, "Paul and the Kingdom of God," in *Paul, Thessalonica, and Early Christianity* (London: T&T Clark, 2002), 233–52, argues that for Paul the kingdom is both present and future and that Paul is dependent on the Jesus tradition as we know it from the Synoptic Gospels.

2. "The Freedom of a Christian," in *Luther's Works* (Philadelphia: Fortress, 1957), 31:355.

Youngmo Cho, *Spirit and Kingdom in the Writings of Luke and Paul: An Attempt to Reconcile These Concepts*, Paternoster Biblical Monographs (Waynesboro, GA: Paternoster, 2005), develops a suggestion made by I. H. Marshall that the Holy Spirit has taken the place of the kingdom of God in the theology of Paul.

In **Sigurd Grindheim**, "The Kingdom of God in Romans," *Biblica* 98 (2017): 72–90, I show that Paul has a dynamic and distinctly ethical understanding of the kingdom as the way in which believers rule with Christ. This article provides more background for my argument in this chapter.

Joshua W. Jipp has reached similar conclusions in his book *Christ Is King: Paul's Royal Ideology* (Minneapolis: Fortress, 2015), in which he argues that widespread concepts of the ideal king serve as an important background for Paul's picture of Jesus.

G. K. Beale, *A New Testament Biblical Theology: The Unfolding of the Old Testament in the New* (Grand Rapids: Baker Academic, 2011), 249–316, 833–84, focuses on the resurrection of Christ as the foundation for the believer's new life in the theology of Paul.

Udo Schnelle, *Theology of the New Testament*, trans. M. Eugene Boring (Grand Rapids: Baker Academic, 2009), 111–21, 133–46, argues that Jesus taught a radically new ethics since the coming kingdom of God restored the will of God as it had come to expression in creation.

To **George Eldon Ladd** in *A Theology of the New Testament*, ed. Donald A. Hagner (Grand Rapids: Eerdmans, 1993), 118–32, 407–11, 521–75, the Christian life is characterized by the tension between the presence of the kingdom of God and the fact that the kingdom is still to be consummated. Because of the inbreaking of the new age, our relationship with God is determined not by the law but by the personal presence of Jesus Christ and the writing of the law on our hearts. Christians are therefore in a real sense able to realize the righteousness of the kingdom (as outlined in the Sermon on the Mount), even if this righteousness will not be fully manifested until the end.

7

Transforming Society

How God's Reign Affects Politics

The early church was an ideal society. When God ruled through the hearts of his people, he created a utopia. People shared their resources. "No one claimed that any of their possessions was their own, but they shared everything they had" (Acts 4:32). "All the believers were together and had everything in common. They sold property and possessions to give to anyone who had need" (2:44–45).

This community knew no class distinctions, no gender conflicts, no ethnic tension, and no tribalism. "There is neither Jew nor Gentile, neither slave nor free, nor is there male and female, for you are all one in Christ Jesus" (Gal. 3:28). The members of this community did not have any conflicting loyalties. The working class did not see themselves pitted against the upper class. When they were led by the Holy Spirit, no one looked suspiciously on those who spoke a different language, had a different skin color, or followed different dietary practices.

All people in this community were equal, and they belonged together as a family. No one held a higher status than anyone else, as all were children of God and related to each other as brothers and sisters. Jesus had taught them, "You are not to be called 'Rabbi,' for you have one Teacher, and you are all brothers. And do not call anyone on earth 'father,' for you have one Father, and he is in heaven. Nor are you to be called instructors, for you have one Instructor, the Messiah. The greatest among you will be your servant. For those who exalt themselves will be humbled, and those who humble themselves will be exalted" (Matt. 23:8–12).

Warnings against This World

The Holy Spirit makes it possible to form such a community in this world, but the New Testament gives us no indication that all of society will be transformed in this way. On several occasions, Jesus warns us that the opposite will be the case. In his sermon on the last things, he prepares his disciples for a tough reality: "Nation will rise against nation, and kingdom against kingdom. There will be famines and earthquakes in various places" (Matt. 24:7). In his Farewell Discourse, he ominously warns them, "In this world you will have trouble." And then he adds, "But take heart! I have overcome the world" (John 16:33).

Should God's people just retreat from this world, then, and accept the fact that it is doomed and beyond redemption? Should they keep their distance from secular institutions, stay out of politics, and focus on saving souls instead? If the world is irreversibly on the way to judgment, should Christians concentrate their efforts on bringing as many people as possible out of the world and into the church? Such an attitude to civil society may claim considerable biblical support, especially from the book of Revelation. In this prophetic book, the kings of the earth are aligned with Satan and anti-Christian forces. There is even a direct call to disengage from this sinful world. When the angel announced judgment on Babylon the Great, the apostle John heard a voice from heaven say: "'Come out of her, my people,' so that you will not share in her sins, so that you will not receive any of her plagues" (Rev. 18:4).

It would be a mistake, however, to understand these words as a blanket call to have as little to do with the world as possible. In the book of Revelation, Babylon stands for the economic power of the Roman Empire (cf. Rev. 17). The Bible frequently warns against riches and their capacity to lure people away from single-minded commitment to our Lord Jesus Christ. John's portrait of Babylon shows the depravity of material exploits, especially as they rely on the exploitation of those less fortunate. The call to leave Babylon is a warning not against engagement with society in general but against the trappings of wealth.

God's Rule Affects Society

In other contexts, the New Testament shows that the proclamation of the kingly rule of God has a profound impact on society. Under the preaching of the apostle Paul, the city of Ephesus experienced a revival that transformed the great metropolis. Huge numbers of people believed the gospel and turned away from the gods of their traditional religion. Such a transformation would not go unnoticed. It would have consequences at every level of society. People would no longer participate in the idolatrous practices that formed the backbone of all communal life. The city's economy would be deeply affected too. The most significant cult in Ephesus was that of Artemis, who was the goddess of the hunt. Her temple provided an important source of revenue for the city. The silversmith trade relied on the demand for silver shrines dedicated to Artemis. When Paul taught people that gods made by human hands were no gods at all, the interest in such shrines would dissipate and a great source of income would dwindle away. Fearing for the future of their livelihood, the silversmith Demetrius roused the crowd into an uproar. Only the clever interference of the city clerk prevented the crowd from turning violent (Acts 19:23–41). The incident shows that the progress of the gospel will not only be felt on the individual level. Its ripple effects are also felt through all of society. It affects religious practices, social practices, and even the economy.

The history of the church has shown what an impact the gospel has had on society. In the Greco-Roman world, unwanted children were often killed soon after they were born. The church was opposed to this practice, and it was outlawed by one of the first Christian emperors, Valentinian I (364–375). Christians founded the first charitable hospitals that served the general public. They were also pioneers in establishing orphanages and institutions to care for the elderly.

The predominant trend throughout history has been for the church to engage with society and with the civil government. Christians know that Christ is lord of all, and they have wished to see his lordship respected in all of society. One of the best-known examples is what happened in the Swiss city of Geneva in the sixteenth century. In 1541, the city officially accepted the Protestant Reformation and adopted a Protestant Church order. The city's government was inspired by John Calvin, who taught that the civil authority was responsible to God for the way in which they ruled society.

The city of Geneva used legislation to ensure the Christian lifestyle of its citizens. It was a legal requirement that everyone go to church on Sunday. The law also included a dress code as well as regulations for social life and how people could furnish their homes in order to avoid ungodly excess. The punishment for the violation of these laws could be severe. In 1553 the Spanish theologian Michael Servetus was convicted of heresy. Because he had denied the Trinity and criticized the practice of infant baptism, he was sentenced to death and was burned at the stake. The Reformers in Geneva had good intentions, but their zeal for the Christian faith was misguided and had disastrous consequences. It was a mistake to try to govern society as if it were the church.

A New Way to Rule

In the Old Testament, God exercised his rule similarly. He chose Israel as his people and gave them his good laws. God's good will was codified in the nation's constitution. To disobey God was forbidden by law, and those who did so were to be punished. If children consistently disrespected their parents, they were rebelling against God's commandment to honor one's father and mother. The laws of Israel commanded that such children should be executed. God told them to "purge the evil from among you" (Deut. 21:21).

In the Old Testament, God's rule was imposed on the people from the outside, through the written law. This institution was a part of God's perfect plan, but it did not result in a society that obeyed God. God's rule did not materialize through the law of Moses. The history of Israel shows clearly that the Mosaic covenant did not bring the kingly rule of God. In the end, the people of Israel lost everything. Their capital, Jerusalem, was conquered by the Babylonians in 586 BCE. God's temple, the building he had chosen for his dwelling, was razed. The people were taken into exile and lost the land that God had given them. The Mosaic legislation had showed them what a society ruled by God would look like, but the sin of the people prevented that society from materializing.

When Christians do not learn the lessons from Israel's history, they fail to understand how God's kingly rule is manifested today. There are many Christians who believe that we can further God's cause by introducing laws in accordance with his will. They are concerned about the immorality that surrounds them, and they think we need legislation to change that. Reading the stories of God's punishment of Israel, they are worried that the immorality of their nation will incur the wrath of God. They fail to consider that God no longer deals with nations the way he dealt with Israel under the old covenant. The history of Israel shows why it was necessary for God to do things in a different way.

The prophet Jeremiah understood what Israel's problem was, and he realized that the nation needed an entirely different kind of constitution. They needed a new covenant that would internalize the law of God.

> "The days are coming," declares the LORD,
> "when I will make a new covenant

with the people of Israel
and with the people of Judah.
It will not be like the covenant
I made with their ancestors
when I took them by the hand
to lead them out of Egypt,
because they broke my covenant,
though I was a husband to them,"
declares the LORD.
"This is the covenant I will make with the people of Israel
after that time," declares the LORD.
"I will put my law in their minds
and write it on their hearts.
I will be their God,
and they will be my people.
No longer will they teach their neighbor,
or say to one another, 'Know the LORD,'
because they will all know me,
from the least of them to the greatest,"
declares the LORD.
"For I will forgive their wickedness
and will remember their sins no more." (Jer. 31:31–34)

Under the new covenant, God's will is no longer imposed on the people from the outside, through a written law. It comes from the inside, from the heart. People do not need someone else to teach them about the Lord because they know him. Their relationship with God is no longer a relationship that is mediated through priests and through a written law code. People know God personally and intimately. They do his will not because they are forced to do so but because they want to. The will of God is no longer external; it is internal.

The laws of society will always be external. Laws may control what people do with their hands, but they can never control what is in their heart. The laws of society may prohibit murder, and they may prescribe the appropriate penalty for those who commit such crimes. In this way, the laws may conceivably induce enough fear that no one will commit murder. But no law can control what is in people's hearts. No law can prescribe that people genuinely love one another.

We can illustrate this with a thought experiment. Let's imagine a society that tries to legislate its way to love and kindness. The governing body of such a society might pass the Altruistic Love Act (ALA). There would be a law prescribing that people had to smile at every person they met. Every day, the police would interrogate all citizens and ask them if they had made sure to smile every time they had an interaction with another person. Those who answered no would go to prison. Anyone who spoke angrily to someone else would be punished in the same way. Another law would state that random acts of kindness were a legal obligation for every adult. At the end of each month, the Internal Revenue Service would require a solemn statement from all citizens. The statement would detail all the acts of kindness performed by each individual. If there were too few of them, that individual would have to do community service, showing kindness to the needy. We could imagine a society that functioned like this, but to imagine it is to realize that it could never exist.

The civil government does not always use punishment to accomplish its goals. The carrot may often be more effective than the stick, and in the case of the government that means money. Tax benefits and direct subsidies are often enough to encourage the populace to adopt the behavior that the government deems desirable. Some habits die hard, however, such as the American appetite for gas-guzzling cars and the Norwegian enthusiasm for international air travel. In any case, whatever may be accomplished through economic incentives is limited to outward behavior. Money does not transform people and make them new. The only thing that happens when you give people money is that they want more of it.

Recent experience in China provides a compelling example of the difficulty of changing the culture in this way. There is a great interest in soccer in China, along with an intense desire to develop a Chinese soccer league that can compete with the best in the world. Offering the world's highest salaries, the Chinese have tried to attract the best talent among international players. The results are unimpressive. China is nowhere near competing with the great nations that have a decades-long culture of soccer enthusiasm. The British periodical *The Economist* coolly observes, "Footballing culture cannot be bought—or regulated into existence."[1]

God's new way of changing societies is entirely different. Jesus does not establish God's kingly rule with external rewards and punishments. His kingly rule comes from the inside. The Holy Spirit is poured into our hearts and makes us want to do God's will. Christ exercises his rule through a different kind of compulsion, the motivation that comes from knowing the love of Christ. "For Christ's love compels us, because we are convinced that one died for all, and therefore all died" (2 Cor. 5:14).

1. "Tackling the Problem? Chinese Football," Espresso, *The Economist*, March 11, 2017, https://espresso.economist.com/0d7f9017fbda691900187b22404b8a1f.

The Role of Government

Is there no place, then, for civil government where God's kingly rule is established? In the future kingdom, there will certainly be no purpose for such government, but we do not yet see the full manifestation of God's kingly rule. When some of the Pharisees asked Jesus about paying taxes, he answered them, "Give to the emperor the things that are the emperor's, and to God the things that are God's" (Mark 12:17 NRSV). With this answer, he made it clear that he had not come to depose the emperor. There was still a legitimate place for the civil government, even as Christ was establishing God's kingly rule.

The apostle Paul elaborates: "For the one in authority is God's servant for your good. But if you do wrong, be afraid, for rulers do not bear the sword for no reason. They are God's servants, agents of wrath to bring punishment on the wrongdoer" (Rom. 13:4). The civil government has a God-given authority to use force in order to ensure law and order. In this way, some restrictions on human sinfulness are put in place. Therefore believers must be subject to the authorities, and they must pay taxes (13:1, 5–7). Those who serve in government should be the object of special prayers. Paul writes to Timothy: "I urge, then, first of all, that petitions, prayers, intercession and thanksgiving be made for all people—for kings and all those in authority, that we may live peaceful and quiet lives in all godliness and holiness" (1 Tim. 2:1–2). While Paul affirms the God-given role of the government, he also leaves no doubt that it is subordinate to God: the government is God's servant.

The fact that those in authority are God's servants does not mean that they are good. In his Letter to the Romans, Paul mentions one example of a person in authority: Pharaoh. Pharaoh was not good, but God accomplished his purpose through him anyway: "For Scripture says to Pharaoh: 'I raised you up for this very purpose, that I might display my power in you and that my name might be proclaimed in all the earth'" (Rom. 9:17). That the authorities are God's servants means that God uses them to bring his own plans to fruition, whether they are aware of it or not.

In his exhortation to the church in Rome, Paul presupposes that the government uses its authority for good. "Do you want to be free from fear of the one in authority?" he asks. "Then do what is right and you will be commended" (Rom. 13:3). Paul does not discuss what a Christian should do when that is not the case. All the biblical authors agree that God "is Lord of all" (Rom. 10:12), and the book of Acts formulates an important principle: "We must obey God rather than human beings!" (5:29). The book of Revelation develops this point further. Believers have a responsibility to disobey the authorities when they are asked to sin against their Lord. Only those who refused the mark of the beast would be saved from God's judgment (14:9–11; 20:4). As God's servants, the authorities are also accountable to God. The book of Revelation paints a graphic picture of the judgment that God will mete out on the rulers of this world when they go against him.

In a modern democracy, every voting citizen is in principle a ruler of their country. The biblical truth that rulers are accountable to God is therefore applicable to everyone. We are responsible to God for the way in which we use our vote, as we are for everything that we do. Every time we vote, we should be governed by the love commandment: "Love your neighbor as yourself" (Lev. 19:18). How this principle translates into support for specific political parties or political ideologies is a question the Bible does not answer. The New Testament does not provide a blueprint for a political program. Faithful Christians will "take captive every thought to make it obedient to Christ" (2 Cor. 10:5) and seek the guidance of the Spirit when they cast their votes. Individual Christians will reach different conclusions, however, and disagreements about these questions should not cause division within the church. Christians are united for a higher purpose than electing the next government here on earth; they are servants of God's government.

Christ's apostles were concerned with something far more significant than politics; they were in the business of bringing genuine change, the change that comes from within and transforms society. This kind of change does not depend on those who hold political power, and it is not brought by the government. This kind of change comes when the church proclaims the kingdom of God.

The civil government has no direct role to play in proclaiming the kingdom of God. No such government must therefore be confused with the rule of God, and we should not think that the government can be used to further God's kingdom. The civil authorities may be an instrument for good but only in a relative sense. If the government promises to bring the good society in an absolute sense, it claims a role that is reserved for God. Such a government represents the antichrist by attempting to take the place of Christ.

God's Universal Purposes

Even though the government does not and cannot exercise the kingly rule of God, it would be a serious error to think that God's purposes do not include the government and society as a whole. His rule is not limited to the church; he rules over all of society and over the government as well. God is the king of the entire universe, and the proclamation of his kingship does not only concern the beliefs and opinions of select individuals. It concerns the whole world, both on earth and in heaven.

In his Letter to the Ephesians, the apostle Paul paints a compelling picture of God's universal purposes. The effects of the gospel will be felt not only by the church but also by the spiritual forces that are at work in the world. God's "intent was that now, through the church, the manifold wisdom of God should be made known to the rulers and authorities in the heavenly realms" (Eph. 3:10).

Paul's language sounds strange to modern Christians as he speaks so naturally about rulers and authorities in heaven. We usually don't ascribe everyday events to the influence of heavenly powers. We think that our political landscape and our cultural values are the result of our own choices and that the only forces that control day-to-day events are human powers (unless we believe that God has intervened and done something extraordinary, like a miracle, but that would be an exception to the natural order of things).

Paul held a different view. He was aware that humans make their own destiny and that events unfold through cause and effect, but he knew that spiritual forces were also at work. Through their influence on people's mindsets, cultural trends, and social conventions, spiritual forces exercise their authority in this world.

In our time, we tend to use different terms for these forces. We speak of the spirit of the times, or the *Zeitgeist*, as the Germans call it. Positively, we may believe in the inevitability of progress; negatively, we recognize the adverse influence of power itself. When social structures and people's behavior change, we may attribute it to the influence of impersonal market forces or technological development. Individual moral choices may be explained as the inevitable result of family background and social context. People's behavior at big sporting events or political rallies shows us that they behave differently in large crowds than they do when they are alone. The explanation has to do with peer pressure and mob mentality. On a number of different levels, we sense that there are forces in our world, forces that cannot be identified with specific human agents, even though they may not operate independently of humans. Their influence cannot be denied. In the New Testament these kinds of forces are referred to as spiritual or heavenly powers and authorities. We should not dismiss what we are told about these forces, even if the apostle's terminology is unfamiliar to us. His point is clear: the purpose of God is not only the salvation of the church but also that the church will make God's plan known to the powers of the universe. God's purposes concern not only believers but also all of creation, both visible and invisible.

Earlier in Ephesians, Paul makes an even loftier statement about the universal nature of the message he proclaims: God "made known to us the mystery of his will according to his good pleasure, which he purposed in Christ, to be put into effect when the times reach their fulfillment—to bring unity to all things in heaven and on earth under Christ" (Eph. 1:9–10). This last phrase is difficult to translate. The Greek term that is rendered "to bring unity" (*anakephalaioō*) often means to draw a conclusion or to recapitulate. Paul's point is that all things in the entire universe have been in a state of disarray because of sin, but now the work of Christ and his lordship bring everything together in a new order. Paul emphasizes that there is no limit to the effects of the gospel. It reaches to all of creation, both visible and invisible. "For in [Christ] all things were created: things in heaven and on earth, visible and invisible, whether thrones or powers or rulers or authorities; all things have been created through him and for him" (Col. 1:16). All creation belongs to Christ, owes its existence to him, and has its purpose in him. Now Christ is reclaiming his creation. God's purpose is that all things will find their appropriate place and function in relation to Christ.

When God reestablishes his kingly rule through Christ, it does not affect only the church. His intention is not merely to carve out a limited territory for himself, the church, in which his rule will be upheld. He extends his reach to the whole world. He is the king of the universe, and in Christ he comes to restore his kingship. A limited role as king of the church will not satisfy him. Now he is making his kingly rule known. He is going to realign the forces that influence the culture on a deeper level than what the government does. These forces will now fulfill God's purposes in society.

The church plays a crucial role in fulfilling God's master plan, as Paul explains to the Ephesians. God intends to make known his wisdom to the rulers and authorities in the heavenly realms by means of the church (3:10). Paul has a beautiful vision for the church's role vis-à-vis the world. The church is instrumental in proclaiming God's purposes not only to believers but also to the powers of the universe. The church is God's agent that makes his wisdom known, the wisdom that concerns the restoration of creation under Christ's lordship. In other words, Christ uses the church to announce his lordship over the universe. To use military language, the church is the army that extends the victory of Christ throughout creation. But military language is misleading. The church does not extend the victory of Christ by coercion, like a military force. The church makes God's wisdom known. It does not enforce it. The victory of the church lies in its ability to embody the victory of Christ and to be a living demonstration of its effectiveness. In this way, the church is more like the king's communications department. It announces Christ's victory and proclaims his rule everywhere.

In Ephesians, Paul explains that Christ has come to bring peace and reconciliation. He has brought peace with God to believers. He has exchanged our
enmity for friendship. Our sins no longer make us God's enemies. Through his
death, Christ has taken our sins away and brought reconciliation and peace.
This reconciliation is demonstrated in the church, as Christ has simultaneously destroyed another kind of enmity: the enmity between people of different ethnic origin, the enmity between Jews and gentiles. "His purpose was to
create in himself one new humanity out of the two [Jews and gentiles], thus
making peace, and in one body to reconcile both of them to God through
the cross, by which he put to death their hostility" (Eph. 2:15–16). The very
existence of the church—consisting of Jews and gentiles, people from different
nations, those who used to be enemies—proclaims the victory of Christ. It
proclaims that Christ has destroyed the enmity. It announces that Christ has
brought reconciliation. It makes known that now there is peace.

Not of This World

The proclamation of the church concerns the whole world, in every nation
and in every aspect of society. God's kingly rule is universal. But we must not
think of God's kingdom the way we think of the kingdoms of this world. In
his conversation with Pontius Pilate, Jesus made this clear: "My kingdom is
not of this world. If it were, my servants would fight to prevent my arrest by
the Jewish leaders. But now my kingdom is from another place" (John 18:36).

Jesus's kingdom and authority are of a completely different nature than
those of Pontius Pilate. Pilate ruled with the power of the Roman army. His
authority depended on his ability to muster a superior military force. The
kingdom of God dwarfs every kingdom in this world, but that does not mean
that God's legions would come and defeat the legions of Rome. "My kingdom is not of this world," Jesus says. It is not a kingdom that rules through
physical strength.

John's Gospel demonstrates the different character of God's power, especially as it portrays Christ's way to his death. John shows that Jesus's
crucifixion is his enthronement. As he walks to the cross, Jesus is in complete
control every step of the way. No one takes his life from him; he freely gives
it up. He tells Pilate, "You would have no power over me if it were not given
to you from above" (19:11). When the soldiers came to arrest Jesus, all Jesus
had to do was to identify himself, and the soldiers were struck to the ground.
According to John, "Jesus, knowing all that was going to happen to him, went
out and asked them, 'Who is it you want?' 'Jesus of Nazareth,' they replied.

'I am he,' Jesus said. (And Judas the traitor was standing there with them.) When Jesus said, 'I am he,' they drew back and fell to the ground" (18:4–6).

The words translated "I am he" (more literally, "I am"; Greek, *egō eimi*) are a translation of God's self-revelation at the burning bush. When Moses asked God for his name, God replied, "I AM WHO I AM. This is what you are to say to the Israelites: 'I AM has sent me to you'" (Exod. 3:14). When Jesus speaks of himself in the same way, he reveals that he is the one who bears the divine name, "I am." All it took for Jesus to defeat the soldiers was to pronounce this name. That is how superior God's power is to the power of human armies.

When Jesus is on trial before Pontius Pilate, John reveals that the real trial plays out at a deeper level. Pilate is the one who is on trial before Jesus. The question is whether he will accept the truth that Jesus proclaims. With his now famous line "What is truth?" (John 18:38), Pilate shows that he is not rising to the occasion.

When Jesus is nailed to the cross, he is crucified as "THE KING OF THE JEWS" (19:19). In John's Gospel, Jesus has repeatedly anticipated his crucifixion, and he has referred to it as his exaltation, the time when he will be "lifted up" or "exalted" (3:14–15; 8:28; 12:32–34).

In Matthew and Mark, the last words of Jesus are "My God, my God, why have you forsaken me?" (Matt. 27:46; Mark 15:34). The contrast to John's Gospel is stark. In John's account, Jesus's final words are "It is finished" (John 19:30). When Jesus breathes his last, his victory is complete.[2] Jesus's crucifixion is therefore his enthronement, and this enthronement teaches us volumes about the nature of Jesus's kingship. He does not rule by force; he rules by sacrifice. He does not use coercion to make people do his will; he draws on the compelling force of love. His kingdom is not of this world!

In the Gospel of Mark, the disciples are given a similar lesson when Jesus is on his way to Jerusalem. After a dispute among the disciples about who would be the greatest, Jesus had to put them straight: "You know that among the Gentiles those whom they recognize as their rulers lord it over them, and their great ones are tyrants over them. But it is not so among you; but whoever wishes to become great among you must be your servant, and whoever wishes to be first among you must be slave of all. For the Son of Man came not to be served but to serve, and to give his life a ransom for many" (Mark 10:42–45 NRSV).

The kind of rule exercised in the kingdom of God is surprising. It is a rule that takes everything we know about authority and turns it upside down. In

---

2. There is not necessarily any conflict between these accounts. As in so many other instances, the evangelists have chosen to focus on different aspects of Jesus's life and death.

our world, the rulers enforce their will on their subjects. In God's kingdom, Jesus does not impose his rule through force. He does not enlist other people in his service to advance his agenda. He enlists himself as the servant of all. He does not draw on the resources of others to use them for his own purposes. He sacrifices all of his own resources so that he can give everything to his followers, even his own life. When he meets people, he does not tell them, "Ask not what your country can do for you; ask what you can do for your country."[3] Jesus comes with an entirely different request: "What do you want me to do for you?" (Luke 18:41).

Jesus's power is different. He exercises his power not by coercion but by showing his love so compellingly that people are won over to become his followers. This is true when Jesus meets individuals, and this is true for Jesus's authority in the church. This is also true when it comes to Jesus's influence on society.

Agents of Societal Change

Throughout history, there have been many examples of how societies have changed through the influence of God's people. The change has not come from the outside—through legislation, coercion, and other incentives—but from the inside. The testimony of the church has brought change into people's lives, societies have been transformed, and new cultures have been created. Below I offer two examples that show that God is in the business of doing the impossible and that he transforms nations and changes societies.

Martin Luther King Jr.

"It is politically impossible," President Lyndon B. Johnson replied when Martin Luther King Jr. demanded voting rights for African Americans. The president sympathized with King's cause, but he insisted that granting voting rights was not realistic. Johnson had spent all his political capital on ending segregation. He simply didn't have any more strings to pull. The vote had to come at a later point in time.

King retorted that justice could not wait. Early the following year (1965), he organized a march from Selma to Montgomery to demand the right to vote. As the marchers crossed the Edmund Pettis Bridge, local law enforcement ordered them to turn around. The protesters refused, and the police

3. From President John F. Kennedy's inaugural address, Washington, DC, January 20, 1961.

responded by attacking them with nightsticks, whips, and tear gas. More than fifty people ended up in the hospital.

Media images of the brutal attacks against peaceful protesters sent shock waves across the land, and there was an immediate outpouring of sympathy for the civil rights movement. Two weeks later, the marchers were joined by thousands of people from across the nation. This time the march to the state capital was allowed to take place, with protection from federal law enforcement. It was only a matter of months before the Voting Rights Act was written into law.

Few movements have changed American society more profoundly than the civil rights movement. Much of its strength lay in the fact that it was a community movement, organized by local churches. It did not depend on clever politicians and their ability to cut deals and ensure that new laws were passed. King was not aligned with any political party and operated primarily outside the political channels. But his influence surpassed even that of the president, and he held a power that proved more effective than political capital. It was a power that consisted in moral authority. The moral authority of King's peaceful protest was so compelling that lawmakers had no choice but to keep up.

King's moral authority came from the teachings of Jesus. He had been inspired by the master who taught us to love our enemies. Anyone who reads King's speeches will be struck by how different they are from the political pitches we hear every day. As an African American, King belonged to a large group of people who had been oppressed for centuries. He sounded a clarion call to resist the injustice and abuse that African Americans experienced on a daily basis. But there was no mentality of "us against them." He did not summon one group of good people to fight against evil people. King did not define his struggle against other people, not even the people who wished to do him harm. His speeches constantly returned to the powerful words of Jesus: "Love your enemies."

A particularly compelling example is found in the speech King delivered on the occasion of Ghana's birth as a nation. Ghana had been colonized by various European nations for centuries but had finally become its own nation in 1957. In his speech, King celebrated the reconciliation between the former colonialists and the new government. He rejoiced in the fact that Prime Minister Kwame Nkrumah had been seen dancing with the duchess of Kent at a state ball. And then he added these beautiful words about the aims of his own activities:

> The aftermath of nonviolence is the creation of the beloved community. The aftermath of nonviolence is redemption. The aftermath of nonviolence is reconciliation. The aftermath of violence is emptiness and bitterness. This is the thing

I'm concerned about. Let us fight passionately and unrelentingly for the goals of justice and peace. But let's be sure that our hands are clean in this struggle. Let us never fight with falsehood and violence and hate and malice, but always fight with love, so that, when the day comes that the walls of segregation have completely crumbled in Montgomery, . . . we will be able to live with people as their brothers and sisters. Oh, my friends, our aim must be not to defeat Mr. Engelhardt, not to defeat Mr. Sellers and Mr. Gayle and Mr. Parks. Our aim must be to defeat the evil that's in them. But our aim must be to win the friendship of Mr. Gayle and Mr. Sellers and Mr. Engelhardt. We must come to the point of seeing that our ultimate aim is to live with all men as brothers and sisters under God, and not be their enemies or anything that goes with that type of relationship. And this is one thing that Ghana teaches us: that you can break aloose from evil through nonviolence, through a lack of bitterness.[4]

Too often our struggle for a better society degenerates into a conflict between those who agree with us and those who disagree with us. Our engagement in politics takes the form of a battle in which we are determined to secure victory for our side and defeat for the opposition. We lose sight of the goal of a better world and focus on gaining a stronger position for our group. Christian involvement in politics has often been little more than another form of tribalism, or identity politics, as it is often called. Progress for Christians is at the same time a setback for atheists. Many times Christians have been engaged by an important ideal, such as the sanctity of life, but too frequently we have come to see our cause as a battle against our perceived opponents. We have seen the political process as a conflict. We have sought a stronger position for people of a Christian conviction like our own or for people of an ethnic background like our own. As a result, we have defined our political engagement as a battle against those of a different ethnicity or a different religious persuasion.

King's speeches are astonishingly free of this kind of identity politics. He did not define his goal as victory for African Americans and defeat for racists. He sought to overcome racism itself. He sought to defeat the very existence of injustice. "Our aim must never be to defeat or humiliate the white man, but to win his friendship and understanding. We must come to see that the end we seek is a society at peace with itself, a society that can live with its conscience. And that will be a day not of the white man, not of the black man. That will be the day of man as man."[5]

4. Martin Luther King Jr., *A Call to Conscience: The Landmark Speeches of Dr. Martin Luther King, Jr.*, ed. Clayborne Carson and Kris Shepard (New York: Warner, 2001), 32–33.
5. King, *Call to Conscience*, 130.

King's commitment was not ultimately restricted to the African American community; he was committed to all of humankind. His dream was the brotherhood and sisterhood of all people, a genuine unity, and such unity could not be built on victory for some and defeat for others. It could be built only on the foundation of reconciliation. And he knew that for there to be genuine reconciliation, those who thought of each other as enemies had to come together in understanding and even sympathy. "Here is the true meaning and value of compassion and nonviolence, when it helps us to see the enemy's point of view, to hear his questions, to know his assessment of ourselves. For from his view we may indeed see the basic weaknesses of our own condition, and if we are mature, we may learn and grow and profit from the wisdom of the brothers who are called the opposition."[6]

King knew that change comes from within. He knew that when people change, societies change. And he knew that the power that changes people is not the coercive force of violence but the compelling strength of nonviolence. He knew that light cannot come from darkness, so he understood that the methods he employed had to be the weapons of light. If he wanted to see a world of greater unity and brotherhood, he had to employ the weapon of love.

> I'm concerned about a better world. I'm concerned about justice; I'm concerned about brotherhood; I'm concerned about truth. And when one is concerned about that, he can never advocate violence. For through violence you may murder a murderer, but you can't murder murder. Through violence you may murder a liar, but you can't establish truth. Through violence you may murder a hater, but you can't murder hate through violence. Darkness cannot put out darkness; only light can do that.[7]

As King's movement showed, this method is truly transformative. It has the power to change societies because it changes people. It overcomes evil with good, as the apostle Paul teaches (Rom. 12:21). King knew what this meant in practice. He said that the method of nonviolence "has a way of disarming the opponent. It exposes his moral defenses. It weakens his morale, and at the same time it works on his conscience, and he just doesn't know what to do."[8]

King's movement brought great changes to the American society. These changes ended up being written into important laws, laws that expressed the ideals of the equality of all people. But the new laws did not change the values of the people. It was the values that changed the laws. This is how the

6. King, *Call to Conscience*, 151.
7. King, *Call to Conscience*, 191.
8. King, *Call to Conscience*, 66.

kingly rule of God brings change to our society: when the people of God live as if there is ultimately only one true king, Jesus Christ, and when they obey this king regardless of personal cost by putting into practice the words he taught. King showed us what it means to love your enemies, and the ripple effects were felt all across the nation, all the way to the White House, and all around the world.

Decades after these events, we can still see the fruits they bore. We can also see clearly that, for all the progress that has been made, the civil rights movement has not yet resulted in the full manifestation of the kingly rule of God. We must still remind each other of King's dream of the day when God's kingly rule is known and felt by all, the day when white and black Americans and people of all nations live together as brothers and sisters. And we must remind each other that it becomes reality one human encounter at a time, when we treat our enemy as our brother or sister.

Laszlo Tokes

God's power to change societies is not limited to democracies like the United States. Nicolae Ceauşescu's Romania was probably one of the most efficient terror regimes in modern history. Ceauşescu ruled Romania with such an iron fist that several thousand people died every year as a direct result of his policies. The whole world was shocked when pictures were eventually released from Romania's orphanages. They showed grotesque images of malnourished and neglected children.

Ceauşescu's brutality and total control were made possible by the secret police, the Securitate, which effectively crushed every attempt at opposition. They had informers in every nook and cranny of Romanian society. Those who refused to cooperate with the Securitate ended up in prison without due process. In the 1980s, of a population of 22 million, half a million Romanians worked for the secret police. As a result, the Romanian society was crippled by fear. Government spies were everywhere, and no one knew who they might be. People could be betrayed by their coworkers, neighbors, friends, even family members. Almost no one dared to say anything against the regime, for fear that someone might be listening.

With such a firm grip on the nation, the evil rule of Ceauşescu seemed to be invincible. In 1989, when other Communist states were opening up, Ceauşescu refused to budge. Through the brutal efficiency of the Securitate, he remained in full control. In Romania, it appeared that the powers of darkness had effectively blocked the progress of freedom and were able to maintain their opposition to God's kingly rule.

Decades of oppression had nearly squeezed the life out of the church in Romania. Pastors who were proclaiming the gospel were persecuted and thrown into prison. Over time, they were replaced by church leaders who were loyal to the Communist regime. Many of them were even enlisted as spies of the Securitate.

A pastor who felt the seemingly unlimited power of the secret police was the young Laszlo Tokes (László Tőkés). He was raised as the son of a pious pastor, and he had learned that a relationship with God was more important than anything else in a person's life. A Christian's commitment to God had to take precedence over all other loyalties, including family, country, and political authorities. As soon as he received his first call, Tokes was questioned by the Securitate for having preached a sermon on Hebrews 13:14: "For here we do not have an enduring city, but we are looking for the city that is to come." A Romanian was not supposed to tell people that they belonged to any other community than the State of Romania. But Tokes did not stop proclaiming that God is Lord above all. He believed that one's Christian faith concerns every aspect of life, not only the few hours people spend in church each week. He threw himself into all kinds of work that could make life better for people in his parish. To him, improvement of people's spiritual life and improvement of the local community were two sides of the same coin.

When he spoke out about the lack of basic resources in the churches, such as Bibles and hymnals, disciplinary action was taken against him. He was not allowed to criticize the leadership of the church and implicitly thereby the mighty Communist State of Romania. Tokes had to leave the ministry, but eventually he was reinstated and allowed to take a call as an assistant pastor on the other side of the country. Away from his constituency and under the supervision of a regime loyalist, he would be easier to control, officials thought. Tokes's attempts at proclaiming the kingly rule of God appeared to be thwarted by the seemingly omnipotent secret police.

In the city of Timişoara, Tokes continued to preach the gospel and help his congregation grow spiritually. During his tenure, the membership of the church doubled, but the internal transformation was more significant. The congregation came together as a family and experienced their unity in Christ. They formed a community that was fundamentally ruled by God, not by Ceauşescu.

Tokes describes two different approaches that Christians demonstrated when they were faced with Ceauşescu's oppression and attempts to quench their faith:

> A typical attitude was that of the conformist, the person who submits to the demands of the regime and practises his or her faith only insofar as the demands of the atheistic state permit. . . .

Between the conformist attitude and the attitude of those who were activists for change there was a great difference. The conformist had made a basic concession to history. He had conceded that the situation could not be changed, and so he changed himself to fit in with it. We who campaigned did so not in order to change ourselves in a negative way, but to change the situation in a positive way. It was a guiding principle in everything we did.

This was our revolutionary ideal; not a revolution of the barricades, but a revolutionary perspective. And, of course, a revolution of the mind, for without changing one's way of thinking one can never arrive at this point.[9]

Tokes chose to obey God rather than humans. He remained loyal to his Lord and did not see himself as a subject of Ceaușescu. He did not organize a violent rebellion against him, but he aimed for a revolution of the mind, a revolution that sprang out of the transformation of the mind in obedience to Christ. His life was lived under God's rule—not only to the extent that Ceaușescu would allow him but completely.

God allowed him to put this way of thinking into practice. As his fruitful ministry once again represented a threat to the authorities, they told him to move out of his home, but he refused. Agents from the secret police were placed outside his home to intimidate visitors. Tokes did not treat them with hostility but persisted in obeying his true Lord, who had taught him to love his enemies. He explains that the weapon of love was the only weapon the secret police did not know how to counter. "Their normal manner was dour hostility. The only effective weapon against them was a kind of Christian tranquility, a spirituality. That perplexed them because they were used to handling people who were frightened and tried to answer aggressiveness with aggressiveness."[10]

In August 1989, the bishop wrote to Tokes to tell him that he had been dismissed from his pastorate and would be evicted from his apartment. Once again, Tokes chose the way of peaceful resistance. He announced to his congregation that he would not obey the illegal order and that he would be forcibly removed on December 15. "Please, come next Friday and be witnesses to what will happen," he told them. "Come, be peaceful, but be witnesses."[11]

On December 15, Tokes's parishioners gathered outside his home to form a human wall around him when the secret police would arrive to abduct him and his family. This peaceful, public protest caught the attention of the people in the city, and the church members were joined by thousands of others. This

9. Laszlo Tokes and David Porter, *The Fall of Tyrants: The Incredible Story of One Pastor's Witness, the People of Romania, and the Overthrow of Ceausescu* (Wheaton: Crossway, 1990), 79.
10. Tokes and Porter, *Fall of Tyrants*, 143.
11. Tokes and Porter, *Fall of Tyrants*, 4.

demonstration stalled the police for two days, but in the end they forced their way through the crowds. When the police entered their apartment, the Tokes family fled into the church sanctuary, hoping the police would respect the sanctity of the church. But this regime had no respect for God. The police broke into the sanctuary and had pastor Tokes violently removed from the altar.

The regime that refused to acknowledge the authority of God appeared to have its victory. But the people who gathered outside had seen that it was possible to oppose Ceauşescu. Tokes had demonstrated that there was an alternative to unconditional submission: peaceful, loving resistance in the name of Christ. The protesters moved to the city square and demanded the resignation of Ceauşescu. The authorities responded in the only way they knew: with violence. Dozens of demonstrators were killed, but by now the people's desire for freedom could not be quenched. The protests moved to the capital, Bucharest. Within a week, Ceauşescu was forced out of office and executed. Timişoara became the first city in Romania to be declared free from Communism.

Through the ministry of Tokes, the kingly rule of God had manifested itself in the church in Timişoara. The shock waves had been felt throughout the land. A nation had gone through a revolution. The powers of evil were defeated. According to Tokes himself, the revolution had begun in the work that God had done in the hearts of his church members. "Long before it leaped into the forefront of world news as an initiator in toppling the Ceauşescu regime, our congregation in Temesvár [earlier name for Timişoara] was a revolutionary organisation. That is what the Church is always called upon to be in whatever time and place. It is a revolution that starts in the souls of people."[12]

The kingly rule of God advances not by the use of military weapons but through hearts that are transformed by the gospel and made obedient to Christ. When people are transformed in this way, societies and nations are transformed too. Not even the power of Ceauşescu's brutal regime could stand against this superior force.

Paradoxical Progress

Events like those in the United States, Romania, and other places have caused many Christians to believe that history will consistently move forward toward the full realization of God's excellent purposes. They have thought that the

12. Tokes and Porter, *Fall of Tyrants*, 98.

unstoppable rule of God will permeate more and more of society, making the world a progressively better place to live, until God's rule manifests itself everywhere on earth. There are good reasons to believe this. God's kingly rule is already among us, and this kingly rule cannot be defeated. The triumph of God's kingly rule has already taken place in Jesus Christ. We are not waiting for any more victories. We are just waiting to see the manifestation of the victory that has already been won.

But Jesus makes clear that God's kingly rule will not keep on advancing until there is no opposition left, at least not on this side of the final judgment. In Matthew 13:24–30 he offers the puzzling parable of the weeds:

> The kingdom of heaven is like a man who sowed good seed in his field. But while everyone was sleeping, his enemy came and sowed weeds among the wheat, and went away. When the wheat sprouted and formed heads, then the weeds also appeared.
>
> The owner's servants came to him and said, "Sir, didn't you sow good seed in your field? Where then did the weeds come from?"
>
> "An enemy did this," he replied.
>
> The servants asked him, "Do you want us to go and pull them up?"
>
> "No," he answered, "because while you are pulling the weeds, you may uproot the wheat with them. Let both grow together until the harvest. At that time I will tell the harvesters: First collect the weeds and tie them in bundles to be burned; then gather the wheat and bring it into my barn."

A little later, Jesus explains the meaning of the parable:

> The one who sowed the good seed is the Son of Man. The field is the world, and the good seed stands for the people of the kingdom. The weeds are the people of the evil one, and the enemy who sows them is the devil. The harvest is the end of the age, and the harvesters are angels.
>
> As the weeds are pulled up and burned in the fire, so it will be at the end of the age. The Son of Man will send out his angels, and they will weed out of his kingdom everything that causes sin and all who do evil. They will throw them into the blazing furnace, where there will be weeping and gnashing of teeth. Then the righteous will shine like the sun in the kingdom of their Father. Whoever has ears, let them hear. (13:37–43)

In the history of interpretation, there has been considerable debate over this parable. Many Christians have read the parable of the weeds and concluded that, until Christ returns, the church will consist of both good and evil people. There will be hypocrites mixed in with the people of God, and we are not supposed to try to root them out. The pure church will not appear on this side of judgment; we should accept the fact that the church is and will be a mixed community, a community consisting of both true and false Christians.

Others have objected to this interpretation by pointing out that as Jesus explains the parable, he does not identify the field as the church. Nor does he say that the weeds are people within the church. Instead, he states that "the field is the world" (v. 38). It is therefore unlikely that Jesus has the church specifically in mind. Rather, he is explaining the nature of the growth of God's kingly rule. While God's kingly rule grows, evil grows as well. In this world, the powers of darkness are present amid the kingly rule of God. The presence of God's kingly rule does not mean the absence of the forces of evil. In this world, they continue to coexist. The powers of darkness are defeated and doomed to destruction, but they are not eliminated.

The kingly rule of God is powerfully present, but the continued presence of evil means that many people fail to see it. The apostle Paul explains that God's power is paradoxically present in this world. In his Corinthian correspondence, he discusses this at length because some Corinthians were "demanding proof that Christ [was] speaking through" him (2 Cor. 13:3). Paul did not appear to be very powerful, and many church members made fun of him: "For some say, 'His letters are weighty and forceful, but in person he is unimpressive and his speaking amounts to nothing'" (10:10).

Many people fail to notice the power of God's kingly rule because it appears to the world as weakness. As Paul explained to the Corinthians, "The message of the cross is foolishness to those who are perishing, but to us who are being saved it is the power of God" (1 Cor. 1:18). The gospel doesn't look like much. It may be mistaken for foolishness and weakness. Jesus looked like a pathetic loser when he was crucified, and the passersby ridiculed him. But in his weakness he performed the greatest feat of strength ever to be conceived, and the Roman centurion who stood guard at the cross was led to confess: "Surely this man was the Son of God!" (Mark 15:39).

We should expect the kingly rule of God to continue to manifest itself in a similar way through the church. It doesn't appear to be very impressive. With another parable, Jesus explains that it is like the mustard seed: "What shall we say the kingdom of God is like, or what parable shall we use to describe it? It is like a mustard seed, which is the smallest of all seeds on earth. Yet when planted, it grows and becomes the largest of all garden plants, with such big branches that the birds can perch in its shade" (Mark 4:30–32). The power of God's kingly rule is hidden under the guise of smallness and insignificance, but make no mistake about it: the kingly rule of God is powerfully at work.

What the parable of the weeds makes clear is that the advance of God's kingly rule does not eliminate the forces of evil on this side of the final judgment. The kingly rule of God is paradoxically present in the midst of evil. But the history of the church shows us that when God's kingly rule is made known, it is as if the powers of evil wake up from sleep. The kingly rule of God is like a potent medicine that is released in the body. As the antibodies are fighting the disease, it feels like we are getting sicker, but the increased discomfort is really a sign of healing. As God's kingly rule manifests itself, it is as if the evil that had been dormant makes its last stand. Until the final judgment comes, we should not expect it to subside.

When we see God's kingly rule in this world, we should not think that evil will disappear altogether. We should expect communities and nations to change for the better as the gospel takes hold among the people, but we should not think that the nations of this world will evolve into societies where nothing but God's peace can be found. We should not look for Christian influence to transform this world into utopia. The weeds will always continue to grow amid the good seed. As the gospel continues to be proclaimed all over the world, we will see more and more people astonish us with their demonstrations of God's love. But unfathomable acts of evil will also be common.

When Christians are confronted with what seems to be an ever-increasing capacity for evil in the world, we should not think that the kingly rule of God is in retreat. Everything is going down just as Jesus predicted. The good seed of God's kingly rule grows, and so do the weeds. The superior power of God continues to be hidden under the appearance of weakness. God's kingly rule is as invincible as ever, and it is always present in the form of the cross. The same cross will in the end ensure the final victory of God's kingly rule.

Further Reading

Regarding the church in the book of Acts, the dominant view has been that Luke shows little interest in political and societal change. Instead, he is concerned to show that the church represents no threat to the political structure of the Roman Empire. In contrast, **C. Kavin Rowe** argues in his book *World Upside Down: Reading Acts in the Graeco-Roman Age* (Oxford: Oxford University Press, 2010) that Acts shows the subversive influence of the church. When people's convictions are changed through the proclamation of the gospel, societies change too.

Scot McKnight argues in *Kingdom Conspiracy: Returning to the Radical Mission of the Local Church* (Grand Rapids: Baker Academic, 2014) that Christ redeems people from the world. With a critique of a form of Christianity that is comfortable in the halls of secular power, he highlights the biblical call for the people of God to live lives that are truly countercultural.

The classic work on the church's engagement with society is **H. Richard Niebuhr,** *Christ and Culture* (New York: Harper Torchbooks, 1951). Through the New Testament and the history of the church, Niebuhr traces five different approaches. In 1 John, some early church fathers (especially Tertullian), the Mennonites, and Leo Tolstoy, he finds the "Christ against culture" model, characterized by the view that there is constant enmity between the church and the world. On this view, the church needs to escape from the world. "The Christ of culture" version is found in gnosticism, Abelard, and liberal Protestantism exemplified by Albrecht Ritschl. According to this model, the church and the best (not necessarily all) values in secular culture lead toward the same goal. Between these extremes, Niebuhr finds three mediating positions, all broadly categorized as "Christ above culture." The synthesis model is represented by Justin Martyr, by Clement of Alexandria, and above all by Thomas Aquinas. Within this model, secular culture is not against the gospel but is perfected by it. The apostle Paul, Martin Luther, and Søren Kierkegaard serve as representatives of the "Christ and culture in paradox" model. They emphasize the dualism between God's righteousness and human sinfulness. The new creation and human evil coexist, and the one does not eradicate the other. Closely related to the paradoxical model, the "Christ the transformer of culture" position gives a different emphasis on the concept of conversion. This view, found in the apostle John, Augustine, John Calvin, and F. D. Maurice, sees the gospel as having a transforming influence on society. Niebuhr sees some value in all of these models, although he favors the "Christ the transformer of culture" model.

In his book *Christ and Culture Revisited* (Grand Rapids: Eerdmans, 2008), **D. A. Carson** evaluates Niebuhr's typology and finds it inadequate. He argues that the "Christ of culture" position does not do justice to the theology of the Bible, whereas the other four views represent different aspects of a model that needs to be developed in light of a fuller appreciation for the biblical story line.[13]

In the three books *Naming the Powers* (Philadelphia: Fortress, 1984), *Unmasking the Powers* (Philadelphia: Fortress, 1986), and *Engaging the Powers* (Philadelphia: Fortress, 1992), **Walter Wink** discusses the New Testament picture of spiritual beings and relates it to a modern understanding of cultural forces and societal structures. He argues that the spiritual powers were originally good, have fallen, and are in need of redemption.

The most influential work from the perspective of Christian pacifism is **John Howard Yoder,** *The Politics of Jesus: Vicit Agnus Noster* (Grand Rapids: Eerdmans, 1972). Yoder argues that Jesus, through his proclamation of the kingdom, calls his

---

13. Another critique of Niebuhr's typology is Craig A. Carter, *Rethinking "Christ and Culture": A Post-Christendom Perspective* (Grand Rapids: Baker Academic, 2007).

followers to restructure social relationships through nonviolence and "revolutionary subordination."

In *Jesus and Empire: The Kingdom of God and the New World Disorder* (Minneapolis: Fortress, 2003), **Richard Horsley** criticizes individualistic, depoliticized readings of Jesus and argues that Jesus must be understood in the context of the Roman oppression of Israel. Jesus's proclamation of the kingdom entails judgment on oppressive rulers and the renewal of Israel. The Gospels originated as texts calling his followers to a social revolution in establishing "just egalitarian and mutually supportive social-economic relations" (105).

From the perspective of liberation theology, **Jon Sobrino** argues in *Jesus the Liberator: A Historical-Theological Reading of Jesus of Nazareth,* translated from the Spanish by Paul Burns and Francis McDonagh (Maryknoll, NY: Orbis Books, 1993) that Jesus's proclamation of the kingdom demonstrates God's preferential option for the poor, aiming to transform all of society and liberate the oppressed.

In his book *The Kingdom of Christ: The New Evangelical Perspective* (Wheaton: Crossway, 2004), **Russell Moore** discusses the significance of the concept of God's kingdom in contemporary evangelical thought and political engagement. He argues that the goal of world history is the final salvation that God will bring.

George Eldon Ladd maintains in *A Theology of the New Testament,* ed. Donald A. Hagner (Grand Rapids: Eerdmans, 1993) that "Paul was not concerned about social structures but only with how the Christian should live out the Christian life within the contemporary social situation" (575).

According to **Thomas R. Schreiner** in *New Testament Theology: Magnifying God in Christ* (Grand Rapids: Baker Academic, 2008), 755–801, because Christians know that God's kingdom is already here but not yet fully manifested, they engage the world with both realism and optimism. Christians confront the world's sins without naïveté and work for righteousness in the knowledge that God ultimately will accomplish his purposes. As aliens in this world, they do not look to the government as the source of the ultimate good but expect God to provide it in the future new creation. At the same time, Schreiner shows that the gospel brings a new social reality that is experienced in the community of the church.

8

Paradoxical Victory

The Future of the Kingdom

A few years ago I heard a young man share about his faith in Christ. His goal in life was not to make a lot of money, he said. He had no need for a nice house with a swimming pool and a Ferrari in the garage because he knew he would have all those things in heaven, when Christ would take him up to his eternal home. This picture of the new creation was inspired by the values of this world, not the teaching of the Bible. The new creation is not modeled after the luxuries of our society. It is created by God, who has better ideas than modern-day designers of consumer products. God knows how to fill his creatures with genuine and lasting joy. If we want to know what his paradise will look like, we should direct our attention to the presence of God's kingdom here and now. The people of God are already experiencing God's kingly rule. They enjoy the benefits of Christ's victory over evil, live in the domain of God's grace, rule over sin, and have tasted the firstfruits of the new creation, the Holy Spirit.

A Preview of the Consummation

When Jesus was about to be taken up to heaven, his disciples asked him, "Are you at this time going to restore the kingdom to Israel?" (Acts 1:6). In his reply, Jesus dismissed any kind of speculation about the times: "It is not for you to know the times or dates the Father has set by his own authority" (v. 7). But that was not all he had to say. Jesus pointed them to the Holy Spirit, whom he was going to give to them shortly afterward: "But you will receive power when the Holy Spirit comes on you; and you will be my witnesses in Jerusalem, and in all Judea and Samaria, and to the ends of the earth" (v. 8).

The kingdom, or the kingly rule, of God becomes a reality through the work of the Holy Spirit. The Holy Spirit is at work in the disciples of Jesus, and in this way God's kingly rule is restored. The disciples do not establish this rule through the use of force or coercion, but they proclaim it when they serve as witnesses of Jesus Christ. Jesus has already brought the kingly rule of God, and the task of the disciples is simply to serve as witnesses to what he has done. The king has come, and the disciples proclaim his kingdom. Jesus rules by the sovereign power of his sacrifice.

This rule is already a reality, a paradoxical reality. In this world the authority of God is hidden under the guise of weakness. The power is just as real, but not everyone perceives its presence. There will come a day, however, when no one will be able to deny or oppose the kingly rule of God. When God's kingly rule becomes visible, every creature will have to acknowledge it. This manifestation still lies in the future, which is why several texts in the New Testament presuppose a future kingdom, even though the kingdom is already present.

Jesus taught his disciples to pray, "Your kingdom come" (Matt. 6:10). This prayer presupposes that the kingdom is not already here; otherwise it would not be necessary to pray for it to come.

When Jesus ate his Last Supper with the disciples, he told them, "Truly I tell you, I will not drink again from the fruit of the vine until that day when I drink it new in the kingdom of God" (Mark 14:25 parr.). Once again, Jesus looked forward to a future that he referred to as the kingdom of God, in which he would once again drink the fruit of the vine. These words do not reveal very much about what the future kingdom will be like, but they teach us an important point: this future kingdom will be the perfection of the world in which we already live. This much we can understand from Jesus's use of the little word "again." Jesus will *again* drink of the fruit of the vine. The same fruit that he was drinking that night with his disciples he will drink again. That God comes to establish his kingly rule means that he comes to reclaim the world he has created. He comes to restore this world to the goodness that characterized it from the beginning. His just and wise rule will ensure that his creation fulfills the good purpose for which it was destined.

When Jesus drinks from the fruit of the vine again, it will also be new. When God establishes his kingly rule, he also creates everything new. As the

Old Testament prophets proclaimed so powerfully, when God comes as king, he will bring the new creation.

We are still looking forward to the day when the new creation will be a fully visible reality, but we can already have a pretty good idea of what it will be like. The new creation is also a present experience. The apostle Paul rejoices that "if anyone is in Christ, the new creation has come: The old has gone, the new is here!" (2 Cor. 5:17). Every follower of Christ already takes part in the new creation. They are still waiting for the full manifestation of the new creation, but they are not waiting for the new creation itself. It has already come. Where Christ is, there also is the kingdom of God, and there also is the new creation.

As the firstfruits of the new creation, the Holy Spirit shows us the characteristics of the new age. "The fruit of the Spirit is love, joy, peace, forbearance, kindness, goodness, faithfulness, gentleness and self-control" (Gal. 5:22–23). In the consummation, we will enjoy this fruit in abundance. The Holy Spirit is the Spirit of Jesus Christ himself. To be given the Holy Spirit means to be given the same Spirit who dwells in God's only Son. It means that we may relate to the Father in the same way that Jesus does. "Because you are [God's] children, God sent the Spirit of his Son into our hearts, crying, 'Abba! Father!'" (Gal. 4:6 NRSV).

Christians Yearn for the Future

God's people find their pleasure in all these gifts already, but the time will come when we will enjoy them in an entirely different way. There will come a time when all the sin and suffering in this world will disappear. Everything that has the ability to distract us from enjoying the gifts of God will cease to exist. Christians who walk closely with their Lord have their eyes fixed on this day, as they are yearning for the visible return of their savior. They cry out with the apostle Paul: "Come, Lord!" (1 Cor. 16:22).

When Christians become too comfortable in this world, they tend to be less focused on the future coming of Christ. The Corinthian church, which gave Paul so much to worry about, did not have much use for the hope of Christ's return. Many of them thought that all the blessings of Christ were for this present life. Some of them even denied the future resurrection, probably because they thought it was a rather crude and naive idea. If people died, were buried, and their bodies decayed, how could they all of a sudden jump out of their tombs and be alive again?

Paul devotes a long subsection of 1 Corinthians to this question (15:1–58). He makes it clear that the future resurrection is an essential truth of the Christian gospel. For Paul, it is fundamental that believers are united with Christ in his death and resurrection. If it were not for Christ's crucifixion and resurrection, there would be no salvation. And if it were not for believers' union with Christ, they could not partake in the salvation he has provided. The logical and necessary consequence of Christ's resurrection is therefore that the believers will also be resurrected. Their resurrection is just as certain as the resurrection of Christ himself.

Paul then goes on to explain how Christ's victory will be made complete in the future.

> But as it is, Christ has been raised from the dead, the firstfruits of those who have fallen asleep. For since death came through a man, the resurrection of the dead also comes through a man. For just as in Adam all die, so also in Christ all will be made alive.
>
> But each in his own order: Christ, the firstfruits; afterward, at his coming, those who belong to Christ. Then comes the end, when he hands over the kingdom to God the Father, when he abolishes all rule and all authority and power. For he must reign until he puts all his enemies under his feet. The last enemy to be abolished is death. For "God has put everything under his feet." Now when it says "everything" is put under him, it is obvious that he who puts everything under him is the exception. When everything is subject to Christ, then the Son himself will also be subject to the one who subjected everything to him, so that God may be all in all. (1 Cor. 15:20–28 CSB)

This glorious conclusion has already been anticipated in the resurrection of Christ. When Christ walked out of the grave, life triumphed over death, the new creation broke through into this world, the age of God's salvation burst forth into human and cosmic history. Christ was the firstfruits, and the firstfruits guarantee that there is more to come. When the new life has appeared, the abundance of fruit will inevitably follow.

The new creation and the establishment of the kingly rule of God are two different ways in which Paul describes the new reality: God's salvation of the world. With both images, he shows that the future salvation is nothing other than the full manifestation of the salvation that is already a reality in Jesus Christ. The fundamental victory has already been won. Paul is not waiting for Christ to win his victory over evil. He knows that Christ has already triumphed. He already reigns, as Paul says: "For he must reign until he has put all his enemies under his feet" (1 Cor. 15:25). As he is reigning, he is putting all his enemies under his feet. The suppression of all Christ's enemies is still ongoing. Christ is no longer engaged in battle; he is simply cleaning up the mess after the battle has been won. He ensures that all enemies are fully subdued so that God may rule without any form of opposition and the kingly rule of God can be experienced everywhere when Christ "hands over the kingdom to God the Father after he has destroyed all dominion, authority and power," and when God will "be all in all" (15:24, 28).

This is what Paul calls "the end," which will come "when he hands over the kingdom to God the Father" (15:24). If Christ is going to hand over the kingdom or the kingly rule to his Father, this presupposes that the kingdom is already his, that he is already ruling. And this is precisely Paul's point. Christ's resurrection is his enthronement. As he is enthroned, his enemies are in the process of being destroyed. First Corinthians 15:26 is translated by the NIV: "The last enemy to be destroyed is death." In the original Greek, however, the verb here is in the present tense, not future tense. A better translation might therefore be, "The last enemy that is being destroyed is death." This reading does better justice to Paul's line of thought. He is not hinting at a vague hope that death will one day be destroyed. He is announcing that Christ is resurrected and has triumphed over death. Therefore, death is in the process of being destroyed. Those who belong to Christ have an assurance: they will be resurrected. Their resurrection is as certain as Christ's own resurrection.

Paul is therefore elated about the future because he knows what the future entails. The gift that Christ has given to him will then come to its full fruition. God's kingly rule will be seen in its full glory. All God's enemies will be destroyed. Every power, every force, every will that stands in opposition to God will be eliminated. God will rule, and he will be all in all.

The first recipients of the Epistle to the Hebrews had lost sight of what Christ was promising them. They had gone through considerable hardship because of their faith (Heb. 10:32–34), and some of them were tempted to give up on the church altogether (10:25). The author of the epistle had to remind them of the kingdom that lay ahead: "Therefore, since we are receiving a kingdom that cannot be shaken, let us be thankful, and so worship God acceptably with reverence and awe" (12:28). This kingdom that cannot be shaken is a kingdom that has been given to the followers of Christ as a gift. It depends exclusively on the eternal and perfect sacrifice that Christ has presented to the Father. That is why the author calls the audience to be thankful and worship God. They have reason to do so. "For by one sacrifice he has made perfect forever those who are being made holy" (10:14).

To help the believers fix their eyes on the eternal kingdom, the author reminds them of the words of the Lord: "Once more I will shake not only the earth but also the heavens" (12:26). He then explains what his words mean: "The words 'once more' indicate the removing of what can be shaken—that is, created things—so that what cannot be shaken may remain" (12:27). God will remove the created things; he will remove the world as we know it, the world that is full of suffering and persecution for God's people. It will disappear "so that what cannot be shaken," the eternal kingdom of God, may remain.

To the author of the Epistle to the Hebrews, this kingdom is clearly something to be expected in the future. It presupposes the removal of the created things as we know them. At the same time, the author makes it clear that this future kingdom is not something entirely new, something of which his audience has no experience. In the very same passage where he encourages them to look forward to this kingdom, he also emphasizes that they have already arrived:

> For you have not come to what could be touched, to a blazing fire, to darkness, gloom, and storm, to the blast of a trumpet, and the sound of words. Those who heard it begged that not another word be spoken to them, for they could not bear what was commanded: "If even an animal touches the mountain, it must be stoned." The appearance was so terrifying that Moses said, "I am trembling with fear." Instead, you have come to Mount Zion, to the city of the living God (the heavenly Jerusalem), to myriads of angels, a festive gathering, to the assembly of the firstborn whose names have been written in heaven, to a Judge, who is God of all, to the spirits of righteous people made perfect, and to Jesus, the mediator of a new covenant, and to the sprinkled blood, which says better things than the blood of Abel. (Heb. 12:18–24 CSB)

In contrast to the terrifying and fearsome Mount Sinai, where the Israelites received the old covenant, the church has arrived at the heavenly Jerusalem, the city of the living God. This is not an earthly city; it is not a part of the created things that will be removed. It is the eternal city of the living God, the place of his dwelling.

We must not think of this city in geographical terms, as a city with buildings of concrete and streets paved with asphalt. The church has not come to a physical city, but the author of Hebrews affirms that the church has arrived in the city of the living God. It is called a city not because of its physical infrastructure but because it is where God dwells among the community of his people. His people have already arrived in this city; they have already been brought into God's presence. They already enjoy the most intimate relationship with him. That is the point that the Epistle to the Hebrews has been making all along: those who believe in Christ have entered into a relationship with God that is far more intimate than anything that was possible under the old covenant.

The letter begins with the sentence: "In the past God spoke to our ancestors through the prophets at many times and in various ways, but in these last days he has spoken to us by his Son, whom he appointed heir of all things, and through whom also he made the universe" (Heb. 1:1–2). In the past, God spoke through mediators, but now he has spoken directly through his Son. In the past, God's relationship with his people was characterized by distance, but now it is characterized by intimacy. In the past, God communicated with his people through the terrifying revelation from Mount Sinai, but now he allows them to live peacefully in his own, heavenly city.

This is the kingdom the believers are waiting to receive, the kingdom they have already entered into, the city in which they already dwell, the neighborhood to which they already belong, the relationship with God that they already enjoy. One day they will enjoy it without the distractions that come from this world as we know it today.

Conflict between the Kingdom of Satan and the Kingdom of God

In the meantime, the powers of evil are mustering all their resources to derail Christ's disciples from the race they have to run. The most elaborate description of this conflict is found in the book of Revelation. John paints a graphic picture of the war between the kingdom of God and the kingdom of Satan. There are cavalry, conquerors, bloodbaths, and horses with heads like lions and tails like snakes. We read about such horror shows that the people on earth call on the mountains to fall down and conceal them (Rev. 6:16). Locusts looking like warrior horses ascend from the abyss. They have power like scorpions and torture people for five months (9:3–11). There is a massacre that causes an area as large as a medium-sized American state or a small country to be flooded with blood (14:20). A rider on a white horse strikes down the nations with his sharp sword (19:15). All the nations of the earth march together toward battle, but they are devoured by fire coming down from heaven (20:7–9).

From the very beginning, however, it is abundantly clear that there is no genuine doubt about the outcome of the conflict. The warring forces are not evenly matched. One of them is so totally superior that there is no room for any real battles to be fought. Already in Revelation 1:5, Jesus is introduced as "the ruler of the kings of the earth." He will not become the ruler; he is not going to battle his way to his position as ruler; he already is the ruler of all the kings of the earth. There is no one who can genuinely challenge him. Those who try are exposed as a pathetic parody.

There is only room for one king in the book of Revelation, the one who is "Lord of lords and King of kings" (17:14; cf. 19:16). This title belongs to Christ. In the book of Revelation, he is characteristically known as the Lamb because he is the one who has been slaughtered and has "purchased for God persons from every tribe and language and people and nation" (5:9). Christ is the Lamb that has been sacrificed for the sins of the world. Like Israel's Passover lamb, this Lamb has brought deliverance to his people.

The people of the Lamb owe their very existence to his act of redemption. As John begins the book of Revelation, he gives praise "to him who loves us and has freed us from our sins by his blood, and has made us to be a kingdom and priests to serve his God and Father—to him be glory and power for ever and ever! Amen" (1:5–6). John echoes the words of God when he established Israel as a nation at Mount Sinai (Exod. 19:6). Now, those who believe in Christ represent God's kingdom. They rule as kings on his behalf and serve him as priests.

As John begins his account of the two kingdoms, the kingdom of God's people is simply "a kingdom." There is still a conflict between their kingdom and Satan's kingdom. As John's story unfolds, this state of affairs will change. A little later, loud voices in heaven will proclaim: "The kingdom of the world has become the kingdom of our Lord and of his Messiah, and he will reign for ever and ever" (Rev. 11:15). God's kingdom will become the only kingdom. "A kingdom" will become "the kingdom." Jesus the Messiah will solidify his universal rule. There will no longer be anyone standing against him, disobeying him, challenging him, or failing to recognize him as the king of kings.

The book of Revelation tells the story of how the world is made subject to the kingly rule of Christ. Its subjection is the inevitable result of the ultimate victory that has been won by the Lamb. The book of Revelation contains no account of any battle, only preparations for battle and the punishment of the losing side. There are references to a victory, but this victory already lies in the past.

As John is given a vision of the heavenly throne, he sees the Lamb, sharing the throne with God the Father (5:13). That vision shows that Christ is equal to God, as he shares the throne with him and rules with him. John learns that "the Lion of the tribe of Judah, the Root of David, has triumphed" (5:5). The lion, evocative of power and might, is the symbol of the Messiah (Gen. 49:9). When John is allowed to see this lion, however, it turns out to be a lamb. The lamb is also a symbol of Christ, but it brings up different associations. A lamb is weak. In Israel, the lamb was an animal that was used for sacrifice. The effect of this combination of symbols is very powerful: the lion is a lamb; the predator is an animal of prey; the triumphant one is a loser; the conqueror is a victim that will be delivered up to be slaughtered.

As we have seen in the rest of the New Testament, the victory that brings the kingdom of God is won in a paradoxical way. It is won through Jesus's apparent defeat when he died on the cross. But his death was his triumph. The Lamb is victorious, and he is worthy to open the scroll that contains the events of the end time. With his death on the cross, he has determined the outcome of all of history. What is going to happen from now on is simply the unfolding of a scroll that has already been written. The events are pre-determined. The punishment of the evil forces is already recorded in the scroll. It just needs to be unsealed and opened. The Lamb is the one to do it, as the heavenly hosts sing: "You are worthy to take the scroll and to open its seals, because you were slain, and with your blood you purchased for God persons from every tribe and language and people and nation. You have made them to be a kingdom and priests to serve our God, and they will reign on the earth" (Rev. 5:9–10). The Lamb's victory is also shared by the Lamb's people. He has made them to be a kingdom, and he will make them reign on the earth.

Persecution and the Antichrist

The churches to whom John was writing did not feel victorious, however. They did not feel like rulers. They felt like the opposite as they were suffering and being persecuted for their loyalty to Christ and for their refusal to participate in the idolatry of their communities, especially the worship of the Roman emperor. In the Roman province of Asia (now western Turkey), where these churches were located, the Roman emperor was worshiped as a god. Pergamum was the first city in the Roman Empire to build a temple specifically dedicated to worshiping a living Roman emperor. Those who refused to participate, Christians who remained faithful to the Lord, were often persecuted.

Christians in the province of Asia were well acquainted with the power of Christ's enemies, who were the powers that represented the emperor in Rome, the powers that ruled with brutality and violence and were trying to compel people to honor the emperor in a way that only God and the Lamb should be honored.

In his first letter, John refers to these powers as the antichrist. The word means both someone who stands against Christ and someone who wants to replace Christ.[1] John also makes clear that there is not just one antichrist but many: "As you have heard that the antichrist is coming, even now many antichrists have come" (1 John 2:18).

In the book of Revelation, the antichrist is portrayed symbolically as a beast coming out of the sea (13:1). The power of such a symbol is that it may refer to more than one individual. As there are many antichrists, so does the beast represent many anti-Christian forces throughout the history of the world. When John explained that people were forced to worship the image of the beast, the first Christians would have understood that he was referring to the emperor in Rome.

Throughout the history of the church, Christians have identified the beast with contemporary rulers, such as Hitler and Stalin. They were not wrong. It is natural for persecuted Christians to respond by turning to the Scriptures. When they read the book of Revelation, they will recognize the characteristics of the beast in the despots that are responsible for their suffering. More important than identifying individuals, however, is the ability to discern the character traits of the beast. The beast claims for itself a role that rightfully only belongs to Christ. It uses its worldly power in its pursuit of this role.

The beast has its power from the dragon (Rev. 13:2), a symbol of Satan (12:9). Together with the great prostitute (17:1), who represents the deception that lures people away from Christ, the dragon and the beast form an unholy trinity. By portraying the powers of evil in this way, John shows us their true nature: they wish to usurp the place of the Triune God. Their sin is the same as the one with which the serpent tempted the first humans: "When you eat from it your eyes will be opened, and you will be like God, knowing good and evil" (Gen. 3:5). Satan and his minions want to be like God, and we can recognize them by their fundamental character trait.

The beast wants to be worshiped (Rev. 13:4). It has crowns on its head (13:1), imitating Christ, who is the true bearer of many crowns (19:12). The number of the beast is 666 (13:18). In the Bible, the number seven is the perfect number, thus representing God. The number six falls one short of seven. The number of the beast is a number that three times fails to reach the number seven. It is the number of someone who aspires to the perfect level of the Triune God, but who falls pitifully short.

In contrast to the Lamb, the beast is a grotesque and terrifying animal. "It had ten horns and seven heads" (Rev. 13:1). It "resembled a leopard, but had feet like those of a bear and a mouth like that of a lion" (13:2). As he was portraying this beast, John realized that the worst predators in nature

---

1. The Greek word *anti* can mean both "against" and "instead of."

do not do it justice. He had to combine three different animals. One image of cruelty was added to another and then yet another.

In many cases the beast asserts itself through the use of brute force; thus the apostle Peter compares the devil to a "roaring lion looking for someone to devour" (1 Pet. 5:8). He is no less active now than he was during the time of the first Christians. As far as we know, there have never been as many Christian martyrs as there are today.[2] These killings are the work of the beast, who tries to force Christians to deny their exclusive allegiance to Christ.

But the devil does not rely only on threats, violence, and outright persecution of the people of God. He is also highly skilled in the art of deception. The apostle Paul reminds us that "Satan himself masquerades as an angel of light" (2 Cor. 11:14). John describes a second beast, exercising authority on behalf of the first beast and performing great signs that deceived the people on earth (Rev. 13:12–14). When the beast returned to power after having been fatally wounded, "the whole world was filled with wonder and followed the beast" (13:3).

The powers of the antichrist are present in the world today whenever Christians are deceived into giving their loyalty to someone or something other than Christ. It may be promises of wealth and success that lure people away from relying on Christ alone. Christ is the only one we may trust for our salvation, but Christians are often tempted to look elsewhere. It may be a charismatic politician who promises security, wealth, and prosperity, and Christians may be misled to think that the success of God's kingdom depends on the success of such politicians. Or it may be preachers promising Christians that they may enjoy the blessings of God's kingdom without having to endure the suffering. Paul and Barnabas told the disciples in Lystra, Iconium, and Antioch, "We must go through many hardships to enter the kingdom of God" (Acts 14:22). It is equally true today. When Christians have no experience with suffering because of their faith, it is an indication that they have not been faithful to their Lord. A Christian who is faithful to the gospel of Christ will be in conflict with the predominant values of the world. A follower of Christ stands up for the vulnerable, the downtrodden, the refugee, and the prison population. They defend ethnic groups that are the object of scorn, contempt, discrimination, and oppression. Christians reject moral values that make individual happiness the ultimate good. They allow their actions to be governed by what is best for others and for the community. These commitments do not make Christians popular in this world.

2. For obvious reasons, reliable numbers are hard to come by. Some missiologists believe that every year as many as 100,000 Christians are killed because of their faith. Others maintain that the number may be closer to 10,000.

In its counterfeiting of Christ, the beast even tries to copy Christ's resurrection from the dead. John says that the beast had been given a fatal wound but was able to recover (Rev. 13:3, 12). Yet its recovery is only temporary: John explains that its authority was restored "for forty-two months" (13:5).

The forty-two months, or three and a half years, represent a time of suffering for the people of God. The number should not be taken literally. It is a symbolic number that evokes a time of great suffering for God's people. From 167 to 164 BCE, during a period of roughly three and a half years, Jerusalem was controlled by the Greek ruler Antiochus IV Epiphanes. He made it illegal to obey the law of Moses and dedicated the temple to the Greek god Zeus. "Three and half years" is therefore a number fraught with emotional significance, much like the date September 11 is in the United States, July 7 is in the United Kingdom, or July 22 is in Norway.[3] It is a time when evil appears to rule supreme and the suffering is extreme.

The beast exercises its authority for three and half years even after it has been given its fatal wound. Jesus has already given the decisive blow to the forces of evil. But, as we know, these forces are still exercising their influence in our world. Their time is limited, however, just as the time of the beast was restricted to three and a half years. In the context of the book of Revelation, three and half years is a very short period. In contrast, those who did not worship the beast "reigned with Christ a thousand years" (Rev. 20:4). To us, it may appear that the oppressive power of the antichrist is indefatigable, but in the big scheme of things, from God's perspective, its time is very short.

It does not seem short to us who live almost two thousand years after John. We still have to witness the seemingly unstoppable power of the forces that make a mockery of God's kingly rule. God's perspective is different. "With the Lord a day is like a thousand years, and a thousand years are like a day," the apostle Peter reminds us. And he adds, "The Lord is not slow in keeping his promise, as some understand slowness. Instead he is patient with you, not wanting anyone to perish, but everyone to come to repentance" (2 Pet. 3:8–9). God is waiting to mete out his eternal punishment because he is merciful. The nature of God is to overcome evil with good, to bring reconciliation, and to transform his enemies into his friends.

In the book of Revelation, we also see how God keeps delaying the final judgment. At first we hear about the seven seals, seals that will unleash God's end-time judgment. With the breaking of the seventh seal, we expect everything

3. Terrorists attacked the World Trade Center in New York on September 11, 2001, and London commuters on July 7, 2005. A lone gunman attacked a youth camp near Oslo on July 22, 2011.

to be over and the end to arrive. But then the whole process starts over again with seven trumpets. These trumpets serve the same purpose of announcing God's end-time judgments, presumably culminating in the end of this world as we know it. But once again we are left in suspense. The seven trumpets are succeeded by seven bowls. It is not until this sequence of final judgments has played out three times that the final showdown happens, and the beast and the dragon are finally dealt with. God waits and waits and waits. His desire is for people to come to repentance. He is a God of reconciliation, and all his actions are governed by this overarching goal: to bring reconciliation, to bring sinful people to himself so that they may be saved.

The Victory of Christ

Paradoxically, the very nature of Christ's victory is that he died for his enemies. In Revelation 5:5 we learn that Jesus the Messiah, "the Lion of the tribe of Judah, the Root of David, has triumphed." Yet this Lion turns out to be "a Lamb," which has "been slain" (5:6). In other words, the victory of Christ was won by means of his sacrifice. He was slain as a sacrifice for the sins of his people.

The people of the Messiah share his suffering, and when they share his suffering, they also share his victory. From the Gospels we know that Jesus won his victory over the evil forces and established the kingdom of God during the time of his earthly ministry. The book of Revelation shares the same perspective. After his account of the seventh trumpet (11:15–19), John gives us a flashback to the decisive event of history: the life of Jesus (12:1–12). This is the time when Satan was defeated.

The great dragon was hurled down—that ancient serpent called the devil, or Satan, who leads the whole world astray. He was hurled to the earth, and his angels with him.
Then I heard a loud voice in heaven say:

"Now have come the salvation and the power
and the kingdom of our God,
and the authority of his Messiah.
For the accuser of our brothers and sisters,
who accuses them before our God day and night,
has been hurled down.
They triumphed over him
by the blood of the Lamb
and by the word of their testimony;

they did not love their lives so much
   as to shrink from death.
Therefore rejoice, you heavens
   and you who dwell in them!
But woe to the earth and the sea,
   because the devil has gone down to you!
He is filled with fury,
   because he knows that his time is short." (Rev. 12:9–12)

Here we also see the characteristic perspective of Revelation: the devil has already been defeated and ejected from heaven, but the time following his defeat is a time of intense activity on his part. "He is filled with fury, because he knows that his time is short." As we have seen in the Gospels, so is Satan's defeat also the time when the kingdom of God has come and the time when the authority of the Messiah is present. The voice from heaven also announces that the people of the Messiah share in his victory. "They triumphed over him by the blood of the Lamb and by the word of their testimony; they did not live their lives so much as to shrink from death." Christ, the Lamb, won his victory over the evil one by giving his blood, by dying on the cross. This victory is at the same time the victory of Christ's followers. The voice from heaven said that "they" triumphed. Their victory is won by the blood of the Lamb, but also "by the word of their testimony; they did not love their lives so much as to shrink from death." In the book of Revelation, John is concerned about one thing: to encourage the believers to be faithful to their Lord even though they have to suffer for his name's sake. He reminds them that their suffering is temporary and that they have an eternal reward. John also warns them of the punishment that will befall those who are not faithful to Christ because they wish to avoid suffering. To get his point across, he teaches them about the value of their suffering. Just as Christ defeated Satan through his suffering, so do they participate in his victory when they suffer for Christ. The voice from heaven describes those who pay the ultimate price: the believers who have to give their lives because of their testimony. But the message also applies to Christians who suffer in a less spectacular way. Their suffering is the way in which they participate in Christ's victory.

The Effective Witness of the Church

In another symbol-laden vision, John shows how believers' suffering brings victory. God announces that he is appointing two witnesses who "will prophesy for 1,260 days, clothed in sackcloth" (Rev. 11:3). The time period of 1,260 days corresponds to the 42 months during which the beast will exercise his authority. This refers to the time when the powers of evil prevail on earth. God still has his witnesses on earth during this time. The two witnesses "are 'the two olive trees' and the two lampstands, and 'they stand before the Lord of the earth'" (11:4). This identification of the witnesses alludes to a prophecy that was given to Zechariah. God let him see two olive trees that represented "the two who are anointed to serve the Lord of all the earth" (Zech. 4:14). The two that are anointed are the king of Israel and the priest in the temple. We recall that the church in Revelation is "a kingdom and priests to serve [Christ's] God and Father" (Rev. 1:6), and that "kingdom" here also means a people who rule as kings (cf. Exod. 19:6). The two witnesses, or the two olive trees, are thus a symbolic reference to the church. The two witnesses are also called "the two lampstands"—another symbol for the church in the book of Revelation (cf. 1:20).

The people of God are kings and priests even in this evil world. As kings, they rule on God's behalf, and as priests, they proclaim God's will. The two witnesses have tremendous power: "fire comes from their mouths and devours their enemies. . . . They have power to shut up the heavens so that it will not rain . . . ; and they have power to turn the waters into blood and to strike the earth with every kind of plague as often as they want" (11:5–6). As everything else in Revelation, these words are to be taken symbolically, not literally. They remind us of Elijah (2 Kings 1:10–14; 1 Kings 17:1) and Moses (Exod. 7:14–24; 1 Sam. 4:8), who also served as God's witnesses.

The two witnesses will eventually be killed by the beast, and they will even be refused a proper burial. Even in their death, they will not escape brutal humiliation under their evil oppressors. But after three and a half days they will return to life and be taken up to heaven (Rev. 11:7–12). Their resurrection and ascension are symbolic, representing God's approval and vindication. In the midst of their suffering and humiliation, God will honor the testimony of the church. He will show that the suffering church was right all along. Just like Christ, who was rejected and mocked by the people but was proved to be God's Son through his resurrection, so also will the church be humiliated and ridiculed on earth, but ultimately believers will be proved to be God's chosen ones.

The testimony of the suffering church will prove to be God's most powerful weapon in the end-time conflict. None of the judgments that are being poured out on the earth in the book of Revelation accomplish God's ultimate purpose. After the many judgments of God, we read that the people did not repent of their sins (Rev. 9:20–21; 16:9, 11). However, when the people see the church's suffering witness and its vindication by God, things are different. When the two witnesses were taken up to heaven, "there was a severe earthquake and a tenth of the city collapsed. Seven thousand people were killed in the earthquake, and the survivors were terrified and gave glory to the God of heaven" (11:13).

When we read that the survivors gave glory to God, many interpreters take it to mean that they now were forced to recognize the truth. They no longer had any choice but to acknowledge that God indeed was the king. Such an acknowledgment, it is argued, is not the same as saving faith, which entails trust in the grace of God. In the end, even God's enemies and the unbelievers will have to accept that God is the one to whom all glory belongs. John does not specify that the survivors came to a saving relationship with God. However, to give glory to God is always a positive concept in the book of Revelation. To give glory to God means to stand in a right relationship with him. Whereas the great prostitute glorifies herself (18:7), only the people of God and the heavenly host give glory to God. "To give glory to God" may also be used as a synonym for repentance (16:9). When we read that the survivors gave glory to God, therefore, we understand that they genuinely repented and turned to God in faith.

The survivors who turned to God included all the inhabitants in the city except the seven thousand who died in the earthquake (11:13). The number seven thousand is the number of survivors at the time of Elijah (who is here used as one of the symbols for the witness of the church). During the time of the prophet Elijah, the spiritual state of Israel was so depressing that Elijah thought there was no one else left who was faithful to the Lord. But God revealed to him that there was a remnant, seven thousand, who had not fallen into idol worship (1 Kings 19:18).

In John's vision, the proportions are reversed. The number seven thousand is no longer the number of the faithful remnant; it is the number of those who suffer judgment. Instead of seeing a small remnant being saved, the church will now see spectacular results of its ministry. The whole population, minus the small number killed, will now accept their testimony. What is the secret to the exceptionally effective witness of the church at this time? Their witness is accompanied by extreme suffering. Just as their Savior triumphed through the excruciating suffering on the cross, so will his church be triumphant through the terrible persecution they will undergo in the end times.

The early Christians were well acquainted with persecution, but the persecution did not stunt the growth of the church. In many cases, the persecution led to even greater church growth. The church father Tertullian famously concluded that "the blood of the martyrs is the seed of the church" (*Apology* 50). The courageous faith of the martyrs made a great impression on people;

they could see that God was present among the Christians and gave them strength to meet their tormentors with love.

Modern times are no different. A striking example is found in the country of Ethiopia. Protestant missionaries from Germany, the United States, Sweden, Norway, Denmark, and Finland came in large numbers to Ethiopia during the twentieth century. They brought the gospel to areas in which the name of Jesus was completely unknown, planted new churches, and experienced encouraging growth. But in 1974 the Communists came to power. They viewed Protestant Christianity as an enemy of Ethiopia and actively sought to eradicate the Protestant churches. Many churches were forced to close. In the Wollega region, the Ethiopian Evangelical Church Mekane Yesus (EECMY) saw the number of open churches reduced from 377 to 22. All over the country, church property was confiscated. Pastors and elders were arrested, beaten, and tortured. Some of them were killed. Young church members were harassed. If they continued to be involved in Christian activities, they were threatened with being sent as soldiers in the war with Eritrea. Most of the missionaries had to leave the country, and they feared that the persecution would snuff out the light of the gospel before it had caught flame in Ethiopia.

They could not have been more wrong. In 1959 the EECMY counted 20,000 members. By 2000 that number had grown to 3.6 million. As it had been in the early church, so was the time of persecution a time of exponential growth for the Ethiopian Christians. The persecution brought them together. They had to rely on each other to an extent they had not done before. Above all, they had to trust in their Lord; they were reminded of their dependence on him every day, even to save their lives. A suffering church is a powerful witness for Christ.

One of the many martyrs was the general secretary of the EECMY, Gudina Tumsa. As a young man, Gudina Tumsa had been radically converted from being a follower of traditional Ethiopian religion to becoming a disciple of Jesus Christ. He courageously proclaimed that Jesus was Lord of all, and he stood firm with the same message when the Communists came to power in Ethiopia. Because he inspired the Christians to show peaceful resistance against the regime, he was closely monitored by the authorities and was arrested twice. When he was released the second time, he knew that he would not survive if he was arrested again. At that point, the president of Tanzania, Julius Nyerere, contacted him and offered him asylum in Tanzania. The president's private plane would wait for him at the airport in Addis Ababa, and Gudina Tumsa was offered a safe escape to freedom. He refused. As an explanation, he told the Tanzanian president: "Here is my church and my congregation. How can I, as a church leader, leave my flock at this moment of trial? I have again and again pleaded with my pastors to stay on." Then he quoted from 2 Corinthians 5:15: "'[Christ] died for all that those who live should no longer live for themselves but for him who died for them and was raised again.' Never ever will I escape," he said.[4]

The last thing Gudina Tumsa wrote before his third arrest was a treatise called "The Role of a Christian in a Given Society." He concluded the treatise by quoting Dietrich Bonhoeffer: "When a person is called to follow Christ, that person is called to die." On July 28, 1979, Gudina Tumsa was on his way home from preaching at a local church when he was abducted by armed men dressed as civilians. No one knew where they were taking him and what they were going to do to him. For more than twelve years, his wife and family did not know whether he was dead or alive. It was not until 1992 that a soldier came forward and testified that he had been present at the execution of Gudina Tumsa. This church leader had been killed the night he was apprehended, but his influence on the church in Ethiopia could not be eliminated. He had witnessed to Christ and the gospel more powerfully through his death than in his life.

Even more recently the Coptic church in Egypt has showed what a powerful testimony the church can have when it responds to persecution with love and forgiveness. Since the so-called Arab spring, which quickly turned into winter again, Coptic Christians have been the target of numerous acts of religiously motivated violence. In Alexandria on January 1, 2011, as Christians were leaving the Saints Church, they were attacked with a bomb. Twenty-three people died and ninety-seven were injured. Since then, many other attacks have likewise claimed dozens of lives.

Faced with such gruesome violence, the leaders of the Coptic church have called on Christians to respond peacefully and lovingly. To explain the needed response, they have quoted the words of Jesus: "Love your enemies and pray for those who persecute you" (Matt. 5:44). In so doing, they give voice to the testimony that is symbolically described in the book of Revelation. Their witness has been effective. Egyptians who convert to the Christian faith risk their lives by doing so. It is therefore impossible to know how many Christian converts there are in Egypt, but reports indicate that the numbers have been on the rise since 2013.

In the end times, God's rule will manifest itself in more and more places, and the beast will become more and more aggravated. Its rage will intensify. Peoples and nations will submit to the authority of the beast, and they will wage outright war against the Lamb (Rev. 17:14). With the kings of the earth

4. Øyvind M. Eide, *Revolution and Religion in Ethiopia: The Growth and Persecution of the Mekane Yesus Church, 1974–85*, with a foreword by Carl Fr. Hallencreutz, Eastern African Studies (Oxford: James Currey, 2000), 177.

behind him, the military strength of the beast will appear to be formidable, but appearances are deceptive. The book of Revelation teaches that the forces that seem to be the most impressive and unassailable in this world ultimately have no power at all. As the beast and the kings of the earth and their armies prepared to march against Christ, they did not even make it far enough to see combat. Before the battle began, "the beast was captured, and with it the false prophet who had performed the signs on its behalf. . . . The two of them were thrown alive into the fiery lake of burning sulfur" (19:20). Christ has already triumphed over Satan and his minions. He already won the battle when he died on the cross. What remains is for the ramifications of that victory to be manifested. The final confrontation between Christ and the antichrist will not be a battle. It will be the time when the forces of evil meet their ultimate demise. They will suffer the full consequences of the defeat that was handed to them when Jesus came to earth.

The Millennium

Following its description of the punishment of the beast, Revelation describes the defeat of Satan himself. An angel "seized the dragon, that ancient serpent, who is the devil, or Satan, and bound him for a thousand years" (20:2). During this time "the souls of those who had been beheaded because of their testimony about Jesus and because of the word of God . . . came to life and reigned with Christ a thousand years" (20:4). Throughout the history of the church, Christians have held different interpretations of this passage. Some take it to refer to an event at the end of history. They see the binding of Satan as an event that is still future, and they look forward to a period when the people of God will rule with Christ. On this interpretation, Christ will return once to establish this millennial rule and then again to bring the resurrection of all humans and the final judgment. Because it presupposes that Christ will come again before the millennium, this interpretation is often referred to as the premillennial view. Others believe that the account of Satan's binding is another flashback to Christ's decisive victory (as 12:1–12 is usually understood). In that case, it is a past event rather than a future one: the rule of God's people is the rule that Christians exercise here and now through their participation in the victory of Christ. This position is usually referred to as the amillennial view because it entails a symbolic rather than a literal understanding of the millennium.[5]

5. The prefix *a-* in Greek is equivalent to the prefix *non-* in English.

It is difficult to decide between these two interpretations. The strongest argument in favor of the premillennial view is that the binding of Satan takes place after the resurrection of those who have given their lives for their faith in Christ. If this is a literal resurrection, then the millennium must be future. Amillennialists contend that this resurrection is a spiritual resurrection, referring to the fact that the followers of Christ have been born again and been spiritually resurrected. Premillennialists retort that John immediately afterward refers to the resurrection of the ungodly (Rev. 20:5). Their resurrection must be understood literally because the ungodly have no part in a spiritual resurrection. Amillennialists agree but point out that John may be playing on two different meanings of the term "come to life" (as he does in John 5:24–29). The discussion does not seem to abate, and Christians will probably continue to disagree about the interpretation of this passage until Jesus comes again.

What we should learn from the account of the millennium is that Christ's victory is secure. He is in total control, even as livid as Satan may be while still at large. Satan's activities should be seen as the desperate acts of someone who is already condemned. His end is already sealed; his judgment is predetermined.

The Consummation

After the judgment of Satan and the ungodly (Rev. 20:7–15), the visible manifestation of God's kingdom follows. All the gifts that the people of God have already received will now be fully seen. Nothing will distract from the fact that God rules. He has reconciled his people to himself so that they may enjoy undisturbed fellowship with each other and first and foremost with God. As we have seen, the followers of Christ enjoy all these gifts already, but at this future time their gifts will shine in sparkling light. In this world, the glory of God's people is concealed under the form of the cross they have to bear. On that day, their glory will shine without any shadow.

> Then I saw "a new heaven and a new earth," for the first heaven and the first earth had passed away, and there was no longer any sea. I saw the Holy City, the new Jerusalem, coming down out of heaven from God, prepared as a bride beautifully dressed for her husband. And I heard a loud voice from the throne saying, "Look! God's dwelling place is now among the people, and he will dwell with them. They will be his people, and God himself will be with them and be their God. 'He will wipe every tear from their eyes. There will be no more death' or mourning or crying or pain, for the old order of things has passed away." (21:1–4)

In the book of Revelation, "the sea" is a symbol for the powers that stand against God and cause fear and disaster among humans. When the powers of evil are fully removed, the consequences of evil will become a distant memory. There will be no more injustice; no one will abuse their power to oppress, humiliate, or discriminate against those less fortunate. Those who have been suffering under the evil rulers of our world will be comforted. God "will wipe every tear from their eyes." Since Christ has dealt with sin once and for all, "'there will be no more death' or mourning or crying or pain, for the old order of things has passed away." While we are in this world, sickness is constantly causing pain and restricting our ability to enjoy the good gifts of God. Death is taking our loved ones away from us. Our desire for love is often unfulfilled. In the new heaven and the new earth, there will be no more loss, no more grief, no more pain, no more heartache.

That God brings a new heaven and a new earth means that the old creation will pass away. But the new creation will not be something entirely different from the old one. The new creation is a renewal of the first one: it transforms the original creation into something even more glorious. God's people will not be transformed into a bodiless existence in heaven, there to float around in a blissful, purely spiritual state. The book of Revelation shows us not that God's people will go to heaven but that heaven will come down to us. The beauty of the gospel is that God is coming down to us; he is not requiring humans to climb up to heaven, and he is not showing us how we may do so. The Bible teaches us that the ultimate sin is to try to ascend into heaven (Gen. 11:1–9; Isa. 14:12–15). It is a characteristic of all false religions that they try to teach people how to improve themselves to the point that they can reach up to heaven. The gospel is a radically different message; it is the good news about the Creator God, who has come down to us. And the book of Revelation shows that God did not come down so that he could bring us back up with him. He came down so that he could stay with us. That is the kind of God we serve, a God who became a human so that he could have fellowship with us; a God who came down to earth so that he could be with us forever; a God who brings heaven down to us; a God who brings his kingly rule and his kingdom to us.

The new creation is more glorious than the old one because the new creation makes it possible for God and humans to have an even more intimate relationship. Before they disobeyed God, Adam and Eve had a good relationship with God and had no need to be afraid of him. This relationship was built around their obedience to his commandment, a commandment they quickly broke. In the new creation, our relationship with God is of a different, much better nature. Our relationship with him is based on his grace and forgiveness;

it is founded on God's demonstration of his abundant love for us, his giving of his Son as a sacrifice for our sins. Before the fall, the first humans knew that God was a loving God, but they had not experienced his love in the way that we have. They had not experienced firsthand what it is like to be the ones who have rebelled against God and spurned his love, only to have God be the one who restores the relationship by making the ultimate sacrifice: giving his Son to die in our place. We had become God's enemies through our own doing, but God made us his friends again by sacrificing his Son. Now we know his love in a way that has never been possible before. Not even the angels have experienced God's love in this way, which is why the apostle Peter says that "even angels long to look into these things" (1 Pet. 1:12).

In the new creation, we know the magnitude of God's love, and we have a relationship with him that is more intimate than anything that could even be imagined in the past. We now know how much he loves us, and in the new creation we will forever experience that love without any interruptions. As the apostle John describes,

> Then he [an angel] showed me the river of the water of life, clear as crystal, flowing from the throne of God and of the Lamb down the middle of the city's main street. The tree of life was on each side of the river, bearing twelve kinds of fruit, producing its fruit every month. The leaves of the tree are for healing the nations, and there will no longer be any curse. The throne of God and of the Lamb will be in the city, and his servants will worship him. They will see his face, and his name will be on their foreheads. Night will be no more; people will not need the light of a lamp or the light of the sun, because the Lord God will give them light, and they will reign forever and ever. (Rev. 22:1–5 CSB)

When God's kingly rule becomes a visible reality, he will exercise his rule through his people, as he intended from the beginning: "And they will reign forever and ever." This time their rule will not be interrupted by their sin. Nor will there be any disturbance from death. The tree of life is found in the city—the tree from the account of the original creation in Genesis. Those who ate from it would "live forever" (Gen. 3:22). After their sin, the first humans were banned from the garden with the tree of life (3:22–24). In the new creation, humans once again have access to this tree, and now the tree is more glorious than ever. It is found on each side of the river so it will always be accessible, and it bears fruit every month so the fruit will always be there for the taking. God gave life when he first created the world; in the new creation he gives life in abundance.

Whereas the picture of the first creation is a garden, the picture of the new creation is a city. It is not a fortress of solitude; it is a community. God has brought down the barrier between Jews and gentiles, black and white, rich and poor, and all other human distinctions. He has brought peace and reconciliation; he has brought together a multitude "from every nation, tribe, people and language" to praise him (Rev. 7:9). Their eternity is spent in a city, in which all people enjoy perfect community under God's rule.

"The throne of God and of the Lamb will be in the city." The entire story of the Old and the New Testaments can be read as the story of God drawing near to humans and of humans' inability to be in his presence. God dwelt among the Israelites in the tabernacle and later in the temple, but the people's sins prevented them from entering into it. No one but the high priest could ever enter into the holy of holies, into God's presence. Throughout the time of the tabernacle and the temple, God was near but yet so far away. In Jesus Christ, God once again has made his dwelling among the people. "He came to that which was his own," John explains, "but his own did not receive him" (John 1:11). Through the Holy Spirit, he made his dwelling in the church, among those who believe in Jesus Christ. In the consummation, the presence of God will be permanent and visible. In John's vision, the measurements of the city are "12,000 stadia [around 1,400 miles or 2,200 kilometers] in length, and as wide and high as it is long" (Rev. 21:16). In the Old Testament, there is only one building that is constructed as a perfect cube: the holy of holies (1 Kings 6:20). In the new creation, there is no temple in the city (Rev. 21:22); the whole city is a holy of holies. God's presence is not confined to a limited space with restricted access. Everyone will be in the intimate presence of God at all times. "They will see his face, and his name will be on their foreheads." Nothing will separate God's people from knowing the presence of God anymore. They will be on the most intimate terms with him, and they will belong to him. We have reason to pray, "Your kingdom come."

Further Reading

The reading of the book of Revelation that is developed in this chapter is influenced by **Richard Bauckham**. In his work *The Climax of Prophecy: Studies on the Book of Revelation* (Edinburgh: T&T Clark, 1993), he emphasizes the significance of suffering for the people of God.

In *Surprised by Hope: Rethinking Heaven, the Resurrection, and the Mission of the Church* (New York: HarperOne, 2008), **N. T. Wright** argues that Christians do not go to heaven when they die but that the earth is renewed when heaven comes down and Christians are raised from the dead.

In *The Book of Revelation: Justice and Judgment* (Philadelphia: Fortress, 1985), **Elisabeth Schüssler Fiorenza** understands the vision of Revelation in political terms. As the kingdom of God, the Christian community stands in opposition to the Roman Empire. This kingdom brings liberation from slavery and oppression.

Dispensationalists tend to read the book of Revelation as prophecies that will be literally fulfilled in the future, before Christ's second coming. **Robert Thomas** is a proponent of this view in his commentary *Revelation: An Exegetical Commentary*, 2 vols. (Chicago: Moody, 1992–95).

In contrast, many modern interpreters maintain that the book of Revelation refers to events that took place when the book was written. **David E. Aune**, *Revelation*, 3 vols., Word Biblical Commentary 52 (Dallas: Word; Nashville: Nelson, 1997–98) is a good example.

While they recognize the connection between the symbols in Revelation and the historical situation in which the book was written, other scholars read the book as describing what Christians will experience throughout church history. **G. K. Beale**, *The Book of Revelation*, New International Greek Testament Commentary (Grand Rapids: Eerdmans, 1999) and **Craig Koester**, *Revelation: A New Translation with Introduction and Commentary*, Anchor Bible 38A (New Haven: Yale University Press, 2014) are good examples of this approach.

Others again, such as **Grant R. Osborne**, *Revelation*, Baker Exegetical Commentary on the New Testament (Grand Rapids: Baker Academic, 2002) and **Paul M. Hoskins**, *The Book of Revelation: A Theological and Exegetical Commentary* (North Charleston, SC: ChristoDoulos, 2017), emphasize that John's visions pertain primarily to the last days before Jesus's return.

Thomas R. Schreiner, *New Testament Theology: Magnifying God in Christ* (Grand Rapids: Baker Academic, 2008), 802–64, describes the future as the fulfillment of the new creation and the kingdom promises, when God will judge the wicked and reward his people.

Scripture Index

Subject Index